THE INTIMATE LIFE
OF AN OTTOMAN STATESMAN
MELEK AHMED PASHA (1588–1662)

SUNY Series in Medieval Middle East History

Jere Bacharach, Editor

The Intimate Life
of an Ottoman Statesman
Melek Ahmed Pasha (1588–1662)

As Portrayed in Evliya Çelebi's
Book of Travels (Seyahat-name)

Translation and Commentary
by Robert Dankoff

With a Historical Introduction
by Rhoads Murphey

STATE UNIVERSITY OF NEW YORK PRESS

Published by
State University of New York Press, Albany

© 1991 State University of New York

For information, address State University of New York Press,
90 State Street, Suite 700, Albany NY 12207

Production by M. R. Mulholland
Marketing by Bernadette LaManna

Library of Congress Cataloging in Publication Data

Evliya Çelebi, 1611?–1682?
    [Seyahatname. English. Selections]
    The intimate life of an Ottoman statesman : Melek Ahmed Pasha
    (1588–1662) : as portrayed in Evliya Çelebi's Book of travels
    (Seyahat-name) / translation and commentary by Robert Dankoff.
        p.   cm. — (SUNY series in medieval Middle East history)
    Selections from the author's Seyahatname.
    Includes bibliographical references and index.
    ISBN 0–7914–0640–7 (CH : acid free). — ISBN 0–7914–0641–5 (PB :
    acid free)
        1. Melek Ahmet Paşa. d. 1662.   2. Statesmen—Turkey—Biography.
    3. Turkey—History—Mohammed IV, 1648–1687.   I. Dankoff, Robert.
    II. Series.
    DR534.M45E82513 1991
    949.61′015′092—dc20
    [B]   90–40379
                                                                               CIP

10 9 8 7 6 5 4 3 2 1

to Claire:
"My eye and soul, my lady love, my royal sultana"
(Fuzuli)

CONTENTS

Illustrations

Maps and Charts

ACKNOWLEDGMENTS

Illustration #4 (Bektaşi Dervish), by Levni, is from Topkapı Sarayı Müzesi, H. 2164, fol. 22v.

The other illustrations are taken from Franz Taeschner, ed., *Alt-Stambuler Hof- und Volksleben: Ein Türkisches Miniaturen-album aus dem 17. Jahrhundert* (Hannover, 1925), as follows:

Illustration #	Taeschner #
1	2
2	3
3	17
5	16
6	25
7	9
8	14
9	19
10	30
11	6
12	32
13	28
14	49

The maps were prepared by Carlene Friedman. The map of the Ottoman Empire is drawn after TAVO, B IX 8 (*Tübinger Atlas des Vorderen Orients*, Wiesbaden, 1979).

I am grateful to Rhoads Murphey, Richard Chambers, and Michael Murrin for helpful suggestions.

R. D.
Chicago, April 1990

INTRODUCTION

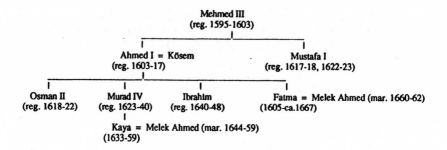

Mehmed III
(reg. 1595-1603)

Ahmed I = Kösem
(reg. 1603-17)

Mustafa I
(reg. 1617-18, 1622-23)

Osman II
(reg. 1618-22)

Murad IV
(reg. 1623-40)

Ibrahim
(reg. 1640-48)

Fatma = Melek Ahmed (mar. 1660-62)
(1605-ca.1667)

Kaya = Melek Ahmed (mar. 1644-59)
(1633-59)

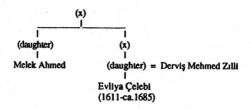

(x)

(daughter)

Melek Ahmed

(x)

(daughter) = Derviş Mehmed Zıllı

Evliya Çelebi
(1611-ca.1685)

THE AUTHOR AND
HIS SUBJECT

Evliya Çelebi was a Turk from Istanbul. His father, Derviş Mehmed Zıllı Agha, chief goldsmith at the Ottoman court, had (according to family tradition) accompanied Süleyman the Magnificent on his late campaigns. His mother was an Abkhazian slave girl, presented to Sultan Ahmed I along with her cousin, Melek Ahmed, who later became one of the great statesmen of the age and Evliya's chief patron.

In the Ottoman system, those men who began their careers as "slaves of the Porte" (kapıkulu)—notably the janissaries, derived mainly from the Balkans, and the military slaves from the Caucasus—had the likeliest chance to achieve high office in the military and political sphere. Such was the case with Melek Ahmed (though he was not technically a military slave, as he was born in Istanbul), whose career followed a typical pattern: upbringing in the Caucasus; introduction to the palace service as a young man (gulam); graduation to officer status (ağa); appointment to the highest offices of the state (paşa).

The military option was not open, at least in principle, to native Turks, who tended rather to seek careers as religious personnel (ulema) or bureaucrats in the financial administration (efendi). But they too could gain entrance to the centers of power by virtue of their skills. Such was the case with Evliya's father, and with Evliya himself.[1] And anyone noted for refined taste and literary accomplishment could gain the nickname of "gentleman" (çelebi).

As a youth of endless curiosity, Evliya explored the variegated metropolis and imbibed tales and accounts of its history, as well as the history of Süleyman's far-flung conquests. He received a thorough training in Islamic and Ottoman sciences, especially Koran recitation and music. With his fine voice and entertaining manner, he attracted the attention of Sultan Murad IV, thus

gaining entry to the palace where his education was refined. He
learned the Koran by heart *(hafız)* and was often called on to
recite. And he was the sultan's boon companion *(musahib)*.

But Evliya's nature was too restless for a sedentary career
as a courtier. His wanderlust was encouraged by the Prophet
himself in a dream which (as he tells us) occurred on the night
of Ashura, the tenth of Muharrem, in the year of the hegira 1040
(19 August 1630)—his twentieth birthday![2] Thereafter, by at-
taching himself to various pashas sent out to govern the provinces, he traveled the length and breadth of the empire, and into
its peripheries. Evliya served his patrons as Koran reciter, caller
to prayer *(müezzin)*, and prayer leader *(imam)*; as boon companion and raconteur; more officially, as courier, tax collec-
tor, or deputy. But he shunned official status. When Melek
offered him the key post of marshal of his guards *(kapıcılar kethüdası)*, he refused (see Chapter 9). He saw himself as a mendicant
(derviş), as "world traveler and boon companion to mankind"
(seyyah-ı alem ve nedim-i beni-Adem). As one of his interlocu-
tors puts it: "Evliya Çelebi is a wandering dervish and a world
traveler. He cries the chant of every cart he mounts, and sings
the praises of every man who feeds him. Wherever he rests his
head, he eats and drinks and is merry."[3] Travel was his true career. And the *Book of Travels (Seyahat-name)* was his life work.

*   *   *

The *Book of Travels* is a vast panorama of the Ottoman
world in the mid-seventeenth century. At this period the Ottoman state was still a great imperial power—geographically it
was at the height of its glory—although cracks and strains were
evident. Evliya's account naturally begins with the capital, also
his birthplace, Istanbul, to which he devotes one entire book
(the work as a whole is divided into ten "books"). Following the
story of the dream (in which the Prophet blesses his travels) the
historical and geographical surveys of the metropolis proceed
systematically and at a stately pace, although with frequent di-
gressions and anecdotal asides. Book I is divided into 273 chapters; the passages translated below (Chapter 1) are drawn from
Chapter 120, "Viziers of Murad IV," and Chapter 138, "Gazas and
Conquests under Murad IV." The longest, Chapter 270, covering
sixty-two folios of text—it would make a book of several hundred
printed pages—is a description of the guilds of the city as they

paraded before Sultan Murad IV in preparation for the Baghdad campaign of 1638. At one point, while discussing the guild of fireworks makers, Evliya mentions a youthful prank in which he launched a spectacular rocket of his own devising from a boat in the Bosphorus, shocking those on the shore. This took place, he tells us, "during the festivities celebrating the birth of Kaya Sultan"—Sultan Murad's daughter who later became Melek Pasha's wife—that is, in 1633.[4]

Book II opens with a reprisal of the initiatory dream. Evliya's first venture outside the capital, beginning (so he tells us) just before his thirtieth birthday in 1050/1640, was to the old Ottoman capital of Bursa. After returning to Istanbul to get his father's blessing, he journeys along the Black Sea coast as far as the Caucasus region, the homeland of his mother's kin, and around to the Crimea. He participates in raids against the infidel (gaza). He suffers shipwreck. He goes to Crete for the Canea campaign, and so is present at the initial Ottoman victory (1645) in the twenty-five-year-long struggle to conquer that island. Returning to Erzurum in the train of the newly appointed governor of that province, his kinsman Defterdar-zade Mehmed Pasha, Evliya accompanies an envoy to Tebriz in the country of the heritical Kızılbaş (i.e., the Safavids of Iran), his first venture outside the Ottoman realm. Later Mehmed Pasha is caught up in one of the frequent Anatolian disturbances of that era, a revolt by a disaffected provincial governor (all such rebels at this time were called celali). The rebel in this instance, Varvar Ali Pasha, refused the command of Sultan Ibrahim to forward the wife of another provincial governor, Ipşir Pasha. The same Ipşir Pasha was sent to put down the rebellion. (He was to play an important role in the later fate of Melek Ahmed Pasha.) Learning of his father's death, Evliya returns to the capital in time to witness the deposition of the extravagant Sultan Ibrahim and the accession of the seven-year-old Sultan Mehmed IV (1648).

In the first part of Book III Evliya accompanies Murtaza Pasha to Damascus, capital of the province of Şam (Syria). Luckily he is back in the capital when his kinsman Melek Ahmed Pasha is appointed grand vizier (1650; Chapter 2). From that time on Evliya is almost constantly in Melek's service, following him to Özü, Silistre, and Sofia (Rumeli province; Chapter 3), and back to Istanbul, where the Pasha serves as deputy grand vizier until the arrival of Ipşir Pasha from Aleppo (Chapter 4). Ipşir "exiles" Melek to Van. On the way there (Book IV) Evliya stops off in Diyarbekir province and has the opportunity to relate some of Melek's exploits when Melek was governor of that province fifteen years earlier (Chapter 5). After reaching Van, Melek takes advantage of his position by mounting an expedition against the rebellious, quasi-independent Kurdish ruler of Bitlis, the flamboyant and wealthy Abdal Khan (Chapter 6). Thus, despite the poor prospects initially, he is able to amass a small fortune—as Evliya remarks, "for Melek Ahmed Pasha the province of Van turned out to be a veritable Egypt."[5]

Evliya once again goes on an embassy to Iran, and takes the opportunity to travel to Baghdad and make an extensive tour of Mesopotamia and Kurdistan, returning to Van only at the beginning of Book V. He is in Bitlis collecting some arrears when Melek is removed from office. After an adventurous escape from Bitlis, Evliya warns Melek not to return to the capital via Bitlis and Diyarbekir, but to take a northerly route through Erzurum, despite the winter season. The remainder of Book V covers the latter part of Melek's career, as governor of Özü (Chapter 7) and Bosnia (Chapter 9), interrupted by the blow caused by the death of his beloved wife, Kaya Sultan (Chapter 8). At the beginning of Book VI Melek is recalled from the Transylvania campaign to marry another sultana, Fatma Sultan, the daughter of his original patron, Sultan Ahmed I (Chapter 10). The unhappy match is short-lived, ended by Melek's death in 1662.

Though left patronless, Evliya rejoices in the lack of family attachments[6] and goes off to join the German campaign. Book VII includes eyewitness accounts of the Battle of St. Gotthard (1664) and the Ottoman embassy to Vienna under Kara Mehmed Pasha (1665), followed by travels in the Crimea, Circassia, and Kalmukia. Book VIII is largely devoted to Greece, including an eyewitness account of the Candia campaign and the final Ottoman conquest of Crete (1669). Pilgrimage to the holy cities of Jerusalem, Mecca, and Medina is the subject of Book IX. In 1672 Evliya finally reaches Egypt, his goal and haven after forty years of travel; and his leisurely description of Cairo in Book X (plus journeys up and down the Nile) recalls his description of Istanbul.

*   *   *

If a travel account can be said to have a hero, that hero must be the traveler himself. While the *Book of Travels* is no exception to this, it can also be said to have another hero: Melek

Ahmed Pasha. For it is not simply a travel account (seyahat-name); it is also a chronicle (tarih) of Evliya's life and times. The narrative thread, accounting for roughly 5 percent of the huge ten-book text, is an autobiographical memoir. And the "hero" in Evliya's life, from his own perspective, is not himself but his patron. Of the various patrons who sponsored Evliya's career Melek Pasha was by far the most important. Their bond of kinship provided the basis for Evliya's attachment to Melek and to his household. Evliya served Melek, not only in religious and official capacities, but above all as confidant—we might say, as friend, although their differences in age and in position clearly made Evliya a subordinate.

One obligation of a subordinate in the Ottoman system was to praise and otherwise to promote the welfare of his superior, to whom he owed loyalty. Evliya fulfills this obligation in the *Book of Travels*. Although not wholly covering up Melek's weak points he tends to portray him in glowing colors. He probably exaggerates Melek's heroic exploits; and in the course of his eulogy after Melek's death, he says that he has gathered the accounts of those exploits in a separate volume, entitled *The Gestes of Melek Ahmed Pasha (Risale-i Menakıb-ı Melek Ahmed Paşa).*[7] *The Intimate Life of an Ottoman Statesman* in some fashion reconstitutes that volume, lost or never written.

What gives Evliya's account its special character is that it goes far beyond the laudatory recounting of public exploits characteristic of Ottoman (and Islamic) biographies and hagiographies. It records how Melek used Evliya as a sounding board for his dreams; how Melek and his wife, Kaya Sultan, related their dreams to each other, and how their dreams reacted to and were fulfilled in events in the world. With these dreams, especially, Evliya comes close to a psychological portrait of his patron and patroness. We gain an acquaintance of their hearts and minds, at a level of intimacy quite unusual, if not unique, in Ottoman (and Islamic) literature.

*   *   *

In the case of most Ottomans, we know very little of their individual lives beyond what we can glean from chronicles and biographical dictionaries; "biographical details on the great men of the empire are characteristically lacking in intimate detail."[8] Melek Ahmed Pasha is an exception only because of Evliya's very rich account.

As with many Ottoman officials, Melek Pasha comes to the notice of the chroniclers only when he holds high office—in this case, during his year as grand vizier.[9] For his fuller career, without Evliya we would have to be content with such notices as the following from the *Sicill-i Osmani:*

The imperial son-in-law *(damad-ı şehriyari)* Melek Ahmed Pasha. He was Abkhazian. Raised in the sultan's harem, he became imperial sword-bearer. In 1048 [text, in error: 1148] (1638–39) he was appointed governor of Diyarbekir, with the rank of vizier. In Zilhicce 1050 (March–April 1641) he was made governor of Baghdad, in 1051 governor of Damascus. In 1053 (1643) he returned to Istanbul and [the following year] married Kaya Sultan. In 1055 (1645) he became governor of Diyarbekir for the second time. He was removed from office in that year, and in 1056 became governor of Diyarbekir for the third [text: second] time. In Zilkade 1058 (November–December 1648) he was made governor of Baghdad for the second time; removed from office in Zilkade 1059. In Zilkade 1060 (November 1650) he was appointed governor of Baghdad for the third time; but the following day he became grand vizier.

In Ramazan 1061 (August–September 1651) he was made governor of Silistre; in '62 governor of Rumeli, removed from office in Zilhicce '63 (October–November 1653). In 1064 he served as deputy grand vizier, and at the beginning of 1065 (November 1654) was sent to Van. In '66 he was appointed to Silistre; in '69 (1658–59) to Bosnia, removed from office in 1072 (1661–62). He died of the plague on 17 Muharrem 1073 (1 September 1662). He was cultured, dignified, gentle, free of defect, compassionate. The Baghdad chronicle notes certain facts, such as that he customarily paid one hundred purses annually from Baghdad into the imperial treasury; that he himself appeared to be abstemious, while his retainers appropriated the wealth of the poor, and he chastised those who informed him. An infant daughter of his sultana, named Afife Hanım Sultan, is buried at Şehzadebaşı.[10]

Evliya's cursory summaries of Melek's career—for example, in Chapters 1 and 10 below—resemble this stereotyped account. In the more detailed sections of Evliya's chronicle we win access to the private side of this public figure: his fears and hopes and dreams; his hesitations as well as his heroics; his religious life and domestic affairs.

*   *   *

In the Ottoman system, relation by family and clan gave the presumption of patronage and favor (though it did not prevent rivalry, as the relation of Melek and İpşir demonstrates). Melek has to assure Köprülü that he will fight against the rebel Hasan Pasha despite their Abkhazian clan ties.[11] The Abkhazians apparently had a reputation for stinginess; Melek was an exception.[12] At one point, when he displayed his typical generosity on the occasion of feasting the Crimean Khan in Ak-kirman in 1068/1657, the people were surprised:

> "Such generosity has never been seen in an Abkhazian," they said. But Melek Ahmed Pasha was not originally Abkhazian. He was born in Istanbul, in Tophane, and since his parents were of Abkhazian origin they sent him, as was customary among the Abkhazians, with his wetnurse to the————clan in the Abkhazian country, at the age of six. Then at age fourteen he was brought to the capital and presented as a gift to Sultan Ahmed along with my own mother, who was the daughter of his maternal aunt. When Ahmed Khan saw Melek he cried, "God knows, that boy is an angel (melek)," and gave Melek into the charge of the chief black eunuch, Büyük Mustafa Agha, while he bestowed my mother upon the chief goldsmith of the Porte, Derviş Mehmed Zılli. I came into being as a result of that union, and this is the source of my kinship with Melek; while the sobriquet "Melek" was the result of Ahmed Khan's pearl-strewn speech.[13]

According to Evliya's family tradition, his own mother and Melek, who were cousins on their mothers' side, were presented to court on the same day during the reign of Ahmed I.[14] And Melek, early in the reign of Murad IV, brought Evliya to the sultan's attention, thus enabling him to be educated at court.[15] Although Evliya provides little information about his relationship with Melek until the year of the latter's grand vizierate, it appears that he was accepted from the start as a member of Melek's household.[16]

Before he began his serious "career" as a traveler, Evliya apparently accompanied Melek at least once to a provincial post, viz., to Damascus in 1051/1641.[17] Several references in Book II seem to corroborate this: Evliya claims to have dined with Haci Baba and Melek in the robbers' den near Ankara;[18] and Ipşir Pasha blames him for serving Defterdar-oğlu Mehmed Pasha: "Why aren't you again with our lord Melek Ahmed Pasha?" he says. "Go again to Melek Ahmed Pasha."[19] Even at this time Evliya was considered to be Melek's protégé.[20]

Melek's wife, the rich and generous Kaya Sultan, made Evliya a special object of her regard. In Book II, again, there is reference to a watch that Kaya gave him "twenty-one years before" (i.e., in 1627?).[21] Kaya was a liberal benefactress to Evliya and was also the patroness of Evliya's sister.[22] Indeed, Melek's other retainers seem to have envied Evliya because of this special favor, and after Kaya's death they felt freer to abuse him.[23] One mark of this favor was an abundant supply of Kaya's hand-embroidered handkerchiefs, which Evliya used as gifts both during her lifetime and well after her death.[24]

*   *   *

As a tried and trusted warrior and statesman, Melek Ahmed Pasha could be sent to troubleshoot in various hot spots of the empire, the frontier outposts, to deal with upstart Kurdish rebels in the neighborhood of the Safavids (Sincar, Chapter 5; Bitlis, Chapter 6); or menacing cossacks (Varna and Özü, Chapter 7); or raiders and rebels on the Venetian and Austrian borders (Dalmatia and Translyvania, Chapter 9).

The rewards for carrying out these duties were substantial, accruing not only from the legitimate revenue of an Ottoman provincial governor,[25] but also from booty, gifts, and other perquisites. Aside from the dangers, however, there were other drawbacks as well, including the great expenses involved and the precarious nature of the posts.

Like other grand statesmen of the day, Melek Ahmed Pasha was obliged to maintain a huge household—a kind of sultanic palace in miniature—as a token of prestige and a basis of power.[26] His retinue consisted of several hundred aghas or "officers," ranging from menial domestics and bodyguards to companions

and agents like Evliya himself and the hapless Kudde Mehmed.
In a famous passage of his didactic work known as *Hayriyye*,
the poet Nabi (d. 1124/1712) advises his son to avoid the lot of a
pasha. To cite E. J. W. Gibb's quaint Victorian translation:

> He wrecks the shrine of Faith, if he oppress;
> If he do not, he bideth portionless.
> Were all the sorrows told he undergoes,
> Cairo and Baghdad were not worth those woes. . . .
> Unless his meinie[27] well he clothe and feed,
> Though he command them, none his words will heed.
> Yet his demesnes suffice not to provide
> All he must lavish upon every side. . . .
> Untold are the expenses of his place,
> To these no limits may he ever trace.
> Kitchens and stables, rations for his rout,
> His servants and his slaves, within, without. . . .
> He passeth all his life in bitter stress;
> Is glory the fit name for such duresse?[28]

A pasha had to steer a course between principle and corruption, between dynastic loyalty and self-preservation. In a violent age, when the exercise of power was erratic and often
brutal, a pasha was in a very precarious position. Melek's reputation for honesty and fair-dealing, and his marriage to the
wealthiest of the Ottoman princesses, made him no less vulner-
able to the whims of grand viziers as ruthless as Ipşir Pasha or
Köprülü Mehmed Pasha and no less subject to the violent currents of Ottoman politics.

Perhaps Evliya's portrait of Seydi Ahmed Pasha—Melek's
friend and fellow-Abkhazian—illustrates this theme best. Evliya
first came into contact with Seydi, then *sancak-begi* of Tortum,
in 1057/1647, when he joined him in raids on the cossacks at
Günye and into Mingrelia.[29] Evliya is fond of quoting Seydi's
barbaric Turkish; he draws a lively and sympathetic picture of
the rough and honest warrior, telling how he even lost some
teeth at Seydi's hands from a playful throw of the jereed-
javelin.[30] In 1071/1661, while Melek was in Tımışvar during the
Translyvania campaign, an order arrived from Grand Vizier Köprülü Mehmed Pasha, who had an old grudge against Seydi, to
have Seydi executed.[31] Melek had had an ominous dream regarding Seydi's fate the previous year.[32] Now Seydi, condemned

to death, entrusted his son to Melek. Evliya's sagalike account of Seydi's bravery in life and death is a moving one. And his description of Melek's reaction on hearing of Seydi's execution is telling. "He summoned all the aghas, made his last will and testament, and distributed the three hundred diamonds that were in his seal-purse, noting down in a register who should get what: ten for his son Ibrahim Beg;[33] ten for Seydi's son Mehmed Beg; ten for his daughter Hanım Sultan; and the rest for his aghas. 'If I die,' he stipulated, 'they are yours; but while I live, I retain possession.' "[34]

*   *   *

Above, I characterized the narrative portions of the *Book of Travels*, using such terms as *chronicle, autobiographical memoir*, and *eulogy* (≈ *menakıb*). To gain a sharper idea of just what Evliya is doing, let us concentrate on the one episode covered in the standard Ottoman histories: Melek's fall from the grand vizierate. We will compare Evliya's account with that of the major historian of the period, Naima.[35]

Naima's account, in the fifth volume of his *History*, is in five sections:

> 1. Restiveness of the *sipahis* over salary delay
> 2. Rebellion of Abaza Hasan
> 3. Unjust execution of Hacı Osman
> 4. Rebellion of Dasni Mirza
> 5. Bazaar revolt

The first and third episodes, which reflect poorly on Melek Pasha's statesmanship, are not even mentioned by Evliya. He names, as the initial reason for Melek's downfall, Abaza Hasan's rebellion, for which he blames Melek's deputies, particularly his steward Kudde. Characteristically, Evliya gives color to the account by quoting the verbal quarrel between Hasan and Kudde, including Kudde's homely proverb (given in the original dialect form) and Hasan's obscene response.

Evliya also exonerates Melek of blame for Dasni (or Dasnik) Mirza's rebellion. He depicts Melek as the cat's paw of his deputies, who by their greed have alienated a public servant, and by their ferocity have driven him to become a rebel or *celali*.

At this point the narrative switches gears and turns into a kind of battle epic, lightened by Evliya's personal touch. Evliya himself joins the fray. In an episode recalling Gideon's spying out the Midianites (Judges 7:9–15), he creeps up to the enemy camp at night where he overhears two young braves, one singing quatrains (in dialect) while grooming his horse, the other telling his friend a dream that, like the quatrains, prefigures their fate. After the fighting, when the rebels are executed, Dasnik's partner with the religious sounding name of Hanefi Halife, who is not mentioned at all by Naima, is revealed in Evliya's account as a holy man, whose execution bodes ill for Melek.

When he turns to the bazaar revolt, Evliya once again depicts Melek as the wholly innocent victim of circumstances and shifts the blame entirely to Melek's officers, especially Kudde. The only implied criticisms of Melek are that he was too weak to oppose his underlings, and that he reacted too impetuously when the delegation demanded justice.

Incidentally, Evliya's judgment here agrees with that of the major Ottoman historians. Haci Halife exonerates Melek, saying that he himself was mild and gentle, but that his deputies (Bektaş Agha, [Kudde] Kethüda Beg, etc.) held sway over him.[36] And Naima faults him only for his quick temper.[37] On the other hand, Eremya Kömürciyan, in his diary, specifically blames Melek for initiating the unjust impositions that alienated the bazaar merchants: "They [i.e., Kara Çavuş, Mustafa Agha, etc.] were not satisfied with silver, gold, and gifts from all sides, but they began to place imposts of linen and cotton on the guildsmen—*from the vizier, whose order it was*. Finally they imposed base money on the guildsmen, demanding one goldpiece for 120 aspers."[38]

In this section as well Evliya inflates the human drama, most clearly in the Telhisi Hüseyn episode, in contrast to Naima's summary treatment: "The vizier, fearing the mob, wrote a note *(telhis)* explaining the situation and sent it with his memorandum-man *(telhisçi)* who, when he set foot inside the palace grounds, was set on by the crowd shouting 'Kill that bastard' *(bre uruň melunı)*. Severely wounded by blows of stones and daggers, he was taken away half-dead."[39] Here, where he claims personal involvement, Evliya builds up the narrative very carefully. He first has Melek Pasha appeal for someone to step forth and act the peace maker. Kudde interrupts with his saber-rattling plan. When Telhisi Hüseyn—too officious and tactless

for the job, as everyone realizes—volunteers, Melek sends Evliya
with him, presumably to act as a restraining influence. Evliya,
anticipating the worst, puts on bazaar clothing (described in
some detail) before entering among the mob. In the event, Evliya's judiciousness fails to save Telhisi Hüseyn; but he himself,
considering discretion the better part of valor, manages to slink
into the crowd and avoid a beating.

There is a telling detail in this narrative: when Telhisi Hüseyn, instead of placating the mob, addresses them rather
roughly, someone cries out, *bizi begnemediñ mi* ("Don't you like
us?").[40] Characteristically, once again, Evliya gives color to the
drama through the use of dialect (in this case, the lower-class
Istanbul *begnemediñ* rather than standard *begenmediñ*). But
there is another point. When Evliya describes a similar episode
that occurred a few years later—how Kara Abdullah tried to pla-
cate the mob during the "plane-tree affair" (Çınar Vakası, 1066/
1665)—he has someone taunt Kara Abdullah with these same
words: *ya siz bizi begnemediñ mi.*[41] It is possible that we have
here a phrase that was commonly used on such occasions. It is
more likely, I think, that we have an example of Evliya's formulaic narrative technique.

Of course, Evliya did not invent the Telhisi Hüseyn episode—its presence in Naima, in however summary a fashion,
proves that it occurred, and we can reasonably credit the ex-
panded and vivacious character of Evliya's account to his actual
presence as participant and eyewitness. But we can also assume
that, in the retelling, Evliya applied the storytelling techniques
which he had mastered as "world traveler and boon companion
to mankind."

* * *

The use of dialect—by the anonymous guildsman taunting
Telhisi Hüseyn, or by Kudde Kethüda provoking Abaza Hasan, or
by the anonymous soldier singing quatrains while grooming his
horse—was interpreted above as one way in which Evliya colors
and personalizes his narrative. Other instances of its use in the
Melek Pasha materials—by Telhisi Hüseyn himself just before he
is attacked,[42] Kudde crying out under torture,[43] the Abkhazian
guards addressing a would-be assassin while squatting outside
the Pasha's tent to "renew their ablutions"[44]—confirm this.

But in all these instances something else seems to be going

on as well. To Evliya's audience, dialect was humorous. And among Evilya's storytelling techniques is the use of humor at points in the narrative that are charged with danger. This is not comic relief, which eases tension after horror or tragedy, but rather its reverse: the comedy is woven into the tense situation and signals that horror or tragedy is to come. The "escape from Bitlis" episode contains several masterful examples: Haydar Kethüda spits a gob of slime "like a mullet-oyster" before he is cut to pieces; Altı Kulaç ("Six Fathoms"), the Khan's goon, approaches "like destiny's cloud" before cutting down Molla Mehmed; Evliya pretends to snore "like a pig" while Nureddehir stands over him with a drawn dagger, then goes to kill his brother.[45] Humor—including the use of dialect—as a counter to fear seems to have come naturally to Evliya, as, just after Altı Kulaç's horrible deed, Evliya, sensing his own danger, "jumped up on the horse without even using the stirrups, and galloped before the Khan, cracking all sorts of jokes, and using dialect to make fun."

Evliya's narrative style, it seems to me, oscillates between anecdotal inventiveness and epic formulaicness. The latter is especially prominent in the descriptions of war and battle, feasts and gift exchanges, and the like. The Sincar episode (Chapter 5) is a good example. Here there is only the slightest pretence to eyewitness. Evliya, responding to Firari Mustafa's insistent queries, elaborates with obvious rhetorical flourishes on one of Melek's martial deeds, which occurred fifteen years before. After the victory, "some of the Yezidis, seeing that their wives and children were taken captive, gouged out their own eyes"—so begins a passage describing the enemy's reaction to their defeat.[46] The self-blinding is a formula Evliya employs as a climaxing device in other battle accounts; for example, at the end of the long siege of Canea on Crete in 1055/1645 the Venetian commander, "witnessing the celebrations, and hearing the Muhammedan calls-to-prayer, and seeing the crosses on the church towers turned on their heads and the green banners of the Prophet waving in their stead, and considering it preferable not to witness this scene, gouged out his own eye with his finger and, damned, died."[47] And following the even longer siege of Candia in 1080/1669 one of the Venetian captains, "considering it preferable to be blind than to see this fortress in the hands of the Turks, stuck his finger into his right eye, gouged it out, and threw it into the sea."[48]

The formulaic character of Evliya's writing is everywhere apparent, not only in narrative style, but at all levels of composition, including orthography and grammar, as well as in the molds into which he casts his topographical and architectural descriptions, his etymological and hagiographical excurses, and so on. At the same time, he can display quite sophisticated literary skills, as in the interplay, in the Sincar episode, between the two time-scales of the narrative; or in the flashback technique employed during Kaya's funeral cortege.[49] The obvious parallel between the Kaya Sultan and Fatma Sultan episodes is another case in point: note their contrasting characters; also the reaction of Mehmed Köprülü at Kaya's death as contrasted with the reaction of his son, Fazıl Ahmed, at Melek's death[50]—although in this case Evliya may simply be reporting what happened.

The question arises, If we are discussing literary techniques, to what extent is Evliya's biography of Melek a chronicle of historical events, and to what extent is it fiction? Clearly some of the episodes are "pure" fiction. The story of the storks and the crows is an Ottoman morality tale, even though the parallel story about Debbağ-oğlu may have a germ of truth.[51] The two accounts of a Bektaşi dervish appearing out of nowhere to comfort Melek at times of stress are surely Evliya's invention, although we can certainly believe that Melek did take comfort in his (Nakşbendi) Sufi connections at such times.[52] Melek's "dream" of the *şeyh* of Urmia is little more than a vehicle for Evliya to display his knowledge of onomancy and to comment on Köprülü's vizierate.[53] The pattern "illness-dream-cure," recurring twice with striking similarity, has a ring of artifice to it, like the appearances of the Bektaşi dervish.[54]

Evliya utilizes dreams to good narrative effect, as in Melek's dreams of the ants (Chapter 6) and the bear (Chapter 9); or the anonymous youth's dream of the candle (Chapter 2). But this does not mean that all the dreams in the *Book of Travels* are fictions. The recording of dreams and the soliciting of dream interpretations were common Ottoman activities.[55] In particular, the two dreams premonitory of Kaya's death—Melek's in which Kaya demands a divorce, and Kaya's in which her *imam's* wife (probably her closest female companion) is arrested for being "bloody"—are so unique and original, and contain such rich psychological insight (Melek's separation anxiety, Kaya's projection of her fear and guilt onto her household companion) that, it seems to me, they can be attributed, at least in conception, only to the dreamers themselves and not to Evliya.[56]

We are not in a position to separate the strands of fact and fiction in Evliya's account more precisely than we have done. Perhaps, when the *Books of Travels* as a whole has been better studied and we know more about Ottoman mentalities and Ottoman realities, we will be in a position to do so. For now, it seems clear that Evliya begins with actual events, then embroiders or "fictionalizes" them to a greater or lesser extent. The result, as illustrated in the materials translated here, is a remarkable portrait of a man and a unique record of his life and times.

Notes

1. Cf. Kunt, *Servants*, p. 17.

2. I 6b.18 (28; Hammer i, 2).

3. V 9b.29 (24–25; cf. *Bitlis*, p. 349).

4. I 182b.32 (Hammer ii, 181; the printed text lacks this part of Book I).

5. IV 284a.6 (not in printed text; cf. *Bitlis*, p. 337).

6. VI 49a.24 (146); cf. II 220b.15 (3; Hammer, 1).

7. VI 48a.7 (see Ch. 10). There is a large literature of the *tezkire* or *menakıb-name* variety. One recently translated example is Cafer Efendi's encomium of Mehmed Agha, chief architect and builder of the Sultan Ahmed mosque; see *Risāle-i Mi'māriyye: An Early-Seventeenth-Century Ottoman Treatise on Architecture*, trans. Howard Crane (Leiden, 1987).

8. Bruce McGowan, "Ottoman Political Communication," in H. D. Lasswell, D. Lerner, and H. Speir, eds., *Propaganda and Communication in World History, Volume I: The Symbolic Instrument in Early Times* (Honolulu, 1979), p. 457.

9. See Naima, vol. 5, pp. 18–102.

10. Süreyya, vol. 4, p. 509.

11. V 69b.21 (236); cf. III 99a.6–8 (beginning of Ch. 2). Cf. M. Kunt, "Ethnic-Regional (Cins) Solidarity in the Seventeenth-Century Ottoman Establishment," *International Journal of Middle Eastern Studies* 5 (1974): 233–39.

12. Cf. III 53a.13f. (143), where Evliya says that high officials like flattery—but Melek Ahmed Pasha was an exception!

13. V 51b.33f. (168).

14. VI 47a, Ch. 10.

15. VI 47b; also I 69a (244; Hammer i, 132).

16. Cf. I 69a22 (245; Hammer i, 133): *her bar silahdar Melek Ahmed Ağa ile görüşürdüm, zira valîdemiz tarafından karabetimiz olması cihetiyle daima hakiri yoklayup hatırum sual edüp ihsanlar ederdi.*

17. VI 47b.12. But note that at V 32a.17 (Ch. 7) Evliya pretends that he had been with Melek in Diyarbekir in 1051. (However, in 1051 Evliya was probably still in the service of Kentenci Ömer Pasha in the Black Sea region; see II 244b.35f. [69f; Hammer, 35f.]) And at IV 344a.1 (426) he claims to have come to Baghdad in Melek's company in 1058. Similarly, at IV 403a.28–29 (not in printed text) he says that in 1059, when Melek was dismissed from Baghdad, "we" spent several hours in the ancient fire temple of Mosul. This apparently contradicts III 51b–53a (138–44), where Evliya gets as far as Aleppo in 1059 (from Syria), then returns to Anatolia. But he affirms several times that he first came to Baghdad in 1059 (IV 348a.3–4, 351a.32, 352b.30, 357a.30 [not in printed text]).

18. II 354a.8 (420; not in Hammer)

19. 366a.28, 32 (453; Hammer, 238)

20. He is called *Melek Ahmed Paşalı Evliya Çelebi* at 374b.1 (477; not in Hammer). Long after Melek's death, when Evliya has an interview with the sultan in 1081/1670, he is introduced as *Melek Ahmed Paşalı Evliya* (VIII 380a.26 [775]); and he identifies himself thus in more than one of his graffiti (see M. Cavid Baysun, "Evliya Çelebi'ye dâir notlar," *Türkiyat Mecmuası* 12 (1955): 257–64). Note also that in a prayer at Mecca for his masters and patrons (IX 345b.19 [752]) the list of patrons begins with Melek Ahmed Pasha.

21. II 374a.33–35 (477; not in Hammer).

22. V 76a.4, Ch. 8.

23. V 79a.32, Ch. 7.

24. They are called *Kaya Sultan yağlığı, Kaya Sultan makraması, destmal-ı Kaya Sultan,* or *Sultanî destmal:* I 192b.margin; II 293a.1, 318b.7, 354b.1, 355b.2,3,7; IV 290a.26; V 50a.31, 51a.30,

64a.1; VI 153a.30; VII 63a.34 (283; trans. Kreutel, 136 and note 2),
73a.2,4 (325), 175b.10 (845); X 183a.3 (391—here [as elsewhere?] for a
type of handkerchief), 399a.17 (858).

25. For a typical example of the period, see I. Metin Kunt, *Bir osmanlı valisinin yıllık gelir-gideri: Diyarbekir, 1670–71* (Istanbul, 1981).

26. For background, see Kunt, *Servants;* Rifaat Ali Abou-El-Haj,
"The Ottoman Vezir and Paşa Households 1683–1703: A Preliminary
Report," *Journal of the American Oriental Society* 94, no. 4 (1974):
438–47.

27. That is, retinue; translating *daire.*

28. *History of Ottoman Poetry* III (London, [1904] repr. 1965),
pp. 344–5.

29. II 328b.13f. (347; Hammer, 191).

30. II 335b.28f. (367; not in Hammer).

31. V 183b.28 (589).

32. V 135a.31f., Ch. 9.

33. Also mentioned at VI 45a.30 (Ch. 10); elsewhere (I 154b.27
[518; Hammer ii, 108], IX 255b.3 [561]) Evliya mentions "a son of Melek
Ahmed Pasha" buried in Damascus.

34. V 186a.2 (597).

35. Evliya: III 98b f. (Ch. 2); Naima, vol. 5, pp. 83–101.

36. *Melek Ahmed Paşa nefsinde halim [ü] selim olduğundan
gayri bunlar teğallub ile sözlerin yürüdürlerdi.* [Katib Çelebi (d. 1657),
Fezleke-i Tarih, ms. Vienna Natl. Libr. H.O.64, fol. 442a.11; cf. printed
edition, 2 vols. [Istanbul, 1286–87), vol. 2, p. 373] Rycaut, p. 13 makes
Bektaş Agha the chief culprit and refers to Melek as "then Prime Vizier,
and yet a slave to the lusts of the *Janizaries.*"

37. Naima, vol. 5, p. 99, line 13: *Melek Ahmed Paşa hiddet ve
sürat-i gazab üzre mecbur idi.* Naima also refers to his quick temper
(acul, acele-i tabʿ) in the colorful incident narrated on p. 61 and again
on p. 91.

38. Eremia Chʿelepi Kʿeōmiwrchiantsʿ, *Oragrutʿiun* (Jerusalem,
1939), p. 20; emphasis added. (Eremya's diary covers the years 1648–
62). The figure 120 agrees with Evliya's at 102a.5f. Naima, vol. 5, pp.
98–99 gives the figure 118.

39. Vol. 5, p. 101.

40. III 103b.7 (284).

41. V 6a.14 (not in printed text).

42. III 103b.17, Ch. 2.

43. III 184b.24. Ch. 4.

44. V 143a.18–24, Ch. 9.

45. V 9a–13b (21–36 [abbreviated]); see *Bitlis*, Part III.

46. IV 215a.30.

47. II 272a.28 (157; Hammer, 81).

48. VIII 329a.32–33 (571).

49. V 78a, Ch. 8.

50. V 78a–b, Ch. 8; VI 45b, Ch. 10.

51. III 143a, Ch. 3.

52. III 175a, Ch. 4; VI 44b, Ch. 10.

53. V 32a, Ch. 7; cf. I 81b, Ch. 1; also III 175b–176a, Ch. 4.

54. III 144a, Ch. 3; V 32a, Ch. 7.

55. For a preliminary survey of the literature, see Cemal Kafadar, "Self and Others: The Diary of a Dervish in Seventeenth Century Istanbul and First-Person Narratives in Ottoman Literature," *Studia Islamica* (1989): 121–50, esp. pp. 130–31; also Orhan Saik Gökyay, "Rüyalar Üzerine," *II. Milletlerarası Türk Folklor Kongresi Bildirileri* (Ankara, 1982), vol. 4, pp. 183–208. For dreams in Islamic culture generally, see the articles gathered in G. E. von Grunebaum and Roger Caillois, eds., *The Dream and Human Societies* (Berkeley, 1966); also T. Fahd, "Les songes et leur interpretation selon d'Islam," *Sources orientales* 2 (1959): 127–58; Barbara Langner, *Untersuchungen zur historischen Volkskunde Ägyptens nach mamlukischen Quellen* (Berlin, 1983), esp. pp. 66–89: oneiromancy. Note Langner's remark (p. 67): "The whole spectrum of religious ideas, personal and political anxieties and hopes of a people at a given point in time is reflected in its dreams. In this respect, it hardly matters for the complete picture of an age which emerges from the mosaic of these dreams, whether they are authentic or made up."

56. V 76a–b, Ch. 8.

THE HISTORICAL SETTING

Rhoads Murphey

While the *Seyahat-name* is essentially a travelogue and *vade mecum* for Ottoman administrators, the passages translated here are written in an autobiographical vein and as a eulogy to Evliya's lifelong patron and friend, Melek Ahmed Pasha. The chronological scope of these segments is relatively short, concentrating on the last twelve years of Melek Pasha's life, between his appointment as grand vizier in 1650 and his death in 1662. A particularly detailed account is given of events in the capital during the short but momentous vizierate of Ipşir Mustafa Pasha during the spring of 1655 (Chapter 4). In this account Evliya provides a panoramic view of the actions of major historical figures, while informing us how these events were perceived by the inhabitants of the city. This is history from the top, but written with an eye to recording the shifting mood of the general populace as well. While the full contents of Evliya's ten volumes give eloquent testimony to the internationalization of Ottoman concerns in the mid-seventeenth century, and although the narrative is peppered with references to Ottoman involvement in far-flung theaters of war in Crete, Dalmatia, and Transylvania, developments on the home front form the principal focus of the narrative in the autobiographical sections of Evliya's work included in this translation. These segments of Evliya's magnum opus are an invaluable source for the study of the Ottoman power structure.

From the dramatis personnae introduced in Evliya's account—some of them celebrities who occupied a place at the center of Ottoman politics, others minor characters, lower-ranking and less visible but nevertheless influential agents, deputies and confidants of the powerful—we can reconstruct the full panoply of Ottoman court life. This permits us to determine who were the real power brokers and who merely figure-

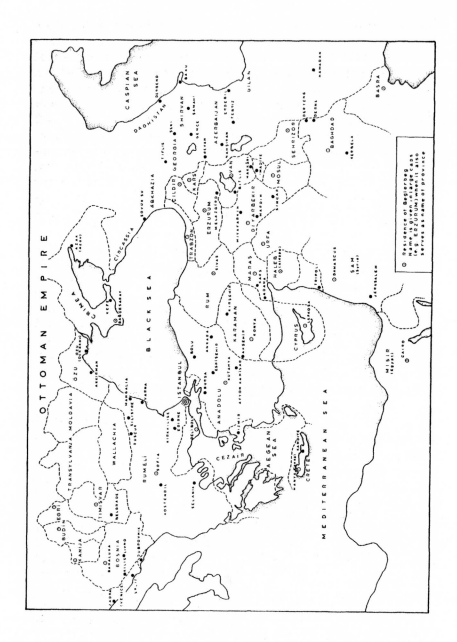

heads, and to penetrate behind the external facade of the Ottoman state apparatus and gauge the strength of the various currents that vied to determine the course it would follow. What was the role played in Ottoman decision making by the deputy's deputy *(kaim makam kethüdası)*? Who was (were) the real power(s) behind the Ottoman throne? Through Evliya's portraits of shadowy figures such as Kudde Mehmed Agha (see Chapters 3 and 4)—described by a later Ottoman historian, Mustafa Naima, as "powerful and wealthy"[1]—we gain an enhanced understanding of the real impetus behind power shifts within the Ottoman bureaucracy. The pressing need to raise funds to finance the war effort in Crete was felt particularly intensely during the early 1650s, and financiers such as Kudde Mehmed were the product of such times.[2]

Evliya's reflections on the current state of the empire have a decidedly partisan ring. Because he populates his narrative with heroes and villains, the modern reader is often left wondering if Evliya has presented the evidence fairly. A case in point is his negative depiction of Köprülü Mehmed Pasha, who was propelled to the head of government in 1656 (see Chapters 8 and 10). Perhaps Evliya felt some resentment at the effective exclusion of Melek Pasha—and, by extension, of all those members of his household, such as Evliya, who had linked their individual fates to the pasha's fortune—from the pinnacle of Ottoman politics during the era of Köprülü dominance. Evliya's views, however, have a depth and complexity that go beyond mere sycophantic praise of his patron, matched by undiscriminating condemnation of that benefactor's rivals.

In point of fact, contemporary opinion was deeply divided in its assessment of Köprülü Mehmed Pasha's vizierate (1656–61). Some authors, in particular the historian Silahdar (d. 1136/ 1723), were in essential agreement with Evliya and characterized the vizierate of the founding member of the Köprülü dynasty as a "reign of terror." Other contemporaries, such as Mehmed Halife (d. 1109/1697) and Abdurrahman Abdi Pasha (d. 1103/ 1692), paint a more flattering and positive portrait of the vizier, while acknowledging that the methods he used to suppress "rebellion" were brutal and ofttimes excessive. This latter group emphasized the positive results of Mehmed Pasha's forceful policies, but even for them his methods remained controversial.

Evliya's own account combines an uncompromising intellectual honesty with a certain lack of objectivity. But it would be a mistake to dismiss the *Seyahat-name* from consideration as a serious historical source simply because its author occasionally indulged in emotional outbursts when he was defending the reputation of his friends and patrons and vilifying their enemies. His partisan remarks enrich rather than distort our understanding of Ottoman realities. Moreover, precisely by recording controversial and deeply felt contemporary opinion Evliya's account achieves its unique standing and value as a source for the study of seventeenth-century Ottoman society and politics.

The Ottoman international and domestic scene in the period leading up to the elevation of Köprülü Mehmed Pasha to the grand vizierate in 1656 was fraught with contradiction and thus eludes easy summary. It is possible, however, to single out several key developments of the period which must have influenced Evliya in the formulation of his views on the Ottoman polity of his day.

The International Scene

From the time of the outbreak of war with Venice over the status of Crete in 1645, the Ottomans' most pressing commitments on the international front were the progress of their naval campaigns in the Mediterranean and developments in a subsidiary theater of war along the empire's land borders with Venice in Bosnia and Dalmatia. The early phases of this war had not been particularly successful for the Ottomans, largely because both the Ottoman regiments (composed of some permanent troops but also many draftees) and the auxiliary forces supplied by Ottoman allies (Crimean Tatars and North African corsairs) lacked the required esprit de corps and unity of purpose. Episodes in this conflict that were either vividly recalled or still current during the vizierates of Melek Ahmed Pasha and Ipşir Mustafa Pasha include the two successive Venetian blockades of the Dardanelles. The first of these lasted for twelve months, from May 1648 to May 1649. The second, involving a far more protracted interruption of the capital's food-supply lines, extended over much of the period between March 1650 and May 1654. In the spring of 1654 the Ottomans succeeded in scattering the Venetian forces in the Aegean, but the success was short-lived. Not until successive campaigns in the summers of 1657 and 1658, securing the islands of Tenedos (Bozca Ada) and Lemnos (Limni), did the Ottomans regain full control over the coastal waters of their own home territories. The Ottoman loss of Klisz (Kilis) and a group of other key frontier garrisons in Bosnia in September 1647 had earlier paved the way for a multipronged attack by the Venetians on Ottoman strategic interests, and prospects for a quick resolution of the conflict seemed remote.

The Ottomans' once dominant position north of the Danube was also under challenge at this time, as Transylvania, in particular, asserted a growing autonomy. The ambition of George II Rakoczy, crowned Prince of Transylvania in 1648, to extend his influence into Poland, which had been weakened by the uprising of the Cossacks under Hetman Khmelnytsky, placed Ottoman diplomacy in an awkward position. With the collapse of the Ottoman-sanctioned Cossack-Tatar alliance of the early 1650s, Khmelnytsky sought the backing of Czar Alexis in a pact signed at Pereyaslav in 1654. Ottoman control in Transylvania was restored by the installation of Michael Apafy,[3] who served an unusually long term as *voyvoda* from 1661 to 1690. But despite later successes in the north, including the establishment of full sovereignty over the region of Kamenets-Podolsk in 1672, the Ottomans never fully compensated for the missed opportunities of the 1650s.

The relative quiet that had prevailed along the eastern frontier with Iran since the signing of an Ottoman-Safavid truce at Kasr-ı Şirin in 1639 gave ample scope for new Ottoman initiatives in Europe. And the major episodes in Melek Ahmed Pasha's career during this period, as outlined in Evliya Çelebi's biography, reflect the actual pattern of Ottoman involvements. Developments in Ochakov/Özü (Chapter 7) and Bosnia and Dalmatia (Chapter 9) were watched closely; and the assignment of a top administrator and veteran warrior like Melek Pasha to these areas (as opposed to his "exile" to Van on the eastern frontier, Chapter 6) is an indication that the Ottomans attached top priority in this period to securing their position along the northern and western frontiers of their empire.

The Domestic Scene

The real source of Ottoman weakness, however, during the 1650s and beyond, lay less in foreign than in domestic problems. The accession in 1648 of a seven-year-old sultan (Mehmed IV, who was to rule until 1687) created the conditions for a prolonged power struggle within the ranks of the state bureaucracy.

Under these conditions, an issue that had already captured the
attention of reform writers in the 1630s—the need for greater
job security for provincial office holders, in particular the *beglerbegis* or governors, and protection against arbitrary dismissal—
was transformed from a topic of mild interest and concern to
one of the burning issues of the day. The revolt of the governor
of Sivas, Varvar Ali Pasha, in 1648 was directly connected with
this issue; and Mustafa Ipşir Pasha, a protagonist in Evliya's
own account,[4] is himself credited with formulating a proposal in
1652 that set a guaranteed minimum term of three years for all
beglerbegis and forbade premature transfers. The uncertain
course of Melek Ahmed Pasha's career in government service,
whose full record is preserved in Evliya's account, provides eloquent testimony to the harmful effects of politically motivated
personnel changes on Ottoman provincial administration.

The case for providing greater job security for provincial
governors had already been convincingly argued by Koçi Beg,
the reformist writer of the 1630s. As long as *beglerbegis* were
not offered security in their positions, he observed, they would
have no incentive to refrain from abusing the peasantry; and he
concluded that, if their security of tenure were ensured, they
would be inclined, both from self-interest and community spirit,
to treat the peasants as solicitously as their own children.

The reduced status, impermanence, and insecurity of provincial office holders were major factors in the steadily deterio-
rating relations between Istanbul and the Anatolian provinces in
particular. The so-called *celali* rebellions of 1591–1609, and
later disturbances in the Anatolian provinces that were essentially identical in character, were related as much to just such
unresolved issues of administrative authority and bureaucratic
control as to the economic factors—subsistence crisis, climactic
change, mounting demographic pressures—to which they are
more commonly ascribed. Evliya's account, focusing as it does
on such administrative issues confronting the empire, provides
a wealth of pertinent material for a fuller understanding of this
crucial period of Ottoman history.

While offering a mine of information on the provinces, the
Seyahat-name also contains many as-yet-unexploited riches for
the social historian of the capital as well. One of the most fasci-
nating aspects of Evliya's account is his depiction of predomi-
nant attitudes in the Istanbul of his day. He records the feelings
not only of the ruling elite but also of the urban masses, whose

colorful and irreverent gibes at their social superiors make very entertaining as well as informative reading (Chapters 2 and 4). He also faithfully records popular prejudices, such as those branding the Istanbul mob as "a fickle and malicious crew" and the Abkhazians as stingy.[5] The attitudes and sympathies of the "man in the street" are further illustrated in Evliya's description of the Istanbulites' reactions to the deaths of their leaders. The spontaneous observance of a three-day mourning period for Kösem Sultan after her murder in 1651 at the hands of the military junta (end of Chapter 2), and their distress at the decease of the popular grand vizier Derviş Mehmed Pasha in 1653 (beginning of Chapter 4), suggest that the common folk were more than passive observers of their predestined fates. Evliya depicts them as politically astute and eager and active participants in the political process.

On most matters Evliya is best left to speak for himself; indeed, it is the evocative power of his historical realism that makes his narrative so appealing today. Two central themes in his biography of Melek Ahmed Pasha do call for some notice: ethics in government; and imperial alliance making and royal marriages.

Ethics in Government

Evliya's account of seventeenth-century Ottoman politics makes oblique reference to this issue, which preoccupied many of his contemporaries. The need for ethics in government became an increasingly insistent theme in Ottoman political writing, beginning with the treatise *Asaf-name* by Sultan Süleyman I's grand vizier Lutfi Pasha. Evliya, in his own role as sultanic adviser and companion *(musahib)*,[6] frequently expresses his revulsion at the moral corruption that flourished at the Ottoman court and his admiration for those who resisted corruption. In Book I of the *Seyahat-name* (68b.29f [243]) he identifies two religious leaders, both of them spiritual advisers to the sultan *(imam-ı sultani)*, as formative influences on his own intellectual development. The first of these, his namesake Evliya Mehmed Efendi (d. 1045/1645), is admired in the standard biographies as a paragon of personal integrity who scrupulously executed the terms of a trusteeship.[7] The second, Yusuf Efendi, served as tutor to Sultan Ibrahim I's sons, three of whom (Mehmed IV, Süleyman II, and Ahmed II) were ultimately to succeed to the throne.[8] Evliya's eulogy of Melek Ahmed Pasha (see end of Chapter 10) is in a like vein; Melek's reliance on "the *ulema*, the pious *şeyhs*, the dervishes, the weak and the poor"—that is, the humble and the community minded, as opposed to the social-climbing coterie with palace connections—earned him Evliya's respect.

Similarly, Evliya's criticism (see Chapter 2) of the high-handed attitude of the sultan's servitors *(hünkâr kulu)*, with their supercilious and unfeeling treatment of the commoners *(halk)*, echoes concerns voiced by contemporary historians. Silent acceptance of such behavior undermined the credibility of the sultan's claim to rule in accordance with a strict standard of justice and equity *(adalet)*. These writers expressed their determination that fundamental tenets of Ottoman administration not be sacrificed to the whims of such self-styled dignitaries, who were themselves no more than coarse upstarts. The general feeling of outrage at the excesses of the palace favorites, in particular the Aghas or high public officials, described in Naima's account of the Dasni Mirza episode of August 1651 (Şaban 1061), is also highlighted in Evliya's narrative. Naima's evocative description of the depressed state of public morale at the height of the "dictatorship of the Aghas" during Mehmed IV's minority gives telling evidence of the rift that had emerged between the rulers and the ruled at this juncture in Ottoman history:

> Although the Aghas [Kudde Kethüda and Bektaş Beg] had already raided all the sources of profit belonging to the state, they were still unsated, but coveted even the poor morsels of the needy. They even dared to interfere with the regime of guaranteed market prices *(narh)*. Thus, while the official price of mutton was eight aspers per *okka*, they raised it to thirteen. In addition, they admonished the sheep drovers throughout the empire to deliver sheep from Erzurum and the other Anatolian provinces, and also from Rumelia and the Moldavian and Wallachian principalities, to the agents dispatched by them from the capital. In consequence, the funds for sheep purchases distributed among the governors and other officials of those provinces were mostly furnished by the Aghas in Istanbul. These funds were exchanged for sheep which were then conveyed—sometimes more dead than alive—to Istanbul where the Aghas disposed of them as they saw fit, keeping the excessive profits all to themselves.[9] They also controlled the flow of Bursa silk and dimity, as well as Chios mastic,

and *halali* cloth, which was forwarded without interruption[10] and by the bailful from Baghdad and Damascus
at the hands of the frontier commanders.

They imposed these goods on the shopkeepers of
Istanbul at a price three times their natural value, and refused to allow anyone outside their narrow circle to participate in this profitable trade. The inhabitants of the city
began to complain about the high cost of bread, meat, and
other basic provisions, but when they submitted petitions to
the authorities, their complaints went unheard. They were
given nonsensical answers instead, calculated to turn their
hearts against the sultan, to the effect that: "This is a city
for the rich, not for the poor; if you can't bear the expense,
go back to your homes in the provinces and content yourselves with cracked wheat and porridge." Others among the
Aghas' devotees—according to the adage, "The emir speaks
truth!"—joined them as accomplices and addressed comments of the following tenor [to the vizier, Melek Ahmed Pa-
sha]: "Your excellency, a pack of country yokels *(etrak)*
abandoned their fields and came to enjoy the delights of the
city where meat and other delicacies were to be had for the
asking. Why should they shy from it now, just because it
costs fifteen aspers? If they don't like it, let them go back
where they came from!"[11]

Incidents such as the Dasni Mirza episode of 1651—
assessed in the light of other basic failures of the government,
such as its neglect of the security of the capital city and its ex-
posing the populace to the effects of the Venetian blockades—
contributed to a confidence crisis of growing proportions. In the
opinion of Evliya and a number of his contemporaries, the credibility gap confronting the sultanate during the 1650s could be
closed only by the resumption of honest government.

For these proponents of ethics in government, statesmen
belonged to one of two classes, the virtuous and the morally corrupt. No one, not even the sovereign himself, was exempt from
being tarred with the brush of these muckraking reformists.[12]
For example, another of Mehmed IV's adviser-companions, the
prominent historian Mehmed Solak-zade (his nickname was
Hem-demi, meaning one who was constantly in the sultan's
company), censured the recently deposed Sultan Ibrahim I for

his unconscionable preoccupation with his personal comfort and luxury at a time when his people were suffering hardship.[13] The same historian praised the sultan's "good vizier" Kara Mustafa Pasha (executed in 1053/1644) for his generous contribution of personal funds toward the building of charitable institutions *(hayrat)* at sites scattered throughout the empire, from the two shores of the capital at Galata and Üsküdar to the Hungarian frontier (Egri) and the far reaches of Anatolia (Sivas-Artukabad and Çorlu-Kuruçay).[14] Similarly, Evliya frequently mentions Melek Ahmed Pasha's charitable institutions, such as those he sponsored in Silistre in gratitude to God for his deliverance from an illness,[15] and in his summation eulogy (end of Chapter 10) he highlights Melek's public generosity along with the abstinence of his private life.

Evliya's caricature of his patron's second wife, Fatma Sultan (beginning of Chapter 10), besides being an entertaining satire on the ways of Istanbul's social elite, also points out by way of negative example the disastrous effects on Ottoman policy of a leadership insensitive to the condition of the poor and unaware of their own obligation to nurture those less fortunate than themselves. Compassion (Ar. *shafaqa*, Tk. *şefkat*) was one of the chief prerequisites for all office holders, according to Islamic principles. Ottoman society was one of self-made men—Evliya's own career amply demonstrates this—but only through universal recognition of an ethic stressing public service, generosity in patronage, and loyalty on the part of the beneficiaries of patronage could such a system become or remain workable.[16] Evliya's insistence on his own incorruptibility—as in his altercation with Melek Pasha's jealous servitors at the end of Chapter 8; or in his fictional but revealing portrayal of Derviş Sünneti in Chapter 4, whom he makes instruct the rowers to "bear witness that I refused to accept the goldpieces and that I distributed them among you, so that the pasha will feel peace of mind, and his heart will be free of any evil suspicion regarding Evliya Çelebi"—should be seen in this light.

Evliya's view on the moral duties and financial obligations incumbent on all holders of high office or prestigious social position is made explicit in the section devoted to the character and accomplishments of Melek Pasha's first wife, Kaya Sultan (Chapter 8). He celebrates Kaya and her husband's generosity to their retainers, and Kaya's munificent benefaction of 20,000

goldpieces on the holy cities of Mecca and Medina. And he exco-
riates the powerful and—in his opinion—morally flawed grand
vizier Köprülü Mehmed Pasha for his confiscatory bent, openly
criticizing him for his morbid avidity and niggardliness and accusing him of ordering the confiscation *(müsadere)* of the de-
ceased princess's worldly goods (some of them her husband's
rightful inheritance) before her body was yet cold.

The public service ethic was such an integral part of the
tradition of Islamic government that, despite their reputation
for despotic and arbitrary rule, even the Ottoman sultans could
not afford to disregard it. Failure to observe the dictates and
conventions of rule in the public interest was sufficient cause to
render invalid the oath of allegiance *(biat)* sworn by high government dignitaries as each new sultan acceded to the thone.[17]
Contemporary readers of Evliya's account would have needed no
reminder of this fact of Ottoman political life, because the
events that had led up to the deposing of Ibrahim I in 1648 were
still fresh in the collective memory.

Imperial Alliance Making and Royal Marriages

The *Seyahat-name* is a uniquely detailed source of information on the character and style of Ottoman royal marriages in
the seventeenth century. Particularly the selections translated
here in Chapters 8 and 10 provide intimate details about the domestic arrangements of the great pashas and imperial sons-in-
law *(damad)* who held top positions in the Ottoman power
structure.[18] The marriage theme forms a natural and recurrent
subject for Evliya to digress on as he weaves his account of the
life of his patron. Melek Ahmed Pasha was twice honored by des-
ignation as imperial consort: first to the child bride Kaya Sultan, daughter of Murad IV, in 1644—by all accounts a love
match—and second to the aging crone Fatma Sultan, daughter
of Ahmed I, in 1662—a kind of shotgun wedding. Though neither match can be considered typical, by comparing the marriage customs of the ruling dynasty in various periods we can
see that seventeenth-century practice differed substantively from
that of earlier eras.

A typical pattern that emerged during the period of rapid
Ottoman expansion in the Balkans was the use of imperial marriage alliances to secure support for the Ottoman cause among

the local dynastic powers in regions with key strategic impor-
tance. Murad I's marriage to Tamara Shishman in 1376 and
successive Ottoman alliances with Serbian royal houses by the
marriages of Beyazid I to Maria Despina in 1390 and Murad II to
Mara Brankovitch in 1435 may all be viewed in this light.[19] Following the return to order after the capture of Istanbul in 1453,
the sultanate achieved sufficient independence and stability to
dispense with such openly opportunistic matches.

   A new pattern in imperial matchmaking that began to
emerge during the first half of the sixteenth century had as its
chief aim securing the undivided loyalty of select members of the
administration while gaining access to their considerable financial and military resources. The malleability of these top-level
bureaucrats was guaranteed by the bonds of filial obligation imposed through marriage to princesses of the royal line. The invi-
tation (actually more a command than a request) to take up a
position as *damad* imposed burdens and responsibilities on the
prospective groom that could never be fully compensated for by
the customary honors and emoluments associated with the office. Holders of the position were judged by the sultan on their
performance both as husbands and statesmen. This new pattern of royal marriage—involving not the sultans themselves but
their dependents, either maiden aunts and sisters or their own
daughters—was regularized during the reign of Sultan Süleyman I (1520–66), in which four of the most influential grand
viziers also had a relationship as *damad* to their sovereign.[20]
The extreme concentration of wealth and power that such
unions brought about is noted with disapproval by sultanic advisers of a later era,[21] but the practice already enjoyed a certain
tenacity deriving from Süleyman's precedent-setting actions.
The elaborateness and expense of the lavish entertainments
staged to celebrate the weddings of the royal princesses,[22] and
the elevation of their grooms to a status nearly equal with their
father's, gave rise to real concern both among political theorists
and the public at large. If the sultan was in general regarded as
the father of his people and "beloved of the country" (*şehriyar*),
these familial feelings did not always extend to his sons-in-law,
particularly when they were perceived to be acting in a need-
lessly wasteful or extravagant manner. One of the character
traits that Evliya and his contemporaries most consistently associated with the "good vizier" was abstinence and avoidance
of ostentation.

Developments in the Post-Ahmedian Era

In several respects the reign of Ahmed I (1603–17) marks a period of bold administrative innovation in the Ottoman empire. The changes in the legal field were especially sweeping. The old Ottoman Legislative Code or *kanun-ı kadim* was subjected to a comprehensive review, and a new legal era was proclaimed with the promulgation of the *kanun-ı cedid*.[23] Sultan Ahmed's "New Code" was the first major revision of Ottoman law since the reign of Mehmed the Conqueror (1451–81) for, despite the attribution of the title *Lawgiver* or *Kanuni* to Sultan Süleyman I, his code was essentially a refinement and codification of earlier legislative activity.[24]

Perhaps the most daring innovation came at the end of Sultan Ahmed's reign when—again for the first time since the reign of the Conqueror—significant changes were introduced relating to the principles of dynastic succession. By effectively eliminating the law of fratricide that had governed the succession for more than a century, the throne was opened up to collateral as well as lineal descendants of the Ottoman house, and Ahmed's eldest son Osman was passed over for the immediate succession in favor of his father's brother Mustafa.[25] Such a departure from past custom was nothing short of revolutionary.

Ahmed also turned to new sources for recruitment into the military services, and Nasuh Pasha, his grand vizier in 1611–14, can take the credit (at least according to Evliya, IV 214b.20; see beginning of Chapter 5) for introducing the new units of Sarıcas and Segbans—composed of Turks, Kurds, and other indigenous Anatolians—to augment the troop strength of the understaffed *beglerbegis* or provincial governors. In a further attempt to expand the personnel reservoir available for assignment to both military and administrative service, the sultan relied increasingly on military slaves *(gulams)* recruited, not from the Rumelian provinces where the *devşirme* or child levy had traditionally been carried out, but from Abkhazia, Circassia, and other regions of the Caucasus.

The long-term effects of such radical departures from traditional administrative practice, first adopted by Ahmed I and continued by his successors, have been considered in a number of scholarly articles;[26] and the transition period has been comprehensively assessed in a recent book.[27] One aspect of change that has been less thoroughly studied is the effect on the character of the sultanate itself of both the broad restructuring in administrative practice and the adoption of new principles of dynastic succession. The exact role that the sultan was being called upon to play in this altered system of government is still understood only imperfectly. Furthermore, any redefinition of the functions of the sultanate implies the need for altering our perceptions of basic traditions, such as decision making through consultation *(müşavere)* with the leaders of the state *(ulu'l-emr)* and the religious authorities or *ulema*, otherwise referred to as *eshab-ı hal ve akd* (lit. "those who loose and bind"), that is, masters of public administration. In what follows we shall address only a minor dimension of the question, and our assessment will fall far short of a comprehensive redefinition.

Among the radical departures from accepted practice first essayed during Ahmed I's reign was to discontinue the venerable tradition of sending out young princes to provincial governorships as part of their training in the arts of sovereignty. This change, combined with the revocation or at least suspension of Mehmed's II's law of fratricide, had the result that the competition for succession, which in earlier periods tended to be confined to the provinces, was now concentrated in the capital. Furthermore, the isolation of the sultan and his government from direct contact with his subjects in the provinces gave rise to an increasing resentment at the disparity between Istanbul, as a center of privilege, and the rest of the empire.

One way to bridge this growing gap and neutralize potentially fractious elements was marriage alliances with members of prominent local or provincial families. An example would be the proposal of a union between the rebel governor İpşir Mustafa Pasha and Ibrahim I's daughter Ayşe in 1655 (see beginning of Chapter 4).[28] Such marriages, by establishing kinship ties with men of wealth and power, also enhanced the power of the sultanate. It appears that concentration of power was a greater motivation than concentration of wealth. As Evliya reminds us in the case of Kaya Sultan and Melek Ahmed Pasha, both parties in these royal alliances usually already possessed considerable independent sources of wealth; generous incomes were bestowed on each of them at the pleasure of the reigning authority, and their union brought about no significant enhancement of these resources or entailment of additional property.[29] Nevertheless, the proliferation of the kind of marriage that instantly propelled the groom to the highest levels of government service exposed the sultan to charges of nepotism. The emergence of a syndrome in Ottoman politics that can be best described as the dominance of the *damads* became increasingly apparent after the reign of Sultan Ahmed I.[30]

Three of Ahmed I's daughters—Ayşe, Gevherhan, and Fatma—contracted multiple marriages that six times during their lifetimes resulted in the promotion of their spouses to the office of grand vizier.[31] A similar pattern is seen in the marriages of the daughters of Ibrahim I (reg. 1639–48), two to grand viziers, three others to admirals of the fleet.[32] Several among this latter group held office during the critical years of the protracted Ottoman-Venetian war over Crete, 1645–69. Such bartering of bride and public office in the same transaction—particularly when the marriages or betrothals were to infant princesses or involved switching partners to make the imperial match possible[33]—was viewed as subversion of accepted norms and strongly criticized.[34] Despite the outspoken criticism of such unusual cases, the practice continued, and we cannot view it as an aberration confined to the reign of Ibrahim I.

The relationship between the sultans and their chief advisers, the grand viziers, had traditionally relied on mutual trust and the expectation of competent performance. Kinship ties greatly complicated this relationship, creating the impression in the mind of the public that the special dispensations enjoyed by the highest class of Ottoman bureaucrats, who were at the same time both viziers and *damads*, amounted to an abandonment of the principle of rule by consent of the governed. A century after Evliya composed his monumental work, the validity of such populist clamorings was eventually acknowledged by sultans such as Mustafa III (reg. 1757–74), who made a conscious effort to restore public confidence in the sultanate (particularly among the rural populations) by public declarations, called *adaletname*, aimed at restoring the reign of sultanic justice.[35] Despite the oft-repeated cliché that the era of the Köprülü viziers (1657–1702) represented a restoration of procedural regularity and bureaucratic order, it seems clear that Evliya's seventeenth-century audience, for whose benefit and entertainment the comical portrait of Fatma Sultan was drawn, still regarded their leaders with some suspicion.

In summary, Evliya's biography of Melek Ahmed Pasha furnishes the reader with a lively and—allowing for creative writing and hyperbole—credible account of Ottoman court life and the life of the households of the great pashas in the second half of the seventeenth century. Evliya provides many intimate details and insights that help us imagine the shape of Ottoman society during that era.[36] And *The Intimate Life of an Ottoman Statesman*—more than previous selections for translation, which have generally focused on a single geographical region—exposes and develops the thematic threads that link Evliya's episodic and, at times, rather disjointed narrative. It is a veritable sourcebook for the study of seventeenth-century Ottoman history.

Notes

1. Naima, vol. 6, p. 60.

2. Naima's assessment is confirmed by archival evidence that indicates Kudde Mehmed's personal fortune at the time of his death included estates in Diyarbekir valued at ninety-five purses or roughly 4 million aspers (see Istanbul, Başbakanlık Arşivi [= BBA], Kamil Kepeci 2468, p. 1). By way of contrast, his contemporary and former patron, the grand vizier Ipşir Mustafa Pasha, left personal property valued at less than one million aspers (see BBA, Maliyeden Müdevver 6597, pp. 28–31, listing property valued at 991,134 *akçe*).

3. Evliya assigns to Melek Ahmed Pasha a (probably exaggerated) role in this event; see VI 12b.8 (56).

4. II 360b–366b (443–54; Hammer, 235–38).

5. See "The Author and His Subject," n. 13.

6. On the duties and prerogatives of the office of *musahiblik*, see I. H. Uzunçarşılı, *Osmanlı Devletinin Saray Teşkilâtı* (Ankara, 1945), p. 75 et passim. Despite the negative remarks directed against the sovereign's boon companions *(nedim, cüce, musahib)* by authors of advice treatises (see in particular R. Tschudi, ed., *Das Asafname des Lutfi Paschas* [Berlin, 1910], pp. 8–9; K. Aksüt, ed., *Koçi Bey Risalesi* [Istanbul, 1939], pp. 20–21), many of the sultans' *musahibs* were highly cultivated and well-trained associates. Evliya's contemporary Solak-zade, for instance (mentioned in the *Seyahat-name* I 152b.5 [509; cf. Hammer ii, 103; and see below] as inseparable from the Sultan) was both an accomplished musician and an author of several books.

7. See Süreyya, vol. 4, p. 158; *Zeyl-i Şakayık* (H. J. Kissling, ed., *Uşaqizade's Lebenbeschreibungen Berühmter Gelehrter . . .* [Wiesbaden, 1965]), pp. 45–47.

8. See Süreyya, vol. 4, p. 656; *Zeyl-i Şakayık*, p. 109.

9. This was a subversion of the usual system, whereby specific quantities of meat were relinquished to meet the requirements of city quarters or communities in accordance with the scale of their respective needs.

10. Understanding *mre* in the text as an error for *merre^ten ba'de uhra*.

11. Naima, vol. 5, pp. 96 (line 12)–97 (line 6) (cf. mss. Paris, Bibl. Nationale, Suppl. 1605, fol. 131b; Istanbul, Topkapı Sarayı, Revan 1169, fol. 541b); cf. Katib Çelebi, *Fezleke-i Tevarih*, 2 vols. (Istanbul, 1286–87), vol. 2, p. 373.

12. For a list of the exemplary qualities of a "good ruler" according to the sixteenth-century moralist *(ahlakçı)* and historiographer royal, Talıki-zade, see C. Woodhead, "Present Terrour of the World?: Contemporary Views of the Ottoman Empire c. 1600," *History* 72 (1987): 27.

13. *Tarih-i Al-i Osman* (ms. Topkapı Sarayı, III. Ahmed 3078, fol. 463b, *sub anno* 1056 A.H.): "His excellency our sovereign being caught up in frivolity and self-gratification *(hava ve heves)* was [completely] unaware of the ruined state of his realm."

14. Ibid., fols. 459a–459b. See the list by Münir Aktepe in *Islam Ansiklopedisi*, vol. 8, p. 738.

15. V 33b.28 (Ch. 7). Other examples at III 119b.35 (337, founding of a saddlery in Silistre), IV 194a.29 (11), 196b.35 (19, repair of Seyyid Battal Gazi *tekye* in Malatya-Aspozu), V 151b.28f. (503, rebuilding of mosque, medrese, primary school, Halveti *tekye*, and bath destroyed by fire in Bosnia-Yayiçse).

16. For traditions of the Prophet enjoining compassion, see A. J. Wensinck, *A Handbook of Early Muhammadan Tradition* (Leiden, 1927), p. 10, s.v. "ADAB." For a discussion of the implications of commensality in the Turco-Ottoman tradition, see R. Murphey, ed., *Kanunname-i Sultani li Aziz Efendi* (Cambridge, Mass., 1985), pp. 52–53, n. 58. For the strong emphasis on communal sharing in both pre-Islamic and Islamic principles governing the moral economy, see also R. Murphey, "Provisioning Istanbul," *Food and Foodways* 2 (1988): 217–19.

17. See El², art. "Bay'a" (E. Tyan).

18. See Alderson, pp. 88–89, 96–99, for a brief and highly schematic overview of royal marriages and an account of the dominant po-

sition held by the imperial sons-in-law *(damad)* in Ottoman political life in the seventeenth century.

19. See Alderson, pp. 166–67 (Tables XXIII–XXIV), 186 (Table LIII).

20. The four viziers in question are Frenk Ibrahim Pasha (grand vizier 1523–36), Lutfi Pasha (1539–41), Rüstem Pasha (1544–53, 1555–61), and Sokullu Mehmed Pasha (grand vizier for Süleyman as well as for his two successors, 1565–79).

21. See in particular the remarks about Sultan Süleyman's daughter Mihrimah Sultan in treatises by Koçi Beg and his contemporaries, cited in R. Murphey, "The Veliyyuddin Telhis," *Belleten* 43 (1979): 551–52, 563–64 (text of Telhis IV).

22. For example, the celebrations held in the hippodrome on the occasion of Ibrahim Pasha's marriage to Selim I's daughter Hadice Sultan in 1524; see the description in Mustafa Celal-zade, *Tabakatü' l-memalik* (P. Kappert, ed., *Geschichte Sultan Suleyman Kanunis von 1520 bis 1557* [Wiesbaden, 1981]), fols. 115b–118a.

23. See EI[2], art. "Ḳānūnnāme" (H. Inalcik)

24. See H. Inalcik, "Süleyman the Lawgiver and Ottoman Law," *Archivum Ottomanicum* 1 (1969): 105–38.

25. Mustafa I actually took the throne twice, once in 1617 when he succeeded his brother, the second time in 1622, four years after being deposed in favor of his nephew Osman, whom he succeeded when the young sultan was murdered in a palace coup.

26. For example, N. Itzkowitz, "Eighteenth-Century Ottoman Realities," *Studia Islamica* 16 (1962): 73–94; M. Kunt, "Ethnic Regional (Cins) Solidarity in the Seventeenth-Century Ottoman Establishment," *International Journal of Middle Eastern Studies* 5 (1974): 233–39; and especially H. Inalcik's indispensable study, "Fiscal and Military Transformation of the Ottoman Empire, 1600–1700," *Archivum Ottomanicum* 6 (1980): 283–337.

27. Kunt, *Servants.*

28. See Alderson, p. 171 (Table XXXVII).

29. On a typical pattern in medieval European marriage alliances arranged by noble families to "increase the possessions of one or both of the partners," see F. Du Boulay, *An Age of Ambition: English Society in the Late Middle Ages* (New York, 1970), p. 184 et passim. It does not appear (at least from Evliya's description) that the match between Melek Ahmed and Kaya was motivated by any such mercenary concerns. Be-

fore Ahmed had ever married, he maintained a personal retinue of 700 military slaves *(gulam, abd-ı müştera)* at his own expense (VI 49a4; see end of Ch. 10). He also spent freely from his own account during the course of military maneuvers and is credited with overseeing expenses of more than 170,000 goldpieces for the maintenance of 7,000 troops during his assignment to the Transylvanian campaign in 1072/ 1662 (VI 44a.16; see beginning of Ch. 10). It should also be remembered that royal marriages such as the one between Melek and Kaya required the groom's payment of a very substantial dowry (V 76b.25; see Ch. 8, n. 8). Such a "downpayment" protected the bride from fortune-hunting suitors and opportunists. In balance, it seems that a fair division of income and assets between the two marriage partners was characteristic of these royal marriages. Alderson's remarks (p. 100), to the effect that the eagerness of the palace to arrange such marriages may have been motivated by a desire to reduce expenses, do not seem consistent with actual practice, at least so far as Evliya's era is concerned.

30. Placing the emphasis on the *damads* themselves rather than on the women who helped them secure their positions helps us avoid the misogynistic terminology that still bedevils the study of mid-seventeenth-century Ottoman politics. The term *kadınlar sultanatı* (Period of the Dominance of the Harem Women)—coined by the early twentieth-century historian Ahmed Refik and referring especially to the reign of Ibrahim I (1639–48) and the first decade of the reign of his successor Mehmed IV (1648–78)—retains its currency even today. (See A. Refik, *Kadınlar Sultanatı*, 4 pts. [Istanbul, 1914–24] and its sequel *Samur Devri* [Istanbul, 1927].) The ultimate source of this antifemale prejudice are opinions voiced in the traditional historiography by authors expressing their moral outrage at aberrant or unusual practices, such as the infant marriages of Ibrahim's daughters and Ibrahim's own contracting of an unprecedented fourteen marriages. The nearly universal contempt for such practices, and a general sentiment rejecting the extravagance, luxury, and licentiousness of Ibrahim's court, are expressed by contemporary historians. (See Solak-zade, *Tarih-i Al-i Osman*, fol. 465a; Naima, vol. 4, pp. 270–72; *Evza-ı garibeden biri . . .* ; Katib Çelebi, *Fezleke-i Tevarih*, vol. 2, p. 323: *Evza-ı garibeden biri . . .* ; Karaçelebi-zade Abdülaziz, *Ravzatü'l-ebrar* [Cairo, 1248], p. 625, *sub anno* 1054, relating the marriage of Ibrahim's three-year old daughter Fatma to the *silahdar* Yusuf Pasha.) These assessments, reflecting broader public opinion, recorded by seventeenth-century historians have been transmitted virtually unchanged to our own time. Viewpoints concerning the unwelcome meddling of women in the affairs of state as expressed by Refik (d. 1937) are not easily distinguishable from the sentiments recorded by Naima two centuries earlier. The most recent accounts of the role of the palace women in Ottoman poli-

tics are essentially biographical (e.g., Çagatay Ulucay's three-part work on the harem, published serially between 1956 and 1980; and Yılmaz Öztuna, *Osmanlı Hareminde Üç Haseki Sultan* [Istanbul, 1988]). In sum, it is fair to say that no in-depth analysis of the role of women in this era of Ottoman history has yet been attempted. Some recent scholarship, however, indicates that the "old school" analysis that once dominated the field is now finally being eclipsed; see L. Pierce, "Shifting Boundaries: Images of Ottoman Royal Women in the 16th and 17th Centuries," *Critical Matrix* 4 (1988): 43–82.

31. See Alderson, p. 169 (Table XXXIV). Ayşe's most illustrious partners were Nasuh Pasha (grand vizier 1611–14) and Hafız Ahmed Pasha (1625–26, 1631–32). Gevherhan held the record among her siblings by her betrothal to three grand viziers: Öküz Mehmed Pasha, Receb Pasha, and Siyavuş Pasha. And Fatma was wed (her fourth marriage) to the former grand vizier Melek Ahmed Pasha in 1662. Fatma Sultan, who died sometime after 1667 (the date of her sixth marriage), was still a presence in Ottoman politics half a century after her father's demise. According to Evliya (VI 32a.26 [103]) Melek was promoted to the post of deputy grand vizier *(kaim makam)* in direct consequence of his royal marriage. However, this may be Evliya's exaggerating of his patron's accomplishments, as it is not mentioned in other sources (see *Silahdar Tarihi*, vol. I, pp. 256–57; *Hadikatü'l-vüzera*, pp. 91–93; Abdi, *Vaka-name* [Istanbul U. ms], fol. 54b).

32. See Alderson, p. 171 (Table XXXVII), recording marriage of Beyhan to Hezar-pare Ahmed Pasha (grand vizier 1647–48); Ayşe Sultan to İpşir Mustafa Pasha (1654–55); Atike, Fatma and Gevherhan to various Kapudan Pashas (chief admirals).

33. The most notorious case of this was Hezar-pare Ahmed Pasha's divorce of Handan-zade-kızı to become the imperial consort of Sultan Ibrahim's daughter Beyhan. Following the divorce, Handan-zade-kızı became one of the sultan's own wives. Such treatment was considered particularly inappropriate in her case because she belonged to a very distinguished family; for an account of some of her forefathers' achievements, see Süreyya, vol. 2, p. 310.

34. See n. 30 above.

35. For a general assessment of Mustafa III's reform efforts, see Mücteba Ilgürel, "Türkler (Osmanlılar): XVII. asır," *Islam Ansiklopedisi*, vol. XII, pp. 321–42 (esp. p. 331); Yücel Özkaya, *XVIII. yüzyılda Osmanlı Kurumları ve Osmanlı Toplum Yaşantısı* (Ankara, 1985), pp. 186–89, 395 (notes 93–113). The latter source describes prevailing conditions in the provinces during the 1740s and 1750s that prompted the issuance of justice decrees. For a selection of passages from these

adalet-names, see also Y. Özkaya, "18. yüzyılda çıkarılan adaletname-lere göre Türkiyenin iç durumu," *Belleten* 38 (1974): 445–91.

36. Cf. G. Duby's classic study, *The Three Orders: Feudal Society Imagined*, trans. A. Goldhammer (Chicago, 1980).

A NOTE ON
REFERENCES, SOURCES,
AND ABBREVIATIONS

References to books I–VIII of the *Seyahat-name* are to the autograph ms. as follows:

Bağdat 304 books I and II   Revan 1457 book VI
Bağdat 305 books III and IV   Bağdat 308 books VII
Bağdat 307 book V   and VIII

References to books IX–X are to

Bağdat 306 book IX   IÜTY 5973 book X

Other page numbers (without a or b) refer to the Istanbul printed text, ten vols. 1886–1938 (references to the first six volumes, which have no scholarly value, are solely for the purpose of orientation).

The sources of the translated sections are as follows:

1. The Reign of Mehmed IV

I 79b.2–81b.9 (277; Hammer, i, 152) Mehmed IV's viziers
   83a–86a (287–99; Hammer, i, 157–63) Wars and conquests during Mehmed IV's sultanate

2. The Vizierate of Melek Ahmed Pasha

III 95b.27–104b.18 (255–89) Vizierate of Melek Ahmed Pasha; appointment to Özü
   116b.30–117a.23 (326–29 Rusçuk and Istanbul: Kaya Sultan intervenes for Kudde Kethüda

3. Governor of Rumeli

143a.27–145a.24 (408–15) Sofia: storks and crows; illness, dream, and cure

4. The Vizierate of Ipşir Pasha

173a.1–185b.27 (491–534) Vizierate of Ipşir Pasha; a Bektaşi dervish; appointment to Van; Kaya's miscarriage; Kudde's torture

5. Governor of Diyarbekir

IV 214a.8–215b.20 (65–68) The Yezidi Kurds of Sincar

6. Governor of Van

235b.27–236b.1 (125–27) Bitlis: Melek Pasha's admonition to Abdal Khan
265a.7–265b.19 (210–13) The Bitlis expedition: Melek's fortitude in adversity; an attempt on his life
266a.5–266b.24 (214–17) His prayer and "inspiration;" a skirmish
267a.32–267b.10 (219–20) His dream of the ants
271a.25–272b.7 (232–35) His disposition of the prisoners; Evliya begs for lives
V 9a.10–15b.32 (41–42) Melazgird: Evliya's dream
16b.18–19a.19 (45–53) Erzurum: Melek gets a prisoner released; meeting with Zurnazan Pasha

7. Governor of Özü

29a.16–29b.20 (84–86) Varna: a cossack raid
31b.13–33b.34 (93–102) Mangalia; illness, dream, and cure
53a.7–64a.32 (172–218) Akkirman; dream and aftermath; Özü and Istanbul

8. Kaya Sultan

75b.13–78b.19 (255–66) Dreams; Kaya's death

9. Governor of Bosnia

78b.23–79b.34 (267–72) Appointment to Bosnia
135a.31–137a.12 (451–58) Livno; dream and aftermath; Vasil the bear
143a.10–143b.7 (477–78) Cetina: an attempt on the Pasha's life

10. Fatma Sultan

VI 43a.24–49a.22 (137–46) Marriage to Fatma Sultan; a Bektaşi dervish; Melek's death; eulogy

The following works are cited frequently according to abbreviation:

Alderson	A. D. Alderson. *The Structure of the Ottoman Dynasty.* Oxford: Oxford University Press, 1956; repr. Westport, Conn., 1982.
Bitlis	Robert Dankoff. *Evliya Çelebi in Bitlis.* Leiden: Brill, 1990.
Bobovi	C. G. Fisher and A. W. Fisher. "*Topkapı Sarayı* in the Mid-Seventeenth Century: Bobovi's Description." *Archivum Ottomanicum* 10, 1985 (1987): 5–81.
Danişmend	Ismail Hami Danişmend. *Izahlı Osmanlı Tarihi Kronolojisi,* III. Istanbul: Türkiye Yayınevi, 1961.
Diyarbekir	Martin van Bruinessen and Hendrik Boeschoten. *Evliya Çelebi in Diyarbekir.* Leiden: Brill, 1988.
EI²	*Encyclopedia of Islam, New Edition.* Leiden: Brill, 1960–.
Hammer	Joseph von Hammer, trans. *Narrative of Travels . . . by Evliya Efendi,* I, i–ii; II. London, 1846, 1850.

Kreutel   Richard F. Kreutel. *Im Reiche des goldenen Apfels.* Graz: Verlag Styria, 1957.

Kunt, *Servants*   I. Metin Kunt. *The Sultan's Servants: The Transformation of Ottoman Provincial Government 1550–1650.* New York: Columbia University Press, 1983.

Naima   *Naima Tarihi,* 6 vols. Istanbul, 1281–83/1864–66.

Rycaut   Paul Rycaut. *The Present State of the Ottoman Empire . . . ,* London, 1668 [repr. 1972].

Süreyya   M. Süreyya. *Sicill-i Osmani,* 4 vols. Istanbul, 1893.

TRANSLATION

1

THE REIGN OF
MEHMED IV (1648–87)[1]

(Among the viziers of Mehmed IV was Melek Ahmed Pasha.) He was born in Tophane in Istanbul. When he reached the age of three he was sent to the——tribe in the country of the Ab-khazians, where he was raised by his wet nurse. At age fifteen he was presented, along with my mother, to Sultan Ahmed. Melek was consigned to the pages of the harem, while my mother was given to my father, and from their union I was born.

Melek Ahmed Pasha's father was Öz-demir-oğlu Osman Pasha's marshal of the guards. He accompanied him during the campaigns of Gence, Şirvan, Şamaki, and Derbend,[2] and he died at the advanced age of 140.

As for Melek, he became Murad (IV)'s sword-bearer and personal companion. On the day of the conquest of Baghdad (in 1638), he was given the governorship of Diyarbekir province, with the rank of vizier. He subsequently held all the Ottoman high offices—some of them three or four times each—with the exception of Cairo and Budin.[3] Finally, having become an old and experienced and pious statesman, he was made grand vizier (in 1650).

During his vizierate he sent 3,000 *sipahis* to Deli Hüseyn Pasha on Crete, awarding him the registry office (making him *defterdar*) and awarding Bıyıklı Mustafa Pasha the rank of vizier with one horsetail. With these reinforcements, and with the imperial Mediterranean fleet that he outfitted and whose like had never been seen, the commander-in-chief Hüseyn Pasha was able to rout those venereal Venetians and conquer Selina and Retimo castles. Messengers arrived at the Porte to announce these glad tidings.

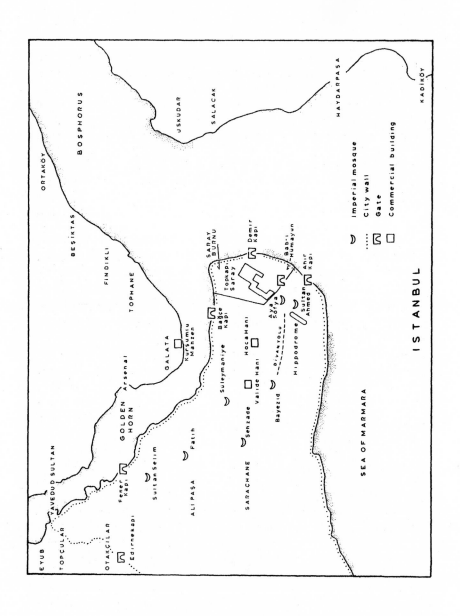

ISTANBUL

The following year he appointed Hüsam-oğlu Ali Pasha chief admiral, outfitting another imperial fleet. It consisted of 300 galleons and galleys, recalling the fleet of Kılıç Ali Pasha.[4] In the evening after the first engagement, when the infidels were put to flight, the imperial fleet anchored in the harbor of Karafoçalar, and the troops all disembarked to carouse in the gardens and the vineyards. At dawn, while most of the troops were on leave and those who were on board were fast asleep, the infidels made a surprise attack and set fire to the entire fleet. Those troops that had remained on board now disembarked, taking forty of the galleys and eleven of the galleons in tow. Our other galleons continued to do battle and managed to destroy twenty of the infidel ships.

When word arrived that the fleet had been routed, each ship fleeing in a different direction, the pasha offered to surrender the seal, but he was reprimanded by the felicitous Padishah and confirmed in his office. He made it a rule to restore to the Bab-ı Hümayun the 700 purses paid annually as stipends to the viziers.[5]

Reason for the dismissal of Melek Ahmed Pasha:[6] The garrison in Azov castle mutinied, killing their aghas and some of their officers (çorbacı) and sent messengers to the Porte demanding their salaries. It being impossible to forward the funds by sea in the winter season, he planned to convert the 300 purses of piasters into gold and send it overland via couriers, first to Crimea, thence to Azov. So he levied the 300 purses upon the merchants and tradesmen of Istanbul. At the same time, the *defterdar* Emir Pasha and Kudde Kethüda and the customs inspector Hasan Çelebi dumped on the tradesmen some items that had been confiscated by the treasury, such as Diyarbekir cotton cloth, red and yellow morocco leather, and druggist's alum, forcing them to pay the market price.

Suddenly one morning, a cry of "Allah Allah!" rose up from the hippodrome and all the tradesmen assembled armed before the Bab-ı Hümayun, demanding justice from the Padishah upon the *defterdar* Emir and the vizier's steward Kudde Kethüda and the customs inspector. When the outcry reached the imperial ears, the Padishah sent three times for Melek Pasha who, fearing the violence of the mob, refused to come. At last the marshal of the palace guards, Ibrahim Agha, and the chief of the pages, came and insisted that he should either respond to the imperial summons or else give up the seal. The pasha immediately com-

plied, handing the seal over to the marshal of the guards, along
with a hundred purses of gold and a sable pelisse for each of
them. He was awarded the province of Silistre. Having been removed from office on the———of Ramazan in the year———[7] he
halted at his palace known as Topçular outside Istanbul.[8] . . .

(Vizierate of Bıyıklı Derviş Mehmed Pasha)[9] By God's wisdom, he suffered a paralytic stroke and was bedridden for six
months, during which time, although he kept the seal, Melek
Ahmed Pasha served as his deputy in the *divan*.[10] Finally, find-
ing no remedy for his paralysis, he died in the year———[11] and
Melek Ahmed Pasha once again became master of the seal. But
after a consultation of all the *ulema* and other worthies, which
lasted for seven hours, on the suggestion of Ahmed Pasha himself, it was resolved that the seal should be sent to Ipşir Mustafa
Pasha in Aleppo. He was a clansman and kinsman of Abaza Pasha who turned *celali* in Erzurum.[12] During the Revan campaign (in 1635) he served as Sultan Murad's stable master. He
subsequently held many of the highest posts, earning a name
for himself when he defeated Varvar Ali Pasha.[13]

The seal having been sent off, Melek Ahmed Pasha served
as deputy vizier in the capital, actually governing as though he
were grand vizier. Ipşir accepted the seal when it arrived, but
instead of proceeding to the capital he tried to stir up trouble on
the Persian frontier, sending orders to (the chiefs in) Kurdistan
to do something contrary to the truce. In this way he raised a
force of a hundred thousand men. He sent a message to the felicitous Padishah that the Kızılbaş had revolted. The Padishah,
for his part, paid no heed to this, but arranged for him to marry
Ayşe Sultan, who was left widowed by Voynuk Ahmed Pasha, and
sent him noble rescripts along with the marriage announcement, insisting that he come to the felicitous threshold.

Left with no choice, Ipşir Pasha put his trust in God and
proceeded to Istanbul, taking seven months to cover the stages
of the journey. Once he reached Üsküdar he halted and refused
to go to the Padishah. The chief black eunuch and the *şeyhülislam* Ebu Said Efendi were sent to Salacak in Üsküdar, thence to
Ayşe Sultan's palace, where they presented Ipşir Pasha with a
sable fur and a jewelled dagger, and invited him to the felicitous
threshold in the name of the sultan. Hinting to his captain
(*bölük-başı*) to detain as hostages those who had come out to
greet him—including Melek Ahmed Pasha, Koca Nişancı Pasha,

Dellak Mustafa Pasha, Defterdar Moralı Mustafa Pasha, and several of the *ulema*—he proceeded via the *bostancı-başı's* caique to Saray Burnu, where he had an audience with the felicitous Padishah. Having been awarded some sable pelisses, and after some discussion, he crossed back over to Üsküdar and ordered a hundred (sheep) to be sacrificed.

The next day, however, he again refused to cross to Istanbul and in fact was about to return to Anatolia. That day the janissaries, who had come out to greet him for the grand procession, all fled back in terror to Istanbul, and the chief admiral, Murad Pasha, moored the imperial barge in the arsenal.[14] At last Ipşir Pasha was prevailed upon to board the imperial barge and cross to Istanbul, along with 80,000 of his soldiers.[15] They paraded in grand procession from Eyub, through Edirne Kapı, to Ayşe Sultan's palace. From there he went to see the felicitous Padishah.

"My Padishah," said Ipşir, "the reason it took me seven months to come to the Porte was that I had to deal with the Kızılbaş uprising. You must confer the province of Van upon your *lala* Melek Ahmed Pasha. That region requires an experienced and noble statesman, one who has held the office of grand vizier."

"O *lala*," replied the noble Padishah, "it is not proper to cast out such an old and meritorious vizier to such a poor province."

"No, my Padishah, it is a fine province. I myself was governor of Van once. It has twenty-seven *sancaks*, and an annual income of a hundred thousand piasters."

"All right, I grant it," he said, and commanded the diploma to be drawn up.

Ipşir-i bi-şir[16] immediately returned to his palace and had one of his chief guards and ten *çavuşes* convey the Van orders. As soon as the pasha read the imperial *ferman*, he kissed it and raised it to his head, saying "To hear is to obey." He awarded the Agha with three purses of piasters and a sable fur, and the ten *çavuşes* with fifty piasters each.

They insisted that he cross to Üsküdar immediately, but the Pasha just as firmly refused to step out the door. He spent the next five days in Istanbul making preparations for the journey. On the fifth day Ipşir went to the sultan and said: "My emperor, your *lala* Ahmed Pasha has disobeyed your order and has not gone off to Van. He must be put to death."

The Padishah immediately sent a *hasseki* summoning Melek Pasha into the imperial presence. After greetings the pasha remained standing. *"Lala,"* said the felicitous Padishah, "I bestowed on you the province of Van. Why don't you go?"

"Once my Padishah has bestowed it, how can I not go? Upon my soul, even if it were a two-house village, I would go."

"My *lala* Ipşir was once governor of Van. It has an income of a hundred thousand piasters."

"Telling a lie is forbidden in the presence of Padishahs and in all the religions. I will tell your *lala* to his face. When this *lala* of yours, Ipşir Pasha, arrived in Van with 150 men, they closed the gates and would not let him in the fortress. They drove him off, branding him as a tyrant. In fact it is an isolated frontier outpost, which cannot even support 200 men. Including perquisites, the revenue scarcely amounts to 7,000 piasters. He is sending me to that province to insult me, and he has misinformed my Padishah about it."

The Padishah immediately called for pen and ink and drew up a noble rescript, appointing (Melek Ahmed Pasha) governor of Van at the rank of commander-in-chief, having power of appointment and dismissal over all high posts in the Anatolian provinces, from Üsküdar as far as Cairo, Baghdad, and Erzurum. As travel expenses he gave him five purses of gold, a hundred files of camels, a hundred files of mules, and one Solomonic tent pavilion. And he gave him a sable robe of honor. "March forth," he said, "may God ease your way, my commander and vizier, with authority to draw the *tuğra*. In the near future, God willing, I intend to mount an incursion in those regions along with my *lala*."

Hearing this, Ipşir Pasha's face turned ashen grey, he was like a zombie. Melek perfunctorily kissed the ground, cried benedictions on the Padishah, and without returning to his palace, boarded the *bostancı-başı's* caique at Saray Burnu, and accompanied by his retinue on a 150 caiques, went straight to Kaya Sultan's garden in Üsküdar. He halted there for a full week to make preparations for our journey. As the Pasha was entering Van in grand procession, after a march of 117 days, a guard named Yıldırım arrived like lightning *(yıldırım)* and informed us that Ipşir Pasha had been killed. . . .

(Second vizierate of Siyavuş Pasha) The first thing he did was to recall Melek Ahmed Pasha from Van. He sent noble orders, and long letters, (urging him to come as quickly as possible to) the felicitous threshold, "so that we can be together—let us be together!"

We got from Van as far as Erzurum, with some difficulty, in the dead of winter, and were obliged to hole up there for a time. By God's wisdom, Siyavuş Pasha had become gravely ill in the capital, and after————days, had died. They accused the *defterdar*, Defterdar-zade Mehmed Pasha, of killing Siyavuş Pasha by having an En'am (Koran, *sure* 6) recited for him.[17] So that noble statesmen was unjustly strangled by those tyrants. It was in Erzurum that we heard of the death of those two viziers, and the appointment of Boynu-egri Mehmed Pasha to the grand vizierate.

In the year————the seal was sent from the capital to Boynu-egri Mehmed Pasha in————.[18] Meanwhile Haydar-ağa-zade served as deputy vizier. Orders reached Melek Ahmed Pasha in Erzurum from Boynu-egri inviting him to the capital. After Boynu-egri had entered the capital in grand procession, Haydar-ağa-zade was appointed governor of Özü. Melek Ahmed Pasha, arriving soon after, had an audience with the felicitous Padishah, and took his seat among the viziers in the *divan*. That very day a noble rescript was sent out concerning Haydar-ağa-zade, and he was put to death in Silivri castle while on his way to Silistre. Boynu-egri thereupon awarded his province, free and clear, to Melek Ahmed Pasha. But when we reached Hacı-oğlu Bazarı (we learned) that Boynu-egri had lost his office because of avarice.

In 1067 (1656) Köprülü Mehmed Pasha was made independent grand vizier. Since the Ottoman state was in turmoil, he killed 400,000 *celalis* in Anatolia, 17 viziers, 41 *begler-begs*, 70 *sancak-begs*, 3 mollahs, and a certain Moroccan cabbalist[19] named Şeyh Salim. He balanced the revenues and expenditures of the Ottoman state, erasing three years of arrears and also accomplished several conquests.

Among the astrologers and the cabbalists, this Köprülü was known as *sahib-huruc*.[20] They discovered the following ominous utterance of Ali, and applied it to Köprülü Mehmed Pasha:

> *Ka'b ismuhu Cisri*
> *Ve-beyne ḫalḳ ismuhu Küfri*
> *Ve-min-'inde' llāhi ḳuṭb aḳṭāb veli ṣaḥīḥ*

The name Ka'b and Mehmed both add up to ninety-two; and Cisri denotes Köprülü.[21] . . .

*   *   ·   *

(Among the wars and conquests during the reign of Mehmed IV:) Defeat of Dasnik Mirza, together with the *celali* Hanefi Halife, in the year————.[22]

Because he was not awarded the aghaship of the Turcomans, he became offended with the grand vizier, Melek Ahmed Pasha, and having gathered a large troop, set out from Üsküdar to raid and plunder Anatolia. They did raid a caravan that they encountered after crossing the Sea (of Marmara) at Hersek Dili. Then they set up camp between the towns of Lefke and Söğüt. The troops of Melek Ahmed Pasha, Bektaş Agha, the janissary agha Kara Çavuş, and the *kul-kethüdası* Çelebi Mustafa Agha caught up with them there and, toward dawn, carried out a surprise attack, crying "Allah!" and striking with their swords. Although taken by surprise, they fought bravely, unhorsing quite a few champions on the vizier's side. But in the end they were overcome and put to the sword, the survivors fleeing into the mountains.

Their swinish commander, Dasnik Mirza, and Hanefi Halife, along with————of their men, having been taken captive, were being conveyed to the Porte. But when they reached the place known as the *bostancı-başı's* bridge, an imperial order arrived. So they were all put to death on that spot, and their heads were made to roll before the Bab-ı Hümayun. That night, by God's decree, a light rained down upon the head of Hanefi Halife—hundreds of people witnessed it. And seventeen days later there was a general uprising, (with cries of) "Allah Allah!" Melek Ahmed Pasha was removed from office and awarded the governorship of Özü. . . .

Defeat of the flotilla of the cursed cossacks, in the fortress of Varna, at the hands of Melek Ahmed Pasha, in the year 1061 (1651).[23]

The ill-omened Ukrainians *(Rus-ı menhus)* set out to raid the walled towns of Varna and Balçık, and landed in the town (of Varna) with seventy *şaykas*. But Melek Pasha's troops, who had arrived there previously, made a surprise attack on the infidels' boats, which were beached on the shore, and captured twenty of them. The other boats put out to sea, leaving all the infidels stranded. Melek Pasha gave battle to those devils and rounded them all up in the hills and the valleys. Seven hundred of them he took captive; 1,000 he dispatched with the sword; and more than a thousand drowned. . . .

Defeat of the Khan of Bitlis, Abdal Khan, at the hands of Melek Ahmed Pasha, in the year 1065 (1655).[24] Such a great battle never before occurred in the province of Van.

Rescue of Özü castle, at the hands of Melek Ahmed Pasha, in the year————.[25] This is a strong fortress on the cossack frontiers, situated where the Dnieper runs into the Black Sea. It was occupied by the cossacks and was rescued at the hands of Melek Ahmed Pasha after a long battle, which will be recorded below.

Defeat of the accursed *tabur* of King Rakoczy, in the province of Poland, at the hands of Mehmed Giray Khan, together with Melek Ahmed Pasha, in the year————.[26] . . .

In the year ————[27] Seydi Ahmed Pasha was appointed to Transylvania as commander-in-chief, and the province of Bosnia was awarded to Melek Ahmed Pasha. . . .

In the year————,[28] when the news reached the sultan that the Venetian infidels had raided the province of Bosnia, he appointed Melek Ahmed Pasha, who was then the governor of Bosnia, to serve as commander-in-chief and to attack the castle of Zadra. . . . In this year I went to our lord Melek Ahmed Pasha, reaching him below Livno castle, and I was honored with his company. Here, too, I participated in a number of *gazas;* but if I were to recount them all, this digest (*fihris*) would turn into a lengthy scroll. Eventually, on Monday, 12 Rebiülevvel 1071 (15 November 1660), Melek Ahmed Pasha was transferred to Rumeli province.[29] . . .

(At Fogarasch in Transylvania)[30] Our lord Melek Ahmed Pasha was assigned Belgrade as his winter quarters. While carousing there he was married off (in absentia) to Fatma Sultan, the daughter of Sultan Ahmed, and an imperial *ferman* arrived (informing him of this and) ordering him to proceed immediately to the capital.

After being conducted to the nuptial chamber, Melek Ahmed Pasha served for three months in the *divan* before he died in the year————.[31] He was buried in the Eyub Sultan cemetery, at the foot of his master Kiçi Mehmed Efendi. And this homeless Evliya was left orphaned. God is generous!

Notes

1. The translations from Book I preserve some of the wording in Hammer's mid-nineteenth-century rendering, while correcting the errors and filling the lacunae. Throughout the translation, gaps are indicated by three dots (. . .); blanks in the original text by dashes (————). Parentheses are used for transitional or explanatory phrases provided by the translator.

2. The reference is to the Caucasian expedition of 986/1578; it is described in more detail at VI 46b (see Ch. 10).

3. Hammer mistranslates: "and having held the governments of Cairo and Budin." The Istanbul printed text (p. 277) makes the same error: *üçer dörder kerre Mısır ve Budin'de mutasarrıf olup.*

4. Kılıç (~ Uluc) Ali Pasha, chief admiral under Murad III, conquered Tunis in 982/1574.

5. Cf. Naima, vol. 5, p. 60, describing a fiscal crisis during Melek's tenure as grand vizier when he suggested that all of the viziers' stipends *(has)* be cut, saving the money for the treasury. At this time the viziers' stipends ranged between twenty and thirty purses (ibid., p. 61); one purse *(kise)* = 40,000 aspers *(akça)*; the term *vizier* included all office holders, both current and retired, with that rank (cf. n. 10 below).

6. Cf. Ch. 2.

7. 4 Ramazan 1061 (21 August 1651).

8. Note Evliya's description of this palace at I 117b.7 (392; Hammer ii, 30).

9. Cf. Ch. 4.

10. Lit. "under the dome" *(kubbe altında),* referring to the domed chamber in Topkapı Saray where the grand vizier met several times a week with the "viziers of the dome," the chief officers of the state who were members of the *divan,* including the *kadı* of Istanbul, the *defterdar,* the *nişancı,* the Agha of the janissaries, the commander of the *sipahis,* and the chief admiral of the fleet (Kapudan Pasha). See EI², art. "kubbe wezīri."

11. His vizierate lasted from 21 Rebiülahir 1063/21 March 1653 to 16 Zilhicce 1064/28 October 1654.

12. Abaza Mehmed Pasha defied the sultanic authority for six years (1032–38/1622–28) as governor of Erzurum; cf. Evliya's account

at I 64a.32–67a.2 (230–38; Hammer i, 122–27), II 286a.2f. (206; Hammer, 109). Ipşir was his nephew.

13. Governor of Sivas (Rum province), turned rebel in 1058/1648 when Sultan Ibrahim ordered him to send ahead the beautiful wife of Ipşir Pasha, then governor of Kütahya (Anadolu province). Ipşir himself was sent to put down the rebellion, and he had Varvar beheaded. Cf. Evliya's account, II 360b–366a (443–52; Hammer, 235–38; both greatly abridged).

14. In his fuller account at III 178a.15f. (Ch. 4), Evliya says that this occurred on the previous day, before Ipşir's interview with the sultan.

15. A huge exaggeration.

16. A playful epithet, meaning approximately: "lacking the milk of human kindness."

17. See V 17a.6 (Ch. 6, n. 23).

18. The appointment was made on 2 Receb 1066/26 April 1656 when Boynu-egri Mehmed Pasha was governor of Damascus.

19. *Ceffar*, a specialist in *cefr* or onomancy; cf. III 176a.9 (Ch. 4, n. 28).

20. Lit. "master of going forth." *Huruc* was a term used for the rise to prominence and independent authority of an upstart, whether negatively (rebel) or positively (conqueror, founder of a dynasty).

21. See V 32a (Ch. 7) for an explanation.

22. 1061/1651; cf. III 99a.15f. (Ch. 2).

23. Cf. V 29a.25f. (Ch. 7).

24. Cf. Ch. 6.

25. 1068/1657; cf. V 60a (Ch. 7).

26. 1067/1656; cf. V 42b (135–37).

27. 1069/1659; cf. V 78b.25 (Ch. 8).

28. 1070/1660; cf. V 137a.12 (457–58).

29. Cf. V 135a–165a (Ch. 9).

30. Cf. VI 28b.20 (92: omitted).

31. 1072/1662; cf. Ch. 10.

2

THE VIZIERATE OF
MELEK AHMED PASHA
(1650–51)

[Undertakings on behalf of the Crete campaign, etc.][1]

A thousand such incidents occurred during the vizierate of
our lord Melek Ahmed Pasha. Most were well-planned and executed, but a few were ill-advised. Because he consulted with the
janissaries *(ocak halkı)*, the wants of the army of Islam were
supplied, the salaries were paid three months in advance, and
there was prosperity on every side. If I were to detail all the
events of his vizierate day by day, I would require a separate volume. Suffice it to say that he remained on good terms with everyone. He himself was mild and gentle, and in his service he
kept men of Aristotle-like wisdom, upstanding and foresightful.

His close companions and advisors included such fine men
of sterling character as his deputy, Kudde Mehmed Kethüda,
from Çermik in Diyarbekir; the great memorandum official *(tez-
kireci)* Gınayi Efendi; the small memorandum official Zühdi
Efendi; the treasurer Ahmed Agha; the seal keeper Osman Agha;
my predecessor Imam Efendi; and the head of the chancellery
Mevkufati Mehmed Efendi.

As for his exterior *(taşra)* servants: as *defterdar* he removed Zurnazan Mustafa Pasha and replaced him with Kırk-
çeşmeli Emir Pasha—in this he was ill-advised, because Emir
Pasha was a greedy, stupid, and negligent man; he made Koca
Ibrahim Agha *çavuşbaşı*—he was a hypocrite and a troublemaker, and used to make the rounds currying favors; as court
usher he appointed Kuska-fırınlı Mustafa Agha from the janissary corps—he, too, was suspicious and hypocritical.

But he was on splendid terms with Bektaş Agha, Kara Çavuş, and Çelebi Kethüda, also with the *şeyhülislam* Bahayi
Efendi. He always consulted with them about affairs and acted
according to their advice.

Concerning the Results of Ill-Advised Action: Reason for the Removal from Office of the Grand Vizier Melek Ahmed Pasha

The initial reason was this: At the time of Sultan Ibrahim
(1640–48) the Turcoman agha, Abaza Kara Hasan Agha, captured a brigand named Kara Haydar-oğlu and (brought him to
the capital) in chains.[2] And at the beginning of the reign of Sultan Mehmed (IV, 1648–87), as part of the *"gaza"* of that sultan,
the aforementioned brigand was strung up at Parmak Kapı, at
the hands of Hasan Agha. As a reward for freeing the Anatolian
provinces of this scourge, Kara Hasan Agha, by royal decree, was
granted the aghaship of the Turcomans in perpetuity for the remainder of his life. Each year he renewed the imperial warrant,
and he deposited the office dues in the imperial treasury. He enjoyed independent authority in this position.

When our lord Melek Ahmed Pasha became grand vizier,
Kara Hasan paid the office dues of seventy purses and renewed
the warrant. Then he took his leave of our lord Melek Ahmed
Pasha, crossed to Üsküdar where he gathered a troop, and was
about to leave to reassume his office of Turcoman agha. But
Bektaş Aghas of the janissary corps along with the janissary
agha Kara (Çavuş), the *kul-kethüdası* Çelebi (Agha), and the Pasha's deputy Kudde Kethüda conspired to take away the aghaship of the Turcomans from Hasan Agha. They give it to Ak Ali
Agha in exchange for 100 purses on the grounds that it was the
time of salary disbursals.

Immediately Abaza Kara Hasan Agha crossed back over
from Üsküdar with 300 loyal and life-risking braves and landed
at Ahır Kapı. He left a hundred men with the caiques and
headed for the pasha's palace with 100 makeshift horsemen.[3]
Meanwhile poor Kudde Kethüda was in attendance with the
grand vizier's private secretary Behceti Efendi. When it was
announced that Abaza Hasan Agha had arrived, there was a
great commotion in the palace, and Kudde Mehmed Kethüda
lost his wits.

Kara Hasan Agha went straight to the pasha. He was ashen
grey. "Look here, my sultan, my dear efendi," he began. "You

took my seventy purses as office dues. I have gone to great expense. And for a long time the aghaship of the Turcomans has been mine by royal decree. Is it fair of you to treat me with such contempt, and to give me a bad name? Are we not clansmen?"[4] And he broke down weeping.

"Hasan Agha," answered the pasha, "let it go for this year. I was under great pressure to give it up. For now I'll give you a hundred purses in place of your seventy. Just be patient for this year."

"I know who is to blame," said Hasan Agha. When he came out he saw Kudde Kethüda. "Look here, Kudde," he cried, "may God not accept my soul if I let you get away with this!"

Kudde Kethüda replied in his Diyarbekir dialect, "Whichever stone is hard, strike your head on it,"[5] and went on to upbraid him roundly. Hasan Agha bared his dagger, grabbed Kudde Kethüda by the collar, and was about to kill him when the others rushed over and separated the two of them.

As Kudde was going in to the pasha to complain, Hasan Agha shouted: "Kudde! your Circassian boy's filth be on my so-and-so[6] if I let you get away with this." He ran downstairs, got on his horse, and undaunted, hastened back to the caïques at Ahır Kapı, and immediately crossed over to Üsküdar.

It was soon bruited in government circles that he had rounded up the sipahis in all of the barracks.[7] At Kudde Kethüda's instigation, Bektaş Agha and the janissary agha and Çelebi Kethüda went to the pasha and pressed for Hasan Agha's head: "He is a rowdy and a brigand, a source of sedition, and deserves to be executed. You had better kill Hasan Agha immediately;[8] otherwise neither you nor we nor the Padishah nor the city of Üsküdar will be left standing." Willy-nilly they obtained a noble rescript condemning Hasan Agha, and the small memorandum official Zühdi Efendi, the imperial sword-bearer, and the captain of the Porte cavalry regiments were preparing to carry out the order. But one of Hasan Agha's friends got word to Üsküdar, and Hasan Agha took flight. This humble one was accused of being the one who sent the warning—but I solemnly swear, by God and the Prophet, that I hadn't the slightest inkling of the matter. The pasha had a wardrobe keeper named Abaza Parmaksız Sefer Agha—he, too, belonged to our mother's clan—and he was the one who warned Hasan Agha to flee. So those people who went to kill Hasan Agha did not find him, and returned disappointed.

Hasan Agha got to Izmid over the mountains in a single day by a forced march. After turning back all the paid cavalry troops he had 1,000 horsemen. By the time he reached Bolu this number had swollen to 3,000. And by the time he reached Osmancık he had an army of 5,000. After joining forces with Ipşir Pasha, the number of their troops was 40,000 or 50,000. They sent a message to the Porte demanding the execution of the *kul-kethüdası*, Kara Çavuş, Kudde Kethüda, the *defterdar* Emir Pasha, and several others indicated by name. An imperial rescript arrived ordering these to be put to death. "I'll give up the seal," said the pasha, "but I won't order these people to be put to death unjustly." And he lay crouching in his lair.[9]

Concerning a Great Catastrophe in the Middle of Şaban 1061 (Beginning of August 1651)

After the flight of Hasan Pasha, Ak Ali Agha was afraid to assume the aghaship of the Turcomans, and the office went vacant. Now two aghas of the *sipahi* corps—Hanefi Halife and Dasnik Mirza[10]—being veterans in state service, had been named candidates for the aghaships of Boz-ulus, Kara-ulus, At-keşan, and Üsküdar of the Turcomans. To obtain a crust of bread (i.e., a livelihood) they were using coercive measures, and several hundred purses of theirs had passed into the public treasury. Nevertheless they were constantly stalled and put off. Finally they, too, feeling frustrated and fearing for their lives, one night disappeared from Istanbul, crossed over to Üsküdar, and took flight.

At this, Bektaş Agha and the janissary agha and the *kul-kethüdası* came to the pasha and said: "These, too, are rebels and *celalis*. Be warned, my sultan; give them no quarter, but put them to death and confiscate their property; or else they might join forces with Ipşir Pasha and Hasan Agha, and this would complicate matters enormously. You must put them to death!"

The magnanimous pasha replied: "With their wealth (having passed into the public treasury), they are a band of servitors (to the state) and unprejudiced Muslims, men of honor and without greed. How can we kill them contrary to the *şeriat*?"

"You must kill them or you will suffer the consequences."

"My good men! Have you learned nothing from the example of Hasan Agha? Even after he had put seventy purses into the public treasury, you took him from the office he had been awarded in perpetuity and gave it to someone who did not deserve it. Now this one is afraid to assume it, and so an imperial service is going vacant. Thus you have turned one man into a *celali* in plain view. What do you want from this Hanefi Halife? By God, soon I too will get burned in your fire! But you will all burn and turn to kebabs."

They got offended at the pasha and went out.

Meanwhile Dasnik Mirza and Hanefi Halife got wind (that they were in danger) and immediately set forth from Üsküdar with 600 mounted men. They made a forced march to the landing at Dil and crossed the Gulf of Izmid in a single night, intending to head for Aleppo and join forces with Celali Hasan Agha and Ipşir Pasha. Word of this reached the pasha, and all sorts of rumors started to fly. The janissary aghas, as soon as they were apprised of these melancholy events, came storming to the pasha demanding that poor Hanefi Halife and Dasnik Mirza be put to death. Reluctantly the pasha signed the memorandum, and an imperial decree was issued ordering their execution.

At once an army was readied, including 200 of Bektaş Agha's men, clad in armor and mail and mounted on Arab thoroughbreds; 300 armed men from the janissary agha Kara Çavuş, mounted on Cilfidan (Arab thoroughbred) steeds; 500 doughty warriors from Çelebi Kethüda, jereed-throwers and reckless braves; and 700 Abkhazian, Circassian, and Georgian soldiers from our pasha, all of them battle-tried and true—a formidable troop! In addition 500 armed braves were assembled from the imperial sword-bearers and *sipahis*, making a grand total of 2,500 light, mounted, hand-picked, sword-thrashing, bloody-eyed soldiers. Abdullah Pasha, protégé of our lord Melek Ahmed Pasha, with his 500 picked Kurdish braves, was put in command. And yours truly, who at that time was still quite spry, along with my eight trusty *gulams* mounted our zephyr-swift steeds and, with the pasha's leave, joined Abdullah Pasha and the rest of Melek Ahmed Pasha's soldiery.

All 3,000 troops embarked at Istanbul in rowboats, caiques, and lighters, and crossed to Üsküdar in a single night. From there we proceeded by forced march to Gebze and pushed on to cross (the gulf) at Dil in one day. At Derbend we inquired of the local inhabitants about Hanefi Halife. They reported that he had come through there with 700 horsemen two days previously, had purchased with aspers two days worth of fodder for the horses as well as food and drink for themselves, and had gone on, intending to hole up in the mountains. On the way they turned back the paid cavalry troops, and were now proceeding, gathering an army as they went.

When we heard this report, as though getting wisdom from Lokman,[11] we cried: "He must be nearby; let's catch up with him before he gathers more verminous troops!" So we pressed on past Derbend and came to the walled town of Iznik. There we purchased two nights of fodder and other provisions and continued by forced march, putting our trust in God. But several hundred of the sleek Arab horses belonging to Bektaş Agha and the janissary agha's troops were overcome by the heat and the forced march; so quite a few men had to stay in Iznik or in the mountains looking after their mounts.

The rest of us, having passed Iznik, were foraging in a meadow when we learned from the passers-by that over 1,000 men had bought provender at Lefke and were on their way toward the town of Söğüt. "Hurry, mount!" cried the marshals. We pressed on past the town of Lefke and now received word that they were camped between Lefke and Söğüt, next to a rice field just to the east of an open plain named Ahmed-beg-çeşmesi, some in the forest, some in the plain with their tents and their muleteers.

As soon as we received this intelligence, our commander Kara Abdullah Pasha mustered the troops and conferred with the officers. It was decided to attack an hour before dawn, and a Fatiha was recited.

At midnight we all rose and set out at a leisurely pace, the army following the scout. I joined the forward skirmishers and our party reached the appointed spot well before the appointed hour. We could make out a sizeable camp of seventy or eighty tents and pavilions. Someone was sent back to report, while we skirmishers moved on ahead. But, because it was still too dark to see clearly, we stopped a little ways off to rest our horses and wait for the remainder of the troops and the appointed hour.

A few of us who had geldings went a bit closer, as your gelding will not neigh and whinny like a stallion and warn the enemy. As we approached unnoticed, we could see that everyone was sleeping peacefully under a tree, sounding slumber's trumpets and dreaming like the seven sleepers of Ephesus. Some were in their tents or out in the open, but most were lying in a covert.

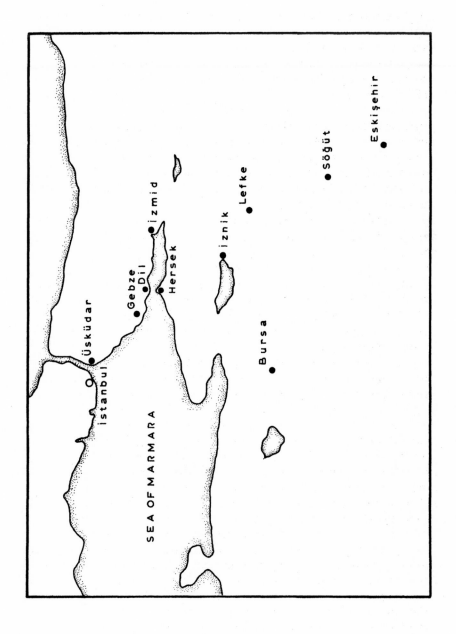

Eskişehir

Söğüt

İzmid

Lefke

Dil
Gebze

İznik

Hersek

Üsküdar

Bursa

İstanbul

SEA OF MARMARA

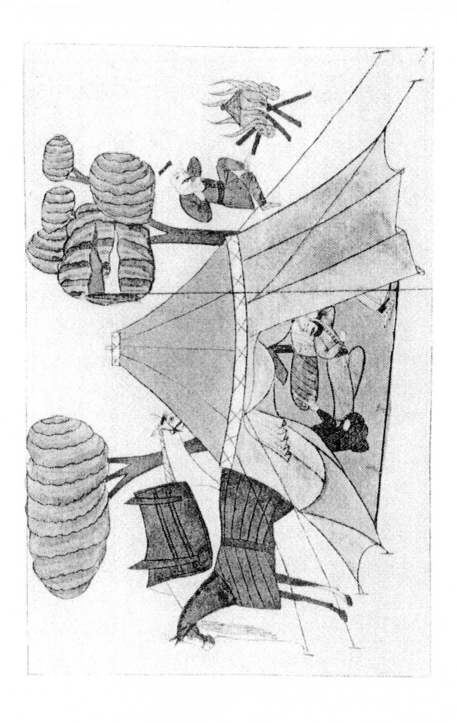

A Marvel

Only there was one brave youth who had risen early. Not yet dressed, he was busy grooming his horse and, in this pleasant meadow, was singing in melancholy voice and to the Beyati measure (makam) the following quatrain:

> *Eyle mi halim felek*
> *Dil bilmez zalim felek*
> *Kesipsen can bağçesinden*
> *İki nihalim felek*
> *Ey felek, ey felek*[12]

> Is this my state, O fate?
> Deaf and dumb, cruel fate.
> You've cut from the garden of my soul
> Two sprigs, O fate.
> O fate, O fate.

Thus he complained of fate in a most philosophical manner. I was quite astounded and wished that things would turn out the best for this young man. Then he sang another quatrain:

> *Baba ki ta bilesen*
> *Ohu ki ta bilesen*
> *Bunda bir iş etgilen*
> *Sinde yatabilesen*

> Until you are with father,[13]
> Until you know the arrow,[14]
> Perform a deed here;
> You can lie down in the grave.

And another:

> *Leleniñ dünyası ne*
> *Aldanma dünyasına*
> *Dünya menim diyeniñ*
> *Gitmişdiñ dün yasına*

> What is Lele's world?
> Be not deceived by his world.
> He who said "The world is mine"—
> You went to mourn him yesterday.

These were the quatrains he sang in heart-rending fashion, weeping the while.

Then he called out to his friend who was sleeping beside him: "Hey, Ali Can, get up! You're sleeping too long. It's nearly morning. All the birds and beasts, sheep and men rise at dawn and pray while the gates of heaven are open. Some pray for this world, some for the next. Get up, you good-for-nothing, let's the two of us pray for martyrdom. Come on, you son of a bitch, get up!"

"May it be auspicious, Veli," said his friend, who was now awake. "I was just having a dream. There was a lighted candle in my hand. You took the candle from my hand, blew it out, and struck me on the head with it. I thought you had split my head open."

"May it be auspicious," the first youth replied. "I couldn't sleep well either, so I got up and groomed my pony. You had better saddle up too, it's nearly morning."

Aside from these two, no one else of their company was awake. Our own group of seven or eight listened attentively to this conversation, then returned to our skirmishing party and reported the quatrains we had overheard. We also sent word to the main body of troops that these people were lying here quiet and oblivious.

As soon as dawn broke our troops came up at a gallop, without looking backward or forward. They rushed right past us crying "Allah Allah!" and fell on that band of sleeping soldiers, toppling all their tents on their heads, and lashing out. Caught unawares, they ran off helter-skelter into the forest, naked and wailing, with our troops slashing them at the heels with their swords.

Now when the attack began, these two youths—the melancholy one who was grooming his horse and singing quatrains, and his friend who woke up and told his dream—had clapped their swords to their waists, mounted their horses bareback, and cut down three of our men each. They certainly were brave warriors! But Melek Ahmed Pasha's Kürd Haydar Agha galloped over and martyred both of them. It is a marvel and a mystery that the one sang, "Two sprigs you've cut from the garden of my soul," and the two of them were killed; and the other one dreamed that the candle he was holding was extinguished and struck on his head, and now his dream had come true: the lantern of his spirit was extinguished, and his head was struck off!

In short, on this bloody field, as the night raiders were making heads roll with their swords, and batting them like polo players with their clubs, it turned out that those two aghas, Hanefi Halife and Dasnik Mirza, had foresightfully set up their tents in the plain and put their gear in the field, while they themselves were lying in ambush, with all their braves fully armed, in the surrounding thickets and forests. Now, while their scullions and muleteers were being butchered in the camp and their tents and pavilions were being pillaged, they crept out of their lairs in the mountains and, as the sun rose, 7,000 or 8,000 fully armed mounted troops came rushing upon us from seven sides like wounded lions rushing out of their dens. They, like raging lions, let out the cry, "Allah Allah!" We on our side also cried, "Allah Allah!" And so the two armies of Islam, both yelling "Allah Allah va-veylah!" joined in the melée, attacking like so many seven-headed dragons.

Hanefi Halife urged on his soldiers crying, "Come on my wolves!" and, bareheaded as he was, knocked over seven or eight men in the battlefield. He had so many arrows sticking out of him, he looked like a hedgehog; but apparently he was protected by his body armor, and his horse had armor as well. Also their horses were rested, while ours were jaded from being ridden for the past two days and three nights and being fed only once each day, so some of them betrayed their masters. The rear of our army was just pouring in and, like a rabble troop, had not yet mustered, while of our forward troops fifty-three men of name had fallen in the first onslaught.

Now Melek's Deli Dilaver Agha rushed upon Hanefi Halife at full gallop and gave him such a mighty Ipşirian blow with his spear that it penetrated his armor, passed through his thigh and stuck in his horse's flesh. The horse reared and withdrew to the side. Immediately Hanefi Halife's companions rushed to his aid and brought him a spare. Meanwhile one of their braves unhorsed our Siyavuş Dilaver Agha with a lance. Dilaver Agha continued shooting arrows on foot until he could rejoin our troop and remount.

Again one of theirs struck our Melek's Deli Şahin Agha with a javelin, so that the point stuck out his back a length of two spans. He managed to rejoin our troop, and they removed the javelin and bound the wound. Now our Elvend Agha unhorsed two of theirs.

By this time the battle had begun to get heated, but—God be praised—not a single musket had yet been fired on either side. Everyone wished to display his manliness; everyone was moved to deeds of valor.[15] God knows that they had been caught by surprise and, with this mighty resistance, our side was about to be victorious. By now, however, the sun was a spear's height above the horizon. Bektaş Agha's and the janissary agha's troops coming up from the rear—God damn them!—found all sorts of excuses for staying back. Some had to tighten their horses' girths; some had to perform the dawn prayer. Also their horses were exhausted. They did wish to display some sort of zeal, so they let out a trumpet blast toward Hanefi's side and began to fire their muskets.

It turned out that Hanefi's side also had 300 Segban dogs[16] drawn up in the forest. They returned the fire, wounding and killing seventy-six of Melek's and Bektaş's and Kara Çavuş's men. Now the battle was becoming heated. The commander, Abdullah Pasha, rallied his *sipahi* soldiery who had come with us, crying: "Come on my wolves!" But what use was all the crying and shouting? Hanefi Halife and Dasnik Mirza were also *sipahis*. Do *sipahis* clash swords with *sipahis*? Those *sipahi* vermin just stood there like lumps. The commander kept shouting at them, "Come on *gazis!*" but they fought only with glances. Then they spurred their horses and started to turn back, with their red and yellow banners fluttering.

"*Gazis!*" cried our commander Abdullah Pasha. "We are 3,000 men; they are 1,000 at most. I know your horses are tired, but why don't we try just once?" He also went over to the janissary Kethüda Çelebi Agha's troops, who were coming up slowly from the rear and were still unbattered, and addressed them: "*Gazis!* What will we tell our lords? Come on, let's attack those *celalis* just once as though we really meant it. May it turn out for the best! Throne or fortune!"

The *celalis*, meanwhile, took advantage of these parleyings and emerged out of the forest in full force. Bektaş's and Kara Çavuş's troops made a beeline to the other side of the hills. But those of Melek and Çelebi Kethüda and Silihdar Sipahi joined forces and charged neck-and-neck, crying: "Allah Allah!" Our skirmishers, too, found new life and came swarming over the corpses, with the marshals sounding their drums and everyone encouraging his fellows with cries of "Come on *gazis*, it's the Day of Kerbela, come on!" God be praised, the breeze of victory seemed to be blowing in our direction. Our men all turned into seven-headed dragons, thirsting for enemy blood. They urged each other on, crying: *"Gazis!* ⬛t's exact blood-vengeance on these *celalis* for our martyrs lying there."

While the others were carrying on their butchery, this humble slave was standing at the foot of Abdullah Pasha's banner, reciting the noble *sure* of Victory (Koran, *sure* 48). What should I see? One of my *gulams* had been mounted crosswise on his horse and was being brought to my side. I forgot all about Victory; in fact I nearly lost my wits. Nothing, whether saddle, sword, or scimitar, was left on the horse. The *gulam* lifted himself a bit and then expired. I secured the horse, consigned the *gulam* to the earth, and resumed the noble Victory *sure* at the foot of the banner; though it seemed to me I was reciting the verse "We belong to God and to Him do we return" (Koran 2:156). Presently I recovered my wits. "Judgment is God's," thought I; "What else is in store?" So I spurred on my horse and joined the fray, performing several deeds of derring-do.

To make a long story short, seven times they attacked us and we attacked them. The battle raged furiously for three full hours. Such courageous and skillful[17] fighting had not been seen since the battle of Azov.[18] But by now, because we had been fighting since an hour before dawn, their horses as well as ours were quite exhausted. As they began edging over toward the hills, our troops took advantage of the situation and renewed the attack. The enemy fled into the sparsely treed forest crying: *"Ormanos keres."*[19] Dasnik Mirza's deputy and his twelve aghas of name and twelve aghas of the interior service fell into the hands of Çelebi Kethüda and were dispatched without ceremony. Once again the *celalis* mustered their energy and struck out from the forest; but when they saw that another seventy of their number had been cut down, they decided emphatically on flight. Our men chased after them and returned with their spears adorned with enemy heads. Bringing these trophies to the commander, they all received handsome rewards and were ordered each to preserve his head.

As we were celebrating this victory, what should we hear but the cry "Allah Allah!" rising again from the hills. Out of curiosity our troops headed into the woods. As it turned out, the regiments of Bektaş and of Kara Çavuş had earlier gone around to the rear of the forest; and, as the fugitives from Hanefi Halife and Dasnik Mirza's troops headed for the hills, they ran into them and began to do battle, raising the cry "Allah Allah!" Now our Melek's troops joined forces with them.

What should we see next but Dasnik Mirza and his forty-six followers being led this way, bound and chained.

"Hey, what about Hanefi Halife?"

"There he is, fleeing."

"He's wounded. Catch up with him!"

Melek's troops galloped off in pursuit and caught up with him in half an hour. So they brought him, too, with his thirteen men, all bound and chained, before the commander.

Until noon there was a continual stream of heads and "tongues" (captive informants) being brought in. Finally we pitched the *celalis'* tents and piled together their effects to serve as booty. We camped ourselves next to the corpses of our martyrs and the dead *celalis.* A day's halt was ordered, and messengers were sent off to the Porte with tidings of victory. Our horses and our *gazis* hadn't a spark of energy or an ounce of strength left. Nevertheless, by order of our commander, our troops mounted the 800 horses taken as booty and, doubling up with their own horses, set off in pursuit of the fugitive *celalis.*

Meanwhile, Kara Abdullah, the commander marked out for victory, immediately drew up orders *(buyurdı)* addressed to the twelve *kadis* (in the vicinity, including those) of Iznik, Lefke, Sögüt, Eskişehir, and Seydi-gazi, ordering them to capture the *celalis* and bring them bound and chained to the Porte. The chief doorkeepers were sent off on the double (to deliver these orders).

Now all the peasants (in the vicinity) who had been hunting game in the hills took the occasion to engage in the manhunt, on the grounds that a general levy had been announced, and for the next twenty-four hours they kept bringing bound captives before the commander—ordinary people, wearing felt caps on their heads, stripped naked, with hands tied and livers branded.

We buried our 170 martyrs on the battlefield, on either side of the main road near Ahmed-beg-çeşmesi. A hundred and forty-six wounded men were attended to by surgeons and loaded onto carts or stretchers. And the 600 *celalis* who were killed—or martyred, from their point of view[20]—were strung out under the trees of this pleasant meadow, adorning the plain like the Tree of Vakvak, so the ground seemed to be decked with mandragora roots.[21] Some had been cut in twain with a single blow, others struck down by the point of a spear, some had been carved to pieces, others split diagonally from shoulder to hip leaving head and arms flying; some had been split down the middle from skull down to waist, others slashed at a slant; some had been shot down with lead, others struck by an archer's arrow, which passed through them like a tailor's needle through satin. In these various ways did they meet their fate, according to God's eternal will. And so we derived a lesson from this battle even greater than at Azov or Canea.[22] It was a marvel, a divine mystery.

For these dead we had peasants dig fifteen pits on either side of the main road and filled them all up to the brim, and their heads were stuck as trophies on our spears. As booty we got 800 horses, a good deal of money, tents and pavilions, and equipment; and quite a few of us got swords, scimitars, chain mail and armor, helmets, muskets, shields, clothing and heavy baggage, and lovely *gulams*. But they had no camels and only twenty files of mules.

In two days we marched triumphantly as far as the place known as Dil, bringing in our train 140 men as informants (*dil*, lit. "tongues") and 70 heads from (prisoners captured in the surrounding) districts. We loaded the informants and all the booty onto boats, crossed (the Gulf of Izmid) at Dil and halted at Gebze. Thence we proceeded to the place known as the *bostancı-başı's* bridge near Üsküdar, where we received a noble rescript from our lord Melek Ahmed Pasha at the felicitous threshold: "You are the commander, Abdullah Pasha: when my noble order reaches you, put to death all of the *celalis* whom you hold captive and convey their misfortunate heads to the Gate of Fortune."

When this imperial command was read out, the soldiers gathered at the bridge head began to grumble. "We have enough heads—may the vizier's head dry up! Let's take all these heads and go directly to Istanbul. Why should we slaughter these miserable creatures? This is manifest injustice."

There was a huge outcry. But Abdullah Pasha said: "I will kill all of these men in accordance with the imperial command."

At this the entire body of *gazis* rushed upon the pasha and cried with a single voice: "We won't massacre a poor band of homeless wayfarers who have been separated from their wealth and their means of livelihood and their honor. We'll bring them to the Porte and hopefully each one will be saved by some means or other."

In the end the commander acceded to the plea of several of the notables. Some of the men were concealed in the vegetable gardens; some were kept hidden in the reed beds below the *bostancı-başı's* bridge; some were disguised and allowed to depart; others were mounted on horses in *sipahi* uniform and brought to Üsküdar, escaping that way. Six of them were requested of the commander, through one pretext or another, by this humble servant Evliya, full of fault, and I set free all six.

The plea on behalf of Dasnik Mirza and Hanefi Halife was not accepted, however. They together with forty-six of their men were lined up along the bridge. Dasnik Beg and Mirza Halife [sic] uttered the witness formula. Then Hanefi Halife said: "O God, in this affair Melek Ahmed Pasha was under constraint, he is quite without fault. O Sovereign and Subduer: You have made manifest in me Your name of Subdual,[23] and from eternity the pen of Your decree has written it on my forehead. My hope from You, Sovereign and Subduer, is that very soon You will kill those who are the cause of my being killed." Uttering a *besmele* and the witness formula,[24] he turned to face the *kıble* and said, "Now take back Your trust, my Lord."

At this point a certain brigand named Ali the Cook bared his sword and was about to raise his hand, when Hanefi Halife rose to his feet and gave that Ali the Cook such a kick that his goose was cooked[25] and his soul left him on the spot. Immediately our commander's sword-bearer—a veritable fool—while mounted on his horse struck Hanefi Halife with his sword. Because his hands were tied, the blow caused him to fall to the ground on his face. All the soldiers could see, plainer than day, that although he had fallen on his face he directed himself toward the *kıble* and was lying on his back! The soldiers gasped in amazement, and some of the sensible ones took to their heels.

Now it was Dasnik Mirza's turn to be cut down. The poor fellow did not say a word. The other forty-six braves were allowed to utter the witness formula one by one, then their heads were cut off and their bodies were buried at the head of the bridge. The heads were conveyed to Üsküdar, thence to Istanbul, where all 814 of them were mounted on spears and paraded from Bağçe Kapı to the sublime *divan* and past the felicitous Sultan Mehmed Khan Gazi. There they were deposited on the ground, to the cry: "Thus at your imperial stirrup may the heads ever roll of those who betray religion and the state!" Finally they were removed to the square in front of Bab-ı Hümayun, where they were trampled in the dust like polo balls beneath the hooves of the passersby.

By God's wisdom: that very night in front of Bab-ı Hümayun, as witnessed and affirmed by several personages of the religious orders, a light descended three times upon the felicitous heads of Hanefi Halife and Dasnik Mirza. The same night, several hundred of the heads were removed and only 100 were left at Bab-ı Hümayun. Also that night, just within Fener Kapı in Istanbul, the infidel quarters known as Bektaş Agha's barracks collapsed. Again that same night small fires broke out in three different places. Quite a few such signs and portents appeared. The gunpowder mill in Macuncu also caught fire.

Reason for the Removal from Office of Melek Ahmed Pasha: Uprising of the Tradesmen

The first reason was his ill-advised and unjustified execution of Hanefi Halife and Dasnik Mirza. The pasha and his followers daily lost favor in the eyes of the janissary aghas and the Istanbul populace. An ominous cloud settled over them.

The second reason was that in the year———the fortress of Azov at the extremity of the Black Sea was besieged by the Cossacks and Muscovites, the Potnaks, Yunaks, and Boynaks.[26] Mehmed Giray Khan[27] managed to escape from Azov while it was under siege by the infidels, and his forty-seven regiment commanders sent calls for help to the effect that "our grain stores and munitions and allowances and provender have run out; we have not received our salaries for a year; if our appointed ration does not arrive we will surely be routed in our straightened circumstance, and we will have to abandon Azov fortress." When their pleas arrived, Melek Ahmed Pasha conferred in grand council with the veteran ministers. The result of their deliberations was this:

If we sent the grain stores and munitions and fodder by sea they would run the risk of storm. Also the Black Sea has been overrun by Azov cossacks and Özü cossacks who are patrolling it with 200 caiques. It is difficult to send reinforcements to Azov (directly; instead) we will order Ibrahim Pasha, the governor of Kefe province, to send the stores and munitions, which can easily be transferred from

Kefe to Azov. As for the salaries: we will remove 70,000 piasters from the imperial treasury, distribute these among
the tradesmen, collect (in exchange) Şerefi goldpieces at the
rate current in the grand market,[28] and send these with
forty-five couriers to the *beg* of Kırk-kilise.[29] He will convey
them to the vizier of Özü, who will give them to the *beg* of
Özü, who will give them to the Crimean Khan. The Khan,
for his part, will bring them to Azov with 5,000 or 10,000
Tatar knights. Documents and reports confirming their arrival will be forthcoming in twenty-five days.

They affirmed that this was the best plan, and sealed it
with the recital of a Fatiha.

So they removed 70,000 piasters from the imperial treasury and gave notice to the tradesmen and their *şeyhs* and
deputies. But certain treacherous efendis in charge of the government, including Kudde Kethüda, the *defterdar* Emir Pasha,
the customs inspector Hasan Çelebi, and Moralı Mustafa Çelebi,
exchanged those 70,000 piasters from the treasury for clipped
and base Moralı (Morea) aspers and gave these to the tradesmen.
What is more, Kudde Kethüda, being from Çermik in Diyarbekir, dumped seventy camel loads of crimson Diyarbekir cotton
cloth and goldsmiths' alum and Kayseri yellow morocco leather
on the guilds, demanding three times their value in return. Also
they demanded gold from the bazaar merchants at the rate of
1 goldpiece for 180 of the clipped aspers or for 120 of the small
aspers.

The tradesmen elders came to the private *divan* of our lord
Melek Ahmed Pasha, rubbed their faces in the dust at his feet,
and said: "My sultan, it is an injustice to us. They dumped Diyarbekir cotton cloth on us for three times its value, also alum
and morocco leather. Now they are demanding gold at the rate of
120 clipped aspers, alleging it is for the Azov salaries. By your
noble head, this is the tyranny of Haccac-ı Yusuf[30] directed
against the poor of the marketplace. You must prevent it. You
must put a stop to it."

"Gentlemen," replied the pasha, "we did not give you Diyarbekir cloth and alum and morocco leather; we gave you 70,000
royal Seville piasters[31] and we demand gold (in exchange) according to the rate current in the grand markets." Turning to
Kudde and the *defterdar* he said, "Why did you force crimson
cloth and alum and morocco leather on these servants of God?"

"My sultan," they replied, "one of the merchants in Hoca Hanı died and this much of his property was confiscated by the state. Since then we sold the cotton cloth and the alum and morocco leather to these tradesmen at the market price. Well then, what is wrong with helping out the Azov treasury?"

The pasha was swayed by their argument. "Go away, people of Muhammed," he said, "let it go at that. Help out the *gazis* and let us send the rations to Azov."

At this the tradesmen raised a hue and cry. "What is this injustice? Are we not the people of Muhammed?" All the white-bearded elders, in their pomp and dignity, and the representatives of the noble *seyyids* came forward and said: "Do not do this, O vizier, prevent this injustice, and put a stop to it."

Now the pasha flew into a rage. He grabbed the rattan staff from the hand of the *çavuş-başı* and drove a group of the servants of God before him in the council hall, thrashing at them wildly. Some threw themselves down the stairs; others got away with a broken hand or foot. The noble *seyyids* and elders, those cunning rascals, cried: "Bear witness! He called us Jews, and attacked and wounded us with a staff. He did nothing to prevent the injustice against us. He does not deserve to be the vizier and the governor. The case belongs to the *şeriat*."

They went straight to the *nakibüleşraf* and to the *şeyhülislam* Aziz Efendi and obtained *fetvas* in their favor declaring that the pasha was an infidel; this was based on (the dictum) handed down in the *Tatar Haniye*:[32] "He who in his wrath scolds a seeker of knowledge by calling him an ass or a pig or the like, has committed infidelity."

The next morning—*a heart-rending event: reason for the removal from office of Melek Ahmed Pasha with the rising of the tradesmen, instigated by Siyavuş Pasha and Ebu Said Efendi*—the tanners from Saraçhane were the first to raise banners and drums, and the shops and the mosques were closed. Crying "let the people of Muhammed rally beneath the standard; let us present a note to the Padishah," 50,000 servants of God— characterized by (the Hadith) "He who earns his living is beloved of God"—all the bazaar merchants, armed and shouting "Allah Allah," came marching wave on wave like a sea.

It was Monday, 4 Ramazan 1061 (21 August 1651)—twelve days after Dasnik Mirza and Hanefi Halife were unjustly beheaded in front of the Bab-ı Hümayun—when the cry "Allah Allah!" was raised aloft in the hippodrome. A great commotion and

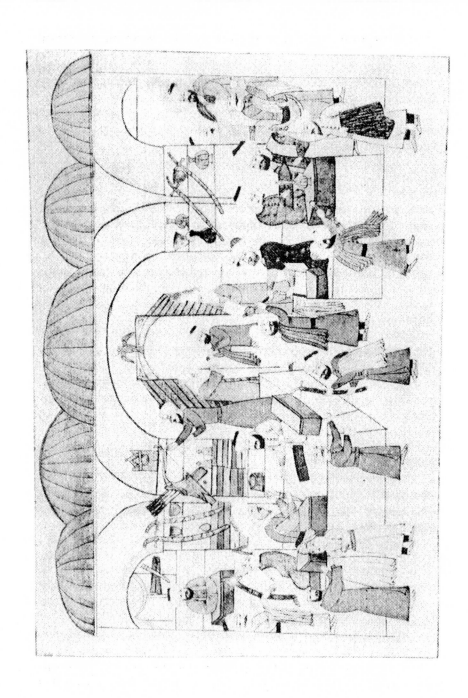

crying and wailing were heard throughout Istanbul, as group after group filled the open area in front of the Bab-ı Hümayun. Aziz Efendi, the *şeyhülislam*, remained inside Aya Sofya mosque. The people were armed with cudgels, clubs, and wooden fire-pokers burnt at the end, and each had a loaf of bread in his bosom. As they raised their cry, the reverberation reached the ears of the Padishah. The Bab-ı Hümayun was shut, and the cannons were ordered readied atop the turrets. A *hasseki* sent from the Padishah appeared from the Bab-ı Hümayun tower. "Servants of God!" he cried, "what is the meaning of this huge gathering?"

"We demand that the grand vizier and others who are oppressing us—the *defterdar* Emir Pasha, the *baş-bakı-kulu*[33] Moralı Mustafa Çelebi, the *çavuş-başı* Ibrahim Agha, the court usher Kuska-fırınlı, Kudde Kethüda, Topkapılı, the customs inspector, the *valide-sultan*, Bektaş Agha, Kara Çavuş the agha of the janissaries, the *kul-kethüdası* Çelebi Agha, Alahoz Mehmed Efendi, Sarı Katib, the *bostancı-başı*, Mevkufati Mehmed Efendi—in short, all 150 men on this list who came prior to Celali Hasan Agha and Ipşir Agha—we demand that they be put to death and that the grand vizier be removed from office and replaced by Siyavuş Pasha."

Word of the affair reached the felicitous Padishah. When the *hasseki-ağa* came through Servi Kapı to report to the Pasha, the felicitous Padishah himself greeted him: "What is the basis for this public disturbance? Have them disperse in an orderly fashion," he said, and went out.

The pasha summoned a group of the protestors, which included the guild elders, the pious *şeyhs*, the *seyyids* with their kohl-shaded eyes, their toothpicks in their turbans, and their prayer-beads in their hands, and also some crass-spoken and dull-minded rowdies. They all came before Melek Pasha to present their plea. "Felicitous vizier," they began, "we are not displeased with you. But we demand the death of Kudde Kethüda and Emir Defterdar. Their oppression of us has passed all bounds. You don't realize that on the pretext of the Azov (salaries) they are amassing a fortune of gold right here in Istanbul."

"Servants of God," replied the pasha, "the sum amounts to 70,000 piasters' worth of gold. Give nothing more than that."

"All right, we'll give that much; may God be pleased with it."

"We have also heard," they continued, "that for a year now pay has not reached the Azov (soldiery) and so they have killed their aghas. Now you, too, kill Kudde Kethüda and Emir Pasha and set our minds at rest. Punish them immediately, or else next time we'll know how to punish them ourselves."

They were quite insistent on the point, but the pasha said: "I cannot kill Emir Pasha, who is one of the noble *seyyids*. It is a matter to be settled by the *şeriat*." He found some mitigating excuse for each one (on the list) and he tried to pacify (the protestors). The equitable ones among them agreed, and fell silent; but the more hot-headed ones shouted: "We don't want discarded goods! We'll take the aspers and piasters in cash and give the gold." The noble Pasha managed to soothe their hearts and win them over, and as they were taking their leave and going down the stairs they were singing his praises.

What should I see next? Seventy or eighty of Ebu Said's and of Aziz Efendi's men instigated the toughs and brigands among the crowd below, and several hundred of them came bounding up the stairs into the council hall, shouting all sorts of abuses at the pasha. He, of course, by God's wisdom, flew into a rage, and once again bandied them with a staff and sent them scurrying back down the stairs. They returned immediately to the Bab-ı Hümayun. Meanwhile the gatekeepers closed the Bab-ı Seadet. Once again the cry "Allah Allah!" went up. The commotion continued for a full three hours.

As we learned later, the *şeyhülislam* Aziz Efendi was sitting inside Aya Sofya with the *ulema*, saying: "The people of Muhammed again went to the vizier to plead their cause. Didn't he heed their warning and remedy their grievances?"

"No, my sultan," they replied, "once again he struck all these noble *seyyids* and servants of God with a stick and wounded them, some almost fatally."

"People of Muhammed!" he cried, "his vizierate is no longer necessary; his removal is necessary. Make your cause known to the Padishah. Cry Allah Allah!" In this fashion he stirred the people to sedition.

Meanwhile he pasha addressed the assembly as follows: "Is there no one among us who is wise and patient and gentle, who can go to this band of rebels and find out the reason for this? After all, when they left us (earlier) they were conciliated." He gazed all around, but no one came forward willing to go.

Now Kudde Kethüda spoke up: "My sultan, there is only one way to deal with these scoundrels. They are nothing but a pack of jackals and grocers *(çakal u bakkal)* and hoarders, saddlers and silk mercers and linen drapers, camel drivers and porters. They aren't about to risk their lives. Not one can go without his Ismehan or his Ümmehan, his Gülistan or his Bustan, his Rabia or his Fatima.[34]

"Here in our palace we have 1,700 paid aghas and their orderlies. In our barracks across the way we have 3,000 warriors—Abkhazians, Circassians, Georgians, Kurds, and Albanians—tried in battle against Dasnik Mirza and Hanefi Halife, and against the Saçlı Kurds whom we massacred in the Sincar mountains in Diyarbekir.[35] We also have 150 halberdiers and musketeers, and 400 aghas of the interior service who will spare neither their heads nor their lives. This adds up to 6,000 soldiers.

"First of all we'll have the gate of Aya Sofya shut, and get word to the *bostancı-başı* to have the *bostancıs* put on the alert with their weapons at hand inside Servi Kapı. Then we'll throw open the palace gate and our 3,000 troops, both mounted and on foot, will march toward Bab-ı Hümayun. They can go up the armory road and attack the crowd from behind. With the Aya Sofya gate shut they'll be caught in the middle of three armies. We'll slash that miserable mob of grocers and jackals with our swords in a way that even Tabanı-yassı Mehmed Pasha did not do to the troops in Aleppo.[36] Those who flee in this direction will meet a shower of lead from the court usher's companions and our men in the barracks. It will give tongues something to wag about for a while.

"Also, my sultan, we'll arm all of our servants and menials. We have a thousand excellent muskets which we took as booty from Mt. Sincar, plus bows and arrows beyond count."

Sparked by this kind of saber rattling, everyone was ready for battle and just waiting for the next step. But then we got wind that Kuska-fırınlı the court usher had slipped out in disguise through the halberdiers' harem gate and ran away. The pasha was vexed at this and cursed him roundly. In the meantime the cry "Allah Allah!" rose up even more loudly before the Bab-ı Hümayun.

A Strange and Wondrous Event:
Telhisi Mazlum[37] Hüseyn Agha

Earlier, when our lord the Pasha inquired who would bring word about the crowd and the commotion, no one volunteered. Now Telhisi Hüseyn Agha spoke up:

"My sultan, 'Haste is from the devil, deliberation is from the Merciful.' Be patient. 'Let us see what image the mirror of fate will show forth.' It is true, my sultan, as the Kethüda Beg has remarked, that these soldiers of ours are skilled and brave Circassian, Georgian, and Kurdish warriors. Now this mob consists entirely of people of little sense. If a thousand of our troops went out the gate behind the harem and shot at them from the direction of the turban makers in the armory road; and if another 2,000 proceeded to the Bab-ı Hümayun via Büyük Demir Kapı and shot at them; and if so many aghas of the interior also poured lead from the windows, taking aim at those before the Bab-ı Hümayun;—for God's sake, not a single one of them would escape alive. Then your name Melek ('angel') would become a bad name, and all the people who now shower you with benedictions would cry curses upon you.

"Before I can let that happen I'll stake my head and my life on your behalf. Let me go to that gathering of rebels. I'll see (what they are up to). I'll listen to what they have to say. And with (God's) grace I'll have something to say to them. I'll maintain a friendly attitude. Just don't forget me in your prayers."

"Well, fine, God save you," replied the pasha. "But my dear Hüseyn Agha, you are much given to technical terminology and fine turns of phrase. I'm sure you know the saying 'Speak to people according to their degree of intellect.' They are a pack of vermin. And since you are somewhat meddlesome, I'm afraid you're going to put your foot in your mouth. What is needed at this juncture is winsome, friendly, and conciliatory talk. Just greet them kindly, then go to the *şeyhülislam*, kiss his hand, and tell him that the demand for gold has been waived in accordance with his request."

So the pasha gave him much wise counsel and, after the customary Fatiha, sent him off with good wishes to the *şeyhülislam*, and greeting to Ahi Baba, the chief of Ahi Evran.[38] Turning to me he said: "You go too, my Evliya. Stick with Hüseyn Agha and counsel him. Don't be afraid of this mob, nothing will happen to you. Go, may God prosper your affair!" He recited another Fatiha, and puffed over me for good measure.

Now since I was already clean-shaven I just removed my turban and replaced it with a tower's cap. I also put on a woolen apron and, tucking up the skirt, went out the palace gate with Hüseyn Agha. There I put on one of my *gulam's* overcoats, beneath it attached a scimitar to my waistband, and muttered: "I put my trust in God."

From the great gate to the harem gate we met no one, because they were all afraid to come beneath the windows of our palace. Hüseyn Agha and I were discussing the wisest course of action, when suddenly we found ourselves amidst a sealike army, a vast jostling crowd of men, all armed and ready. The fumes from the matchlock fuses were overwhelming, and the glare from mail and armor and swords and shields was blinding.

When I saw this huge mob I was taken aback. For his part, Hüseyn Agha proceeded through the rabble with pomp and grandeur—with his wool lined ermine stole and his courtier's turban, and with twelve servants in his train, all grandly attired in multi-colored garments of rich fabrics—bestowing salaams on both sides, until he reached the ablution fountains before the Bab-ı Hümayun.

"Halt there, agha! Where are you going?"

"I'm going up ahead to your ringleader." When he said this I nearly fainted.

"We're the ringleaders. If you have something to say, say it to us."

"Damn you! I'll say what I have to say to a man who speaks like a man."

He was about to go on ahead when someone cried: "Don't you like us, you cuckold? What's this nonsense you're spouting?"

"Gazis!" I cried, "it's not that he doesn't like you, only that he is going to the grand müfti, the pillar of our religion. The vizier gives you his greetings. He says that he has waived the imposition of gold, in accordance with the request of the people of Muhammed. And he has sent this agha to our şeyhülislam in Aya Sofya."

"God be pleased with the vizier," they cried. And on every side they said: "Fine, fine. Let the agha pass."

A path was opened and Hüseyn Agha started to go ahead. But then he stopped and cried out: "You men! Why have you gathered for this sedition? Didn't Kadi-zade preach every Friday from the pulpit of this very Aya Sofya, and wasn't that the reason the coffeehouses were closed and public gatherings were forbidden?[39] So why have you assembled? Disperse! Go each man his way! Otherwise they are going to fire the cannons atop the turrets of Bab-ı Hümayun; and the soldiery stationed in the vizier's palace will hem you in from two sides. If that happens you will all be killed!"

When I heard him say this I stayed back a little.

Suddenly one of the troops knocked off the courtier's turban from Hüseyn Agha's head with the butt of his musket. Hüseyn Agha, who was a Laz, upbraided the man in his peculiar dialect: "Look here, you gallows-bird. I am the padishah's memorandum writer *(telhisçi)*. I make peace between padishahs. I come here to pacify you and you knock the turban from my head!"

When he began striking the man I realized that it was a spark to dry tinder. So I withdrew and concealed myself in the crowd.

"Hey, shoot this pimp! Kill him!"

First they struck Hüseyn Agha with hands and fists, then started pounding him with cudgels. When he tried to run away they grabbed the ermine stole from his back and, holding him by the belt, dragged him over to the ablution fountains, shouting "Hey, kill this pimp!" As they set on him with swords, Hüseyn Agha ran for his life down the slope toward Melek Pasha's harem gate. They slashed and wounded him in several places. Someone snatched the memorandum purse out of his bosom, along with his watch, knife, and dagger. Then the murderers fled, fearing that they would be shot at from Melek's palace; and Hüseyn Agha, in the throes of death, was left in the open before the harem gate.

Now I came rushing down the slope to our palace gate. "Hey, Yıldırım Kapıcı ("Gatekeeper Lightning"), open the gate, it's Evliya Çelebi!" I shouted until I nearly had a hernia. Eventually they let me in. I went straight to the Pasha and told him what had happened. "He's lying there now, at his last gasp, just in front of our interior aghas' windows."

"You see," cried the pasha, "didn't I tell you he was meddlesome? Well, we belong to God. But perhaps he'll survive."

"My sultan," someone reported, "we just looked, and really, he is in the throes of death."

"Damn it," cried the pasha, "isn't there any brave soul who will bring him inside? I'll give 100 goldpieces." Some men went off.

I looked out the aghas' window. There was Hüseyn Agha muttering: "How could this happen, how could this happen?"

Just then a man picked up a rock from the ground—it was the size of an Isa Çelebi loaf baked in Tophane—and raising it to his shoulders, came over to Hüseyn Agha. "You tyrant!" he shouted. "Damn you, you old fool.[40] Aren't you the one who robbed me of my office as castle warden of Günye, through the influence of Sarı Gınayi Efendi? Now you got what you deserved." And he brought down the rock on Hüseyn Agha's chest.

After the fellow ran away Hüseyn Agha, by God's command, managed to get up on his feet. He collapsed, got up again, and kept falling and rising like a drunken man. At last a *gulam* named Abdurrahman came up like Hızır,[41] clapped his master on his back like a burlap sack, whisked him over to our palace gate, and got him inside. They bound his wounds right away and buried him up to his throat in horse dung until the surgeon arrived.

At this juncture, just as the palace gate was opened and the pasha's armed soldiery was about to march against the rebels— *by God's wisdom*—seventy or eighty doorkeepers entered in the company of the imperial marshal of guards, Ibrahim Agha, who approached the pasha and said: "Come along, his majesty the world-refuge Padishah wants to see you."

"Agha," said the pasha, "how can I get through this throng of rebel vermin? Please tell the Padishah that I kiss his foot, and politely inform him of our situation." He removed the seal from his bosom and handed it to Ibrahim Agha.

"God forbid, my sultan," he said, "I did not come here to get the seal."

"Now," replied the pasha, "take these 1,000 goldpieces and go inform him of the situation. May your service endure." And he sent him off.

Outside, the crowd kept up their shouting. To make a long story short, three times the marshal of guards came from the felicitous Padishah, along with the chief *hasseki-ağa* and the privy chamberlain, to summon the pasha. But he cited the koranic verse (2:195) "And do not with your own hands cast yourselves into destruction," and said: "I will not cast myself into destruction. I cannot go to the Padishah's presence if I have to pass through this mob. 'Opposing the commonality is from the force of error.'[42] I simply cannot go."

The fourth time the chief deputy of the palace guards came, accompanied by the privy chamberlain Hasan Agha, and said: "Either come to the imperial presence—and we swear by God that you will not be harmed—or give up the seal."

The Pasha thanked God and said: "Aghas, I tried three times to give my Padishah the seal, but he refused to take it.

Now let him just give me a crust of bread—I'll go to serve in any province." He handed over the seal to the chief deputy of the palace guards and gave each man a purse of gold and a sable robe, saying: "I rub my face at the felicitous foot of my Padishah."

On their way back they cried: "Look here, we have the seal from the vizier. Disperse, people of Muhammed!"

But they only increased their outbursts shouting: "We demand the death of the seventy men."

The Bab-ı Hümayun was now opened and the *şeyhülislam* Aziz Efendi was summoned within to confer with the Padishah. He proceeded to the royal presence in the company of about 150 *ulema* and elder officials. The seal was then conferred upon Siyavuş Pasha, who emerged in procession through the Bab-ı Hümayun to the acclamation of the public. "God bless you," they cried. "Now kill the seventy men on our list and prove that you are an independent grand vizier." Finally, the whole rebellious crowd dispersed.

That very hour Bektaş Agha and the janissary agha and the *kul-kethüdası* arrived, with 500 or 600 armed mounted men each, to confer with the pasha. "My sultan," they said, "why did you give up the seal without informing us? We would all have given our lives for your sake." They upbraided him in this fashion, and wept.

"Look here, aghas, may God be pleased with you," replied the pasha. "In the fourteen months that I have been grand vizier[43] I maintained good relations with all of you and I served Islam to the best of my capacity. God be praised, I have gotten out of it safe and sound. Now you look to save your heads!"

"Whatever we did we brought on ourselves,"[44] they said. Weeping some more, they and the pasha quitted one another of the due of bread and salt (i.e., their obligations of service) and they took their leave. To spite Siyavuş Pasha they marched right in front of his gate without going in to congratulate him. Siyavuş Pasha was chagrined at this.

The next day the privy chamberlain brought a noble rescript (order from the sultan) to the following effect: "My *lala* Melek Ahmed Pasha, I have bestowed upon you Egypt or Baghdad or Budin or Özü province. Whichever province you may desire, it is granted as a benefice, without office dues. Inform (me of your choice)."

The Pasha chose Özü. He was given three purses of gold, fifty files of mules, fifty strings of camels, and a royal tent-pavilion. After visiting the felicitous Padishah to take his leave, he went to the grand vizier Siyavuş Pasha. The feigned affection demonstrated by both men was marvelous to behold. They gave each other a thousand words of caution and counsel, after which came sherbets and incense, and Siyavuş Pasha gave our pasha a sable robe and two purses of gold, before they kissed and took leave of one another.

Finally, after paying his respects to the *şeyhülislam*, the pasha did not return to the palace (in Istanbul). Rather, he uttered a *besmele*, went straight out Edirne Kapı, and halted at his palace known as Otakçılar. Kudde Mehmed Kethüda marched with the pasha's horsetail banners and his soldiery, and playing his military band, to Topçular and halted there. Our lady Kaya Sultan moved quarters as well, following our lord the pasha,[45] and all other preparations for the journey were completed.

Meanwhile, on Wednesday, 6 Ramazan 1061 (23 August 1651) another great tumult arose in Istanbul and the gates were shut. Bektaş Agha had been awarded the *sancak* of Bursa, the janissary agha had been given Erzurum, and the *kul-kethüdası* Çelebi (Agha) had been given———. Now Bektaş Agha was bound and fettered, mounted on a porter's packhorse, and dispatched by Siyavuş Pasha, who also had the janissary agha killed. When Sarı Katib got news of these disastrous events he stabbed himself with a knife, thus committing suicide. Several hundred other men were eliminated as well. All the wealth belonging to Bektaş Agha, Çelebi Kethüda, and the janissary agha———[46] was confiscated and delivered to the imperial treasury. This included money that had been buried and was now dug up.

That very hour the Mother of the World—wife of Sultan Ahmed (I); mother of Osman (II), Orhan,[47] Bayezid, Murad (IV), and Ibrahim; the grand Kösem Valide—was strangled by the chief black eunuch Div Süleyman Agha.[48] He did it by twisting her braids around her neck. So that gracious benefactress was martyred. When the Istanbul populace heard of this they closed the mosques and the bazaars for three days and nights. There was a huge commotion. Several hundred people were put to death, secretly and publicly, and Istanbul was in a tumult.

When our lord Melek Ahmed Pasha learned these sad events, he remarked concerning Siyavuş Pasha: "In order to be grand vizier for fifty or sixty days, he unjustly killed our poor

lady, Mother of the World, the mother of our lord Sultan Murad and of Sultan Ibrahim. But Siyavuş Pasha won't prosper. Only may God not cause his mother to weep; may his brother Hüseyn Agha get well; and may God get him out of the vizierate safe and sound. He has become vizier in the midst of a great abyss." When he uttered these words Melek Pasha's eyes turned to bowls of blood.

The following day ten overbearing *çavuşes* came, sent by Siyavuş pasha, and insisted that we leave immediately for Özü. "It is for the Padishah to command," said the pasha; "have the horsetail banners go out right away." While the *çavuşes* were present he sent the banners to the Çekmeces; then he gave them presents, and they departed.

[On the way to Özü they halt at Rusçuk.]

While we were enjoying the pleasures of Rusçuk, a chief doorkeeper named Bayram Agha, along with forty chamberlains, brought the pasha noble rescripts from the felicitous Threshold, demanding that Kudde Kethüda be sent to the Porte in chains. Acceding to the imperial command, Melek Ahmed Pasha confined Kudde to the Rusçuk citadel and immediately had letters prepared that he entrusted to me, saying: "Get ready, my Evliya, you are going to my Kaya Sultan." . . .

When I arrived at Kaya Sultan('s palace) in Topçular she took me in the harem and questioned me from behind the lattice. . . . I recounted in detail how Kudde Kethüda was confined in chains in Rusçuk citadel through the agency of the chief doorkeeper and chief barber Bayram Agha. Upon hearing this, Kaya Sultan did not cry out; instead she let loose her hair, flew into a royal rage, and nearly turned into a witch. "I swear by God, Evliya Çelebi, even if I must spend 2,000 purses for the sake of the pasha's steward, come what may, I will not let him into Siyavuş's clutches!"

She got into her coach and drove straight to Siyavuş's wife, Hanıma Sultan, Receb Pasha's daughter. "Hurry," she said, "call your husband." Siyavuş Pasha entered the harem and welcomed her. "You tyrant Siyavuş!" she cried. "You murdered my grandmother, your lord Murad's mother (Kösem Sultan). And you have robbed my husband of whatever lofty position he has gained. Finally you even took the seal (of the grand vizierate). And now you want to imprison his steward and kill him. Aren't you and my pasha kinsmen? Weren't you valet to my father Sultan Murad, God rest his soul, when he was sword-bearer? Don't you have claims on each other reaching back forty or fifty years? Release my pasha's steward! Otherwise, by the soul of my grandfather (Sultan Ahmed I) I will curse you, and you will get no pleasure from this seal."

To this outburst of wrath Siyavuş replied: "My sultan, your pasha owes the Padishah 1,000 purses. They were taken by the hand of Kudde Kethüda. Let him come and pay up; then he may return to his pasha."

"My pasha deposited 3,000 purses in the inter-porte treasury as 'bureau gifts.' He has paid the debt—he even went 1,000 purses over. Check the imperial register. If my husband owes anything to the imperial treasury, *I* will pay it. What do you want from my pasha's steward?"

Still in a rage, she got up and went to the *valide-sultan*, then to the felicitous Padishah himself, and to the chief black eunuch Div Süleyman Agha, the one who had killed the old *valide*. She went the rounds of quite a few other places before returning to her palace.

Three days later Kudde Kethüda was brought by coach and delivered in chains to the sword-bearer's headquarters, where they imprisoned him and demanded 1,000 purses. That same day, due to Kaya Sultan's instigation, the world came tumbling down on Siyavuş Pasha's head. When he arrived at the imperial *divan*, the chief black eunuch Div Süleyman Agha wrested the seal from him by force, saying: "Give me the seal, you foolish boy!" He gave it to Gürcü Mehmed Pasha. . . . Gürcü Pasha released Kudde Kethüda from prison, and he returned to the pasha without paying a cent.

Notes

1. See I 79b (Ch. 1).

2. Evliya recounts this episode at II 372b.30–374b.26 (472–79; not in Hammer); cf. Naima, vol. 4, p. 375; vol. 5, pp. 83ff.

3. *Ariyeti atlılar*—that is, horsemen on borrowed horses?

4. Lit., "What about zeal for our clan?" *(aşiret gayreti yok mu)*. Melek Pasha, like Kara Hasan, was of Abkhazian origin.

5. *Her kansı taş katıdır başını aña urgilen. Kansı* (for *kankı*, modern Turkish *hangi*) and the imperative in *-gilen* are dialect features (cf. IV 207b.24 for *-gilen*). For the expression, cf. Aksoy II, 708 (#5054): *Hangi taş pekse (katıysa) başını ona vur.* [Ömer Asım Aksoy, *Atasözleri Sözlüğü* I–III (Ankara, 1981)] The sense is, Do your worst, you will fail in your scheme against me.

6. *Seniñ Çerkesiñ necaseti benim fülanıma olsun.* Kudde's "Çerkes" is later mentioned as one of the Diyarbekir rebels whose heads were sent by Murtaza Pasha and displayed before the sultan at Bursa in 1069/1659 (see V 84b.34–85a.1 [288]).

7. Lit "inns" *(han);* cf. I 143a.26–29 (476; Hammer ii, 81): *bazısına üç ayda bir ulufe için sipah tayfası gelip sakin olurlar.*

8. The text has *bu ayda* "this month," which I interpret as an error for *bu anda* "immediately."

9. *Busuda pinhan oldu;* that is, he lay low and watched what would happen next.

10. Evliya's various spellings of the two names are reduced in the translation to these two forms. Naima, vol. 5, pp. 92f. makes no mention of the first and states that the second, whom he calls Dasni Mirza, was a *beg* of the Mirdasni clan. For the Dasni Kurds, see J. S. Guest, *The Yezidis* (London and New York, 1987), pp. 42f. And see Evliya, V 2b (7: abbreviated).

11. An ancient sage of the Arabs, mentioned in Koran 31:12f. "To get wisdom from Lokman" is to learn something from the horse's mouth.

12. The elaborate word play, the ambiguities of the orthography, and the eastern Anatolian dialectal forms *(kesipsen, oḫı, etgilen, menim)* make these *manis* (quatrain folksongs) difficult to interpret. For previous attempts (all based on the Istanbul printed text), see Evliya Çelebi, *Seyahatname: On yedinci asır hayatından lâvhalar,* ed. M. N. Özön, vol. 1 (Ankara: Akba, n.d. [1944]), p. 117; Z. Danışman, trans., *Evliyâ Çelebi Seyâhatnâmesi,* vol. 7 (Istanbul, 1970), p. 156; L. Sami Akalın, *Türk Manilerinden Seçmeler,* I (Istanbul, 1972), p. xxvi. The second of these three *manis* is also found at V 72a.13 (244).

13. Or, "Father, you are with a book" *(Baba kitab ile sen).*

14. Or, "Read so that you will know."

15. Cf. the famous verses of Kör-oğlu, the *celali* rebel and minstrel: "The musket was invented and manliness was destroyed; / The curved sword must rust in the scabbard" *(Tüfek icad oldu merdlik bozuldu / Eğri kılıç kında paslanmalıdır).*

16. There is an untranslatable word play here: *seg-pay segban-ı pay-taban.*

17. The text has *er ama avz;* read *az ama uz.*

18. Evliya describes this battle, which he witnessed in 1050/1640, at II 259b f. (113–22; Hammer, 59–64).

19. A gypsy expression (cf. VI 54a.1 [159: omitted]) called up here by association with the word *ormanlar* ("forest").

20. *Beynehu ve beyne'llah şehid.*

21. Vakvak is a legendary tree with human heads growing on its branches. The mandrake root is shaped like a human torso.

22. For Azov see n. 18 above. Evliya describes the Canea campaign which he witnessed that same year (1050/1640–41) at II 268b f. (142–65; Hammer, 74–88).

23. *Kahr*—relating his violent subjugation to one of the "beautiful names" of God: el-Kahhar.

24. *Şehadet kelimesi*, that is, the creedal formula: "I bear witness that there is no god but God and that Muhammed is His Prophet," which Muslims are supposed to utter when they die.

25. Lit., "he did not linger *(tehallüf)* at all."

26. Terms for Christian frontier warriors of various kinds.

27. That is, Mehmed Giray IV, brother of the reigning Crimean Khan, Islam Giray III.

28. One Şerefi was equivalent to 160 aspers at this period; see Mantran, Table 2 (opp. p. 244). [Robert Mantran, *Istanbul dans la seconde moitié du XVIIe siècle* (Paris, 1962)]

29. Present-day Kırklareli in Turkish Thrace.

30. The Umayyad governor of Iraq (d. 95/714), notorious for his harsh measures.

31. One "piastre espagnole (sévillane-mexicaine)" was equivalent to ninety aspers at this period; see Mantran, n. 28 above.

32. That is, *el-Tatārḥāniyye*, a compendium of Hanefi law by ʿĀlim b. ʿAlāʾed-dīn el-Ḥanefī, d. ca. 752/1351.

33. He was an official of the Ottoman finance department *(defterdarlık)* responsible for the collection of tax arrears.

34. The names, presumably, of their wives.

35. In 1050/1640; see Ch. 5.

36. Refers to an event in 1043/1633 during Murad IV's eastern campaign undertaken by Tabanı-yassı Mehmed Pasha (grand vizier, 1041–46/1632–37).

37. An epithet meaning "oppressed, injured."

38. Ahi Evran is the patron saint of the Turkish tanners' guild and, by extension, of the entire Turkish guild organization. Ahi Baba is the title of the şeyh of the tekke of Ahi Evran in Kırşehir and, by extension, of the şeyh's delegates to the Turkish guilds. Here it probably refers to the chief of the Turkish guilds in Istanbul. See EI², s.vv. "Akhi Baba" and "Akhi Ewran" (both by Fr.Taeschner); and see I 193b.23 f. (594–95; Hammer ii, 206). At I 194a.26 (595: ommitted; Hammer: abbreviated) Evliya says: "Because these tanners are a brave and rough crew, all the guilds, numbering ———, look to them, and always call their chief 'Ahi Baba.' They were the cause for our lord the late Melek Ahmed Pasha's removal from the vizierate in the year 1006 (sic; error for 1061). They are indeed so riotous and unruly that if they were to join forces they would be capable of deposing and enthroning padishahs."

39. Kadi-zade was appointed preacher of Aya Sofya in 1041/1631 and died in 1045/1635–36. He was a popular fundamentalist preacher, leader of a movement condemning all innovations, including coffee and tobacco, because they were without religious sanction and therefore contrary to the Sunnah (sünnet). Cf. Madeline C. Zilfi, "The Kadızadelis: Discordant Revivalism in Seventeenth-Century Istanbul," *Journal of Near Eastern Studies* 45, no. 4 (1986): 251–69.

40. Pir ev oğlu (?—reading and interpretation of this phrase uncertain; perhaps an error for pir oğlu).

41. An immortal saint (or, according to some, prophet) and a popular savior figure. Cf. EI², art. "al-Khadir" (A. J. Wensinck). [To the bibliography there, add F. W. Hasluck, *Christianity and Islam under the Sultans*, 2 vols. (Oxford, 1929), Index (Khidr); H. S. Haddad, " 'Georgic' Cults and Saints in the Levant," *Numen* 16,1 (1969): 21–39; Altan Gökalp, "Hızır, İlyas, Hidrelles: Les maîtres du temps, le temps des hommes," in R. Dor and M. Nicholas, eds., *Quand le crible était dans la paille* (Paris, 1978)]

42. Umuma muhalefet kuvvet-i hatadandır, a proverbial expression; also quoted at I 22a.2 (omitted in printed text and Hammer; here gulu-yı 'am instead of umum), II 361a.5 (omitted in printed text and Hammer), VII 25b.34 (117), 99a.19 (462). It is cited in Agnellini's 1688 collection of Turkish proverbs in the form: Cümleye muhalefet kuvvet hatadandur (Italian trans: L'esser contrario à tutti è peccato). See

Vladimir Drimba, "XVII. yüzyılda yayımlanmış bir Türk atasözleri ve vecizeleri denemesi," *Türk Dili Araştırmaları Yıllığı Belleten* 1985 (Ankara, 1989), 9–26, p. 17.

43. According to Danişmend, p. 417, Melek Ahmed Pasha's vizierate lasted one year and seventeen days (or nearly thirteen lunar months), from 7 Şaban 1060 to 4 Ramazan 1061 (5 August 1650 to 21 August 1651). At III 179b.35 (514; Ch. 4) Melek claims that he was grand vizier for sixteen months, and at V 19a.6 (53; end of Ch. 6) he claims that he was grand vizier for a year and a half.

44. Preceding this there is another phrase, unpointed and hard to interpret; a conjectural reading is *biz bize biz sokup* ("We have stuck the awl into ourselves").

45. That is, from Üsküdar to Eyub, as the pasha would now be in the Rumelian provinces.

46. His name is given above at 102b.2 as Kara Çavuş.

47. A son named Orhan does not appear in Alderson, Table XXXIV.

48. For this incident, cf. Naima, vol. 5, pp. 110–11; and see M. Cavid Baysun, "Kösem Sultan" in *İslam Ansiklopedisi*, vol. 6, pp. 920–21.

3

GOVERNOR OF RUMELI
(1652)

[At the end of Zilhicce 1062/beginning of December 1652, following the dismissal of Gürcü Mehmed Pasha as grand vizier and the appointment of Tarhuncu Ahmed Pasha, Melek is removed from Özü and appointed governor of Rumeli province (capital: Sofia).]

A Marvel

Upon the lead-tiled roof of the ancient mosque named the Gentleman's Friday Mosque (Çelebi Camii), which is in front of the pasha's palace in the city of Sofia, a pair of storks made their nest and deposited their eggs. One day a notorious rogue named Debbağ-oğlu ("son of the tanner") climbed up to the roof of this mosque, removed the stork eggs, and put crow eggs in their place. Eventually these hatched and two crow chicks emerged, according to the verse:

Beyza-ı zağı kosañ tavus-ı kudsi altına
Zağdır peyda olan biñ dürlü tedbir eyleseñ

If you put crow eggs beneath a blessed peacock
What hatches are crows, despite a thousand schemes.

When the father stork returned from his foraging, what should he see but two black crow chicks squirming in the nest. He gave the mother stork a sound drubbing with his beak, then flew up and began to cry and wail as he soared about over the entire city of Sofia. Thousands of storks assembled and flew straight to Çelebi Mosque, landing on the domes and covering the roof so that you could not see a single lead tile. All these birds came forward one by one to peer into the nest and take a look at the grafted crow chicks. They raised such a hue and cry on the mosque dome that it frightened the wits of the passersby. None of the birds ate or drank that day; they just kept up their crowing and cawing. So there was no peace of mind in Sofia on that day. All the people stopped what they were doing to watch the storks.

Finally, the crowd of storks killed the crow chicks. Then they rushed upon the mother stork, accusing her of adultery, and cut her to pieces with their beaks. After some further stork talk they gave the father stork another mother stork as his mate, and all flew back to their own nests.

The townsfolk marveled at this incident, and our lord Melek Ahmed Pasha, too, was quite astounded. "Have that scoundrel who exchanged the eggs brought here immediately," he said, "we'll punish him." But then he decided to bide his time saying, "Be patient, God almighty will punish that rogue as he deserves."

A few days later—*by God's wisdom*—that notorious outlaw who had exchanged the stork eggs—he was a Segban servant named Uşkurta Debbağ-oğlu—was tipsy and went to visit his lady friend. Just as he was shuttling on her loom like a master weaver, the lady's husband suddenly entered and saw that the workshop was in full swing. This householder bared his sword in a fit of zealous rage, rushed upon his wife and on Uşkurta Debbağ-oğlu, and led them outside wounded and manacled, crying, "See, O people of Muhammed!"

When they reached Bana-başı, the gathering place of Sofia's mystics and lovers, some Zadra janissaries were squabbling over a woman, and it turned out that this woman was the original whore of that very Debbağ-oğlu who had exchanged the stork eggs. So now Debbağ-oğlu freed himself from his captor and began trying to rescue his whore.[1] In the midst of the struggle the janissaries bared their swords and cut up both Debbağ-oğlu and his whore and left them in Bana-başı.

A band of youthful tanners from the town brought Debbağ-oğlu's corpse to the pasha's palace, crying, "The janissaries killed our Çelebi, here is his corpse!" Because the pasha was rather displeased at this plea for justice, the tanner youths put Debbağ-oğlu's corpse under the eaves of the mosque in front of the pasha's palace.

So you see the divine plan! Because this Debbağ-oğlu took the stork eggs and put crow eggs in their place, when the crows hatched, all the birds cut the female stork to pieces and dropped them from the eaves of the mosque. A few days later—according to the verse, *Muntakımdır bir adı Kayyumuñ* ("Avenger is one name of the Eternal one")—God had *him* cut to pieces, as well as his whore in place of the female stork and had them leave Debbağ-oğlu's corpse in the very place where the storks had left the stork. For God is just.

When the pasha heard of this he said, "I ought to have punished him, but I cast him to God, and a few days later God punished him. He got what he deserved. Have that damned fellow's corpse removed from the courtyard of the mosque, shrouded in a mat, and buried." So the tanner brigands took away the hide of the tanner's son and brought it to Bana-başı to be tanned. It was quite a spectacle. Many moral lessons can be drawn from this event.

After the Debbağ-oğlu affair our lord the pasha banished all the prostitutes of Sofia from the town.[2] A few of them, by leave of the *şeriat* and for the reform of the world, were strung up like chandeliers to adorn the town at the street corners in the silk market. The notables of the province were grateful that their town was now tranquil and free of prostitutes. But the rogues and the brigands, for the sake of their carnal pleasures, bruited it about that the town's resources had grown scarce, and there would now be famine and dearth, even plague.

And indeed—*by God's wisdom*—the plague did begin to spread in the city from day to day. By the end of a month, 500 people, men and women, were dying from it daily. It reached the point that thousands of people fled from Sofia to other regions. Seventy-seven of our fortunate lord's renowned aghas, among his highest officers, died. The pasha, too, had to take to his bed from illness. His head swelled up like an Adana squash, his tongue was scorched and turned black, his ears oozed with pus. More than once he was on the verge of death.

During this period the good-natured pasha learned that Gınayi Efendi, who was our head of chancellery, was very low spirited. He got upset at this, and whenever he thought about Gınayi Efendi he would always ask for his welfare and send him load after load of various foods and drinks, accompanied each time by a purse of "bath money" to cheer him up. One day he even sent him a splendid Circassian slave girl.

Meanwhile the pasha, too, was failing rapidly, only the last spark of life remained. I recited the noble Yasin (Koran, *sure* 36) several times. We were all in a quandary; the aghas were quite despondent; the physicians gave up their treatment; and the pasha's servants despaired of his recovery. That day, however, the pasha has a nosebleed, after which he felt somewhat better.

The following morning I went to the pasha's bedside, kissed his noble hand, and was gently rubbing his blessed right hand when he addressed me in a thick voice: "My Evliya, the vision I have seen, you have seen, too. Tell it to me."

"it is no vision (*vakıa*) that I see my sultan, it is a fact (*vakı*) that I see him now in health." But as I said this my blood-tinged tears streamed down my cheeks.

"No Evliya," he said, "tell me the dream that you saw this night." And he began to recite a Fatiha.

Just as he was reciting the Fatiha I recalled that I had indeed seen a marvelous dream that night, and that at the end of the dream I saw the pasha, who said to me, in my dream, "My Evliya, in the morning tell me this dream which you just saw." I had forgotten it because of my gloomy thoughts. But in the morning, as I was rubbing his noble hand and he said, "Tell me the dream you saw this night," he was clearly referring to that dream.

A Marvel: The Genuine Dream of This Humble One,
Evliya the Unhypocritical.[3]

"My sultan," I began, "this night in my dream we were all in Istanbul. You had constructed a galleon in Bağçe Kapı,[4] but where it stood on the land its bow and stern reached up to the sky. People were gathered all round this galleon, wondering how it would be launched safe and sound. A dervish of the Nakş-bendi order came up and said, 'God willing, this galleon will be launched safe and sound onto the sea of the world, and will be brought back to land.' He recited a Fatiha amidst the crowd and departed.

"Thousands of people thronged around your ship as, with a cry of 'Allah!' it was launched safe and sound. A cannon salute was fired. Your ship was towed across (the Golden Horn) and berthed with seven anchors in front of Kurşumlu Mahzen.[5] Everyone came to view your ship and to pronounce advice about it, saying, 'This part should be like this, and that part like that.'

"Then a hairy Frankish physician approached and said, 'I have seen many ships in this sea, but I have never seen a ship so well outfitted, with such strong timbers, and so sound both within and without. However, it is too top-heavy in the bow, and there is no ballast in the hold. It won't withstand the storms of this sea. Its underside must be rubbed with oil and caulked. Sacrifices must be performed and blood made to flow from its rudder case. And its mast is much too top-heavy for this galleon, it has to be cut down. Then this ship might survive the storms of this world.'

"After the Frankish physician had given these prescriptions and departed, by God's wisdom a great storm arose. Your ship could not lie steady on its seven anchors. Five of them broke away, and your ship was left on two anchors, tossing and spinning in the waves. When it was about to founder, the sailors on board began to wail and cry for help. At this the *bostancı-başı* set out from Saray Burnu by imperial order, with his troops loaded onto ten caiques, and surrounded your galleon.

"As they were boarding your ship, who should I see but the Frankish physician, the one who was there before. He was speaking to the *bostancı-başı* and saying, 'My sultan, if you wish to save this ship you have to cut down its mast, because the mast is far too top-heavy for this ship.' So the *bostancıs* and halberdiers all began to hack away at the mast with their axes. The moment the mast fell into the sea, the storm subsided. So your ship was saved, and it lay steady in front of Kurşumlu Mahzen."

The pasha, who had been listening avidly as I recounted my dream in all its details, told his servants to lift him out of bed. They sat him in a corner of the room, propped up with cushions. He spoke moaning and humming like a bee: "In my sleep I was directed to question Evliya about the genuine dream. This was the dream I meant when I said, 'You saw me this night in your sleep, tell me the dream.' Now may this genuine dream be auspicious, a dream such as the prophet Joseph saw and interpreted. I have formulated an interpretation, by divine inspiration which flashed upon my heart. A Fatiha on this intention!"

All present recited a noble Fatiha, and the aghas rejoiced and thanked God that the pasha was feeling somewhat better. *A marvel: interpretation of the dream.* Despite his weakened state, Melek Ahmed Pasha interpreted this humble one's dream. He began with a *besmele* and went on thus:

"That galleon which I had built in Bağçe Kapı is the ship of my body. Bağçe Kapı ('Garden Gate') refers to the garden (*bağ*) of the Ottoman state. I grew up and was nourished in that paradisical garden for forty-seven years, from the time of Sultan Ahmed Khan. In that noble harem I was anointed with divine love, and in the council chamber I became a servitor of the noble cloak of the Prophet. I always lay down and rose up on the sea of love in that abode of felicity.

"You said that the galleon's bow and stern reached up in the air. Now my head is swollen and full of air. Those people swarming about the ship and wondering how it would be launched safe and sound are my servants, wondering how their lord will find health in the sea of the world. A Nakşbendi dervish said that this ship would be launched safe and sound and would be brought back to land. Now I belong to this order of the Hocagan.[6] Through their spiritual effort I will regain my health and I will be launched and be brought back from fortune to fortune (or, from reign to reign).

"Thousands of people surrounded my ship and launched it on the sea, crying 'Allah Allah!' while a cannon salute was fired. This refers to all the people who have experienced my bounty. They will cry benedictions in the name of 'Allah Allah' and the cannons will announce the news of my recovery.

"My ship was towed across and berthed with seven anchors in front of Kurşumlu Mahzen. Now my administrators are towing me to the path of Truth. They are bringing me to Kurşumlu Mahzen which is the Treasurehouse of the Unknown. There I will lie berthed, held fast by anchors rather than by my seven men. Kurşumlu Mahzen is the storehouse (*mahzen*) of my religion and my faith. My religion is weighty as lead (*kurşum*) and I am harbored in my faith, having put down the anchor of steadfastness.

"Everyone was giving advice about my ship, saying, 'This part like this and that part like that.' Now my friends are worried about my treatment and saying that I must do this or that. A Frank came and examined my ship. 'I have seen many ships,' he said, 'but never one like this.' That refers to all the learned physicians who say, 'I never saw a sickness like this one.' His saying, 'I never saw one so well outfitted and so sound both within and without' means that I am pure in belief, stocked with weapons of righteousness, and free of guile both within and without. His saying, 'But it is too top-heavy in the bow' means that I am too concerned with worldly pomp, that I have too many servants and a swelled head. His saying, 'There is no ballast in the hold' refers to my being hungry because of my regimen. His saying 'It won't withstand the storm' refers to all the people rushing at me and proposing impossible treatments and cures, and indicates that you should not take the pasha out into the storm of Fate.

"He said that the ship's underside needs to be oiled. In point of fact, my own underside is so full of sores from lying in bed the past seventy days, it does need to be rubbed with oil. And he said we should make sacrifices and let blood flow from its rudder case. Now my head is the rudder of the ship of my body, so the meaning is that the physicians will apply cups and let blood, and when I regain my health I will perform a sacrifice. As for his saying that the mast is too top-heavy for this ship and has to be cut down: this is a sign that my health is bound up with the loss of one of my men, one of the pillars of my administration.

"The fact that five of the seven anchors broke indicates that five of my anchormen have died and I am left with only two administrators. The sailors on board crying that the ship is sinking stand for my servants who are afraid that their pasha is dying. The *bostancı-başı* setting out from Saray Burnu and cutting down the ship's mast indicates that a *hasseki* of the *bostancıs* will come from the Padishah expecting news of my death, but he will see that one of my men, one of the pillars of my fortune, has died. And the fact that the storm subsided when the mast was cut down is a sign that I will be saved only when one of my chief officers has died.

"So the meaning of my ship being subject to a great storm is just that the boat of my body has been so terribly sick. Their saying that the ship nearly foundered refers to the fact that a day or two ago only the last spark of life remained in my body. And the fact that a Frankish physician boarded my ship with the *bostancı-başı* means that Kaya Sultan is sending a physician along with a halberdier. This skillful physician will care for my body, and when I regain my health I will love the physician from the bottom of my heart and will award him handsomely.

"But—and God knows best—the major sign is this: the mast of my body's ship will be cut down, it will be separated from the ship of the flesh, it will be carried off for my sake, and I will be delivered from sickness, God willing."

He recited a Fatiha and continued: "Well, my Evliya, since you are my faithful friend and ancient companion you saw this dream for me. On the same night I, too, was directed in my sleep to question Evliya about the dream he saw. That is why today I questioned you about the fact (*vakı hal*) of this dream vision (*vakıa*). Now this humble one has interpreted it in this fashion, by divine inspiration; may it be auspicious." Weakened by so much talking, he leaned back on the cushion with a moan and fell asleep.

All the aghas, both of the inner and outer services, and the other people present were amazed at the Pasha's interpreting the dream in this fashion. "Bravo!" they cried, "a hundred thousand bravos, O Melek Ahmed Pasha, you are truly intimate with the mysteries. May God grant you health!" They also showered me with benedictions, crying, "Truly, Evliya, you are a real man and a pure world traveler to have seen such a genuine dream." They showed sincere affection.

Later, when the Pasha awoke, he turned to the treasurer, Sakallı Imam Mehmed Efendi, and said, "I have been starving now for seventy days; bring me a little nourishment." After eating a piece of bread, some chicken soup, and a bowl of sherbet, by God's command the pasha immediately came alive. That very hour he had 7,000 goldpieces brought out from his treasury. He bestowed a thousand on his aghas of the interior; a thousand on the chief doorkeepers of the exterior; a thousand on those deserving consideration; a thousand on the *muteferrikas*; a thousand on the irregulars and conscripts (*delis* and *gönüllüs*); a thousand on the cooks, tasters, pantrymen, muleteers, grooms, and torchbearers; and a thousand on the homeless and destitute of the city of Sofia. To me in private he gave 300 goldpieces and a sable fur that he himself used to use when making his ablutions.

Notwithstanding his gradual recovery and daily improvement by God's decree, a Frankish physician also arrived, sent by Kaya Sultan in the company of a halberdier and his court agent, the treasurer Ahmed Agha. The pasha put on some of the clothing sent by Kaya Sultan and had the rest put away in his room or in the wardrobe. The physician began to treat the pasha. But the pasha was also astounded, because, by God's wisdom, three days after the day on which the dream was interpreted, our lord the pasha's head of chancellery Gınayi Efendi—who was the apple of his eye, his friend and companion for the past forty years—passed away. May God have mercy on his soul.

Notes

1. *Orfana*. At III 140b.18 (401) Evliya explains that in Sofia this term simply means "servant girl" and not "prostitute" as elsewhere.

2. At 140b.15 Evliya says that Melek Pasha tried to put a stop to the widespread practice of loose women going out at night "to do their laundry," but the notables of the province did not consent.

3. *Evliya-yı bi-riya*, a common self-designation, but here with a play on *rüya* "dream."

4. Two years prior to this, when Melek was grand vizier, he had a huge galleon built at Bağçe Kapı (on the Stambul side of the Golden Horn) for the Crete campaign; but when it was launched it sank and 150 men were drowned (III 97a.25–27 [261]). According to Naima, who reports the incident, fifty men were drowned, and Melek, witnessing the event, burst out weeping (Naima, vol. 5, p. 72).

5. A lead-covered grain magazine in Galata; cf. I 177a.margin (568; Hammer ii, 167).

6. For the dervish order of the Hocagan~Nakşbendiye, see J. Spencer Trimingham, *The Sufi Orders in Islam* (Oxford, 1971), Index, s.v. Naqshabandiyya; also Hamid Algar, "The Naqshbandi Order: a preliminary Survey of its History and Significance," *Studia Islamica* 44 (1976): 123–52. In Evliya's time the Ottomans considered the Nakşbendis (including the Mevlevis) as one of the two principal orders, the other being the Halvetis (including the Bektaşis); cf. I 116a.25f. (389; Hammer ii, 29), 147b.18–22 (490; Hammer ii, 91), X 108a.6–12 (236); Rycaut, p. 136.

4

THE VIZIERATE OF IPŞIR PAŞHA (1653–54)

In this year, on the first of Ramazan (1063/26 July 1653), by order of the sultan, our lord Melek Ahmed Pasha entered Istanbul and was appointed second vizier in the *divan*, with a stipend amounting to forty *yüks* of aspers.[1] It was during the vizierate of Bıyıklı Derviş Mehmed Pasha. For four months our lord entered the council chamber night and day and was on fine terms and had good brotherly relations with Bıyıklı Derviş Mehmed Pasha. Our lord was given the governorship (*sahib sancağı*) of (Afyon) Karahisar as an imperial grant. He sent about 3,000 of his aghas to his fief, thus freeing himself of encumbrances, and enjoyed himself in his twelve *yalıs*, including those at Fındıklı, Beşiktaş, Ortaköy, Üsküdar, and Eyub. And I too went on pleasure outings—free of care, along with friends—to Eyub, Kağıdhane, Akbaba, Beg-koz, Kanlıca, Hisar, Üsküdar, Çamlıca, Kadıköy, Sarıkadı, Alemdağı; or else we pursued our pleasure in Göksu; and especially in the Hisar cherry season, we gorged on the crimson fruit and the juicy ruby-colored cherries in Istinye, Yeniköy, Tarabya, Kefeliköy, Büyükdere, and Sarıyar.[2]

This season of pleasure was not ours alone. For during the vizierate of this Bıyıklı Çerkes Derviş Mehmed Pasha, in the reign of Sultan Mehmed IV, in that auspicious (*meymun*) year, all the peopled danced and pranced like monkeys (*maymun*). There was a carnival atmosphere. For during the vizierate of Gürcü Mehmed Pasha[3] the people were in mourning, because of a dearth in the treasury and an abundance of death by plague. And after that, when Tarhuncu Ahmed Pasha was grand vizier,[4] there were austerities due to poor harvests and to infidel incursions in the Aegean Islands, and the people in their straits called on God the Straitener. So when the vizierate fell to Derviş

Mehmed Pasha, who was a jovial and generous nature, free of guile and jealousy, the people breathed a sigh of relief, and all the Muslims in their relief called on God the Reliever. They celebrated each day as though it were New Year's Eve. Even the Persian Shah and the infidels of Vienna and Germany and Venice hung their heads in silence. The treasures of Croesus were unearthed that had been buried by the earth-worshipping sects. Everyone rejoiced.

But, "There is no turning back His decree, and no preventing His judgment." By the eternal will of the Owner of this workshop and the Creator of the eighteen worlds, in the year——on the——th day of the month of——Derviş Mehmed Pasha failed to appear in the imperial *divan*. After the session he summoned our lord Melek Ahmed Pasha to his palace, and I accompanied him there. We found him in a sorry state. God preserve us, he had suffered a stroke; one arm was paralyzed, and nose and mouth were awry. The learned doctors and physicians consulted and, after a great deal of doting and discussion, prescribed all sorts of remedies, none of which had any effect. Finally Melek Ahmed Pasha addressed me as follows: "Evliya, you have in your possession certain charms and spells and cures. Why don't you recite some of them over our brother here? Perhaps they will cure him of this disease."

So I knelt down, took the grand vizier's paralyzed hand in my hand and, with a *besmele*, recited this Persian spell:

Ṭābe serānī 'azemtü 'aleyküm
Yā mihter-i perriyān
Sukkān-i ḥirbizān
Bişīzān künī 'arş-ı Ḥudārā fermānest
Bidih mīn Ḥudārā fermānest
Ṣad hezārān ve çehār hezārān peyġamberān Ḥudārā
   fermānest
Evvel Ādem āḥir Muhammed
Ve yā dīv-i ḥākim-i Süleymān 'aleyhi's-selām
Eger muġān est
Eger mürteżā künī est
Eger rāfiżī est
Eger mecūsī est
Eger sıklān-i cin est
'Azemtü 'aleyküm in küntüm müslimīn
Bişnī bişnī necā-yı berānest

Necā-yı Mūsā-yı peyġamberānest
Necā-yı ʿĪsā-yı bni Meryem est
Necā-yı mürsel-i peyġamberānest
Eger kibriyā nenci
Biḥaḳḳiʾn-nūr
Ve-eẕilliʾl-ḥurūr
Rivāyetiʾn-nār
Ẕālike rabbuʾl-ʿālemīn
Feʾncu ʿĪsā rūḥuʾllāh ve kelimetüʾllāh
Hāẕā veʾl-feraḥ-i incīl
Ve ḥaẕretiʾn-nāzil
Vekkil Mūsā ve Zuʾl-ḳarneyn ʿaleyhiʾs-selām
Velā ḥavle velā ḳuvvete illā biʾllāhiʾl-ʿaliyyiʾl-ʿaẓīm[5]

Three times I recited this spell while passing the amulet with my left hand over his palsied mouth and all of his limbs. One of the conditions for the efficacy of this spell, however, is that the reciter must strike the palsied man's face three times with his own shoe, holding it in the left hand. But because he was after all a grand vizier, I could not very well strike him with a shoe, so I touched him three times with an old slipper instead. Next I tried this spell of the Moroccan şeyh Tancavi:

Heşāşi hüşeyşi ṭuşeyşin
Ecib yā şarġım hindī
Ente ve ḥuddāmek mineʾr-raḥāniyyeti veʾl-eraẕiyyeti
Ve ente yemīnehü yā şarfiyāʾīl yā şarfiyāʾīl
Ecib ecib yā ecinneʾs-selāṭīn
Velā ḥavle velā ḳuvvete illā billāh
Tedrūs bedrūs fī ḳavmi naḥmūs
Üskün taḥteʾl-melikiʾl-ḳaddūs[6]

After this I recited the Muavvizeteyn (two final sures of the Koran) three times, puffed on Mehmed Pasha's face and limbs, said some prayers, and fell silent. By God's command, he stopped drooling at the mouth, claimed to feel somewhat better, and awarded me with a sable fur cape and a purse of piasters. And so for seven days I continually recited spells in the manner indicated above.

Finally our lord the pasha tore himself away from Mehmed Pasha, went straight to the felicitous Padishah, and reported the grand vizier's condition. The noble Padishah sent the chief eunuch with numerous gifts to inquire about the grand vizier's health. "I am on my death bed," he replied. "Make my brother Melek Ahmed Pasha my deputy vizier in order that the affairs of the Muslims not be neglected." He had the chief eunuch draw up a memorandum to this effect and, it being accepted, in the year———on the———th day of the month of ———our lord Melek Ahmed Pasha was officially appointed deputy vizier in the place of Bıyıklı Çerkes Mehmed Pasha. He donned a sable robe of honor at the hands of the felicitous Padishah, and undertook the affairs of the Muslims. But he constantly went to inquire after Derviş Mehmed Pasha's health, and, although he was on his death bed, continually sought his advice in retirements and appointments and all other important matters.

Things went on in this manner for six months. Every three months the salaries had to be paid. Provisions for the arsenal had to be got ready on time. Treasure and troops to the tune of 3,000 soldiers had to be sent to Crete.

Meanwhile the grand vizier sometimes seemed to recover, sometimes suffered a relapse. His final illness came on just when he felt somewhat better and had a meal of the type he was used to—being a Circassian and having grown up among the Tartars—a meal consisting of the flesh of a fat horse, koumiss or mare's milk, and a Circassian cheese pastry. Now all these foods are binding. The fact is that foods of a dry humor are very harmful to the disease of paralysis, which rather requires a constant diet of laxatives and purgatives. As a result, his condition grew daily worse. Finally, he summoned our pasha and the rest of the viziers and emirs and deputies to his side, and uttered his final testament:

"First of all, my servants are killing me for lack of water.

"Bury me next to my brother viziers in front of the prayer niche at the Ali Pasha mosque.

"Use 40,000 goldpieces to erect a life-nourishing fountain at my tombstone.

"Distribute 40,000 goldpieces to my aghas and to my personal retinue, and another 40,000 for Mecca and Medinah."

Three days later he passed away. The entire populace of Istanbul fell into mourning. Eventually, by the command of God and in accordance with his final testament, he was buried within a casement in front of the prayer niche of Ali Pasha mosque, which is on the Divan Yolu, and a small fountain was erected at his tombstone. But the rest of his property was sequestered, contrary to his last will. The chronogram above the casement of his tomb is this verse by Fuzuni:———. If I were to record his estate to the extent I am familiar with, it would be as long as that of Sinan Pasha, the conqueror of Yemen. But it would serve no useful purpose to do so. The length of his vizierate, including the six months on his death bed, was———.[7]

After his death, all the viziers and deputies and *ulema* and grandees gathered in the Padishah's presence and discussed to whom they should award the vizierial seal. At that time our lord Melek Ahmed Pasha was among the candidates. He dismounted, leaping like a veteran acrobat, and entered the Padishah's presence at the place known as Çemen Soffa. The privy chamberlain Rum Hasan Agha conducted him to the throne. The pasha, being unaccustomed to kissing the ground, merely uttered a benediction, saying: "*Es-selam aleyk*, my Padishah!" and was awarded the privilege of kissing the imperial fingers. Having attained his desire, and taken precedence over the other viziers, he stationed himself grandly and sedately at the very top row. At once the felicitous Padishah graciously rose to his knees and said: "Look here, my viziers. It is my special desire and wish— emanating not from the suggestion of anyone else, nor from the desire to curry anyone's favor, but emerging rather from my own innate disposition and inborn conception—to bestow my noble seal and my grand vizierate upon my *lala* Melek Ahmed Pasha."[8]

At this our lord Melek Ahmed Pasha jumped up three times, placed his hands on the ground, and said: "My Padishah, in order that your pearl-strewn speech not be scattered in vain, I accept your noble seal. However, as long as such brigands and rebels and outlaws, such *celalis* and Segbans and Sarıcas, as İpşir Pasha and Seydi Ahmed Pasha and Tayyar-oğlu Ahmed Pasha and Mirza Pasha and Kara Hasan Pasha are scouring Anatolia and looting it from end to end, as long as they are harrassing so many thousands of Muslims, grinding so many Ottoman subjects and their wives and daughters into the dust, and laying waste to the countryside—while all this is going on, no vizier can take possession of the seal, get a firm grip on affairs, administer justice, and raise revenues. From month to month, all of your *kuls* seek their salaries; the imperial arsenal is in need of supplies; and every year expenditures mount to 47,000 Rumi purses.[9] Meanwhile, not a single asper enters the treasury from all the imperial grants and imposts of Anatolia. The whole eastern region has turned into 'warring kingdoms'.[10]

"My Padishah! According to the humble opinion and limited intellect of this lowly slave, the best thing to do would be to bestow the noble seal upon your *lala* Ipşir Pasha. Have him proceed to the capital immediately, so that the Muslims in Anatolia may be secure from the depredations of those evildoers. He is a veteran vizier, wealthy and experienced. Let him come and outfit a great fleet, let him drive a sea of men to Crete from Anatolia and Rumelia; let him take charge himself as commander-in-chief; let him conquer Crete with its fortress of Candia; let him conquer the island of Corfu, and the fortress of Zadra, so that the lanes to Egypt by land and by sea will be made secure and peace will prevail; and let your *lala* Ipşir Pasha also for once be possessor of the seal, that he may know the meaning of the seal of Solomon, and may experience its flavor."

After so many words of counsel, he fell silent.

Reply of the Universal Padishah, Sultan Mehmed IV

"Look here, *lala*. Innumerable heads of *celalis* and brigands have rolled and tumbled at this court. God willing, those, too, will soon be punished, and all the Muslims will be delivered from their depredations, just as you desire."

The felicitous Padishah, quite enraged, got to his feet and with his own blessed and noble hand gave the seal to our Melek Ahmed Pasha, and clothed him in a sable robe of honor. "Go forth," he said, "may God on high assist you in all your endeavors, may the Lord Creator succor you and bring all of your undertakings to a successful conclusion. Now show me how you will strive on behalf of the clear Religion, and struggle for my imperial sake; how you will build up the treasury, and pay all my office holders their salaries, from 1 to 1,000, and from 1,000 to 100,000."

He showered him with praises and benedictions, and the notables on every side shouted, "God bless you!" Thereupon the felicitous Padishah cloathed our lord in another sable cloak, so that day he acquired two fur pieces.

The pasha, to be sure, put the seal inside his bosom, but it was as though a stinging scorpion entered his bosom, he took no joy in it at all, in fact he was quite dejected. For he was thinking how to raise money for the treasury. Ten days remained be-

fore the distribution of salaries; but there were only seventeen
purses at the imperial gate; the wicked infidels were overrun-
ning all the islands in the Aegean; while on this side the imperial arsenal lacked provisions and supplies; and in Anatolia the
depredations of the *celali* vermin prevented a single copper coin
from entering the treasury. Perplexed and overcome with a thousand such gloomy thoughts, and unable to refuse the seal, he
kissed the ground and withdrew to the council chamber where
for a full seven hours he consulted with all the viziers and deputies, the *şeyhülislam* Ebu Said Efendi, the *nakibüleşraf*, the
two *kaziaskers*, the chief eunuch, the privy chamberlain Hasan
Agha, the *bostancı-başı*, and the other courtiers.

At the time of the late-afternoon prayer he happened upon
the Padishah once again at the place called Çimşirlik. "My Padishah," he said, "we have decided that the best plan is to send
the seal to your *lala* Ipşir Mustafa Pasha."

"What are you saying, Melek *lala*?"

"I swear by God, my Padishah, this is the best plan." And
he quoted the hadith: "What the believers think to be best is the
best with God."

He took the seal from the Pasha, immediately gave him the
substitute seal from the treasury, said, "You are my honored
minister and my grand deputy," and cloathed him in a sable
robe of honor. So on that day the pasha donned three sable furs.

In the year———on the———th day of the month of———[11]
the pasha became independent deputy vizier, and returned to
his palace happy and smiling. As for the noble seal, Dergah-i-
ali———Agha conveyed it to Ipşir Mustafa Pasha in Aleppo. Our
lord the pasha also sent quite a few valuable congratulatory gifts
with Ak Agha to Ipşir Pasha in Aleppo. That same blessed
month Ayşe Sultan, daughter of Sultan Ahmed,[12] was given in
marriage to Ipşir Pasha, and tidings to that effect also went via
the agha to Aleppo.

The pasha now conferred several high posts and in seven
days brought out 4,000 salaries and office expenses, thus paci-
fying all the *kuls*. But Ipşir Pasha did not allow any of the
agents to assume their posts, and afterward the agents re-
claimed their office dues from the pasha by right of the *şeriat*,
so the Pasha incurred a loss of 1060 Rumi purses, which he had
to turn over to the claimants.

On the twentieth of the month, our former agha, Kulaksız
Abaza Şahin Agha, arrived with the gypsy *harac*; but our lord

the pasha did not allow Şahin Agha to take possession of the gypsy *harac*. This was the beginning of the falling-out between our lord and Ipşir Pasha.

Now everyone who arrived (at the capital) brought news of Ipşir Pasha's rebellion in Aleppo. They said he had raised a sea-like army. The sultan kept sending sergeants-at-arms and valets and palace guards with urgent appeals, inviting Ipşir to come immediately to the Threshold of Felicity. But he did not set foot outside Aleppo, and he kept on building up his army. Once a memorandum arrived to the following effect:

"The petition of this worthless slave to the court of my Padishah is as follows: The ignoble, head-shaven Kızılbaş[13] have driven off several hundred thousand sheep from the region of Pinyanişi in the province of Van, and they have killed several hundred Kurdish notables and laid waste to numerous villages and towns. They have committed all sorts of acts contrary to the truce established by Sultan Murad.[14] Because this lowly slave is investigating affairs in that region, I am unable to come to the court. I am now gathering an army and, with your imperial command, am about to set out in that direction as commander-in-chief. God willing, my Padishah, too, will direct the reins of a sealike army toward these regions in the spring, and we will take the lives of thousands of these ignoble wretches and will recover Revan and Nahşivan and Şirvan and Azerbaijan, which your uncle Sultan Murad conquered but which the Kızılbaş took back.[15] Now I have mustered 40,000 musketeers and Segbans and Sarıca *gazis*, and I have with me seventy *begler-begs* and seven noble viziers. I am prepared, if necessary, to come with this company and to rub my face on the imperial Threshold."

News of this message left all of the courtiers in a quandary. The chief admiral, Kara Murad Pasha, kindled the fire of sedition in the janissary corps, saying: "Do you see? He will surely massacre you with 40,000 musketeers!" All sorts of rumors, grounded and ungrounded, began to fly in Istanbul. And the courtiers, once drunk with power, now reeled about in a daze, as though they were genuinely intoxicated. Seventy-three individuals to my knowledge—including our lord the pasha's steward Kudde Kethüda, the *defterdar* Moralı Mustafa Pasha, Mevkufati Mehmed Efendi, Topkapılı, and the customs inspector Hasan Agha—conspired together and, for 2,000 purses, demanded the seal on behalf of the *defterdar* Moralı Mustafa Pasha. But the felicitous Padishah categorically refused. "Just let my *lala* Ipşir Pasha come!" he said. Even our lord Melek Ahmed Pasha took fright and sent Ipşir Pasha quite a few letters of conciliation, but he received only derisive replies. In short, tranquility had fled Istanbul, confusion reigned, there were thousands of jangling voices and clashing rumors.

One day, while all was quiet and the gatekeepers were guarding the gates, and our lord the pasha was in his private chamber with his melancholy thoughts, he engaged me in conversation, saying, "What's new in the world?"

"You're in charge," I replied, "you know what's new."

Just then we heard a voice outside the door crying "Allahu Hak."[16] *Marvel of marvels, concerning the states of the noble dervishes.* All of a sudden Telhisi Hüseyn Agha came inside, and there were three of us in the room. Among the things said was this: "Ipşir Pasha is coming with his henchmen and bandits, a huge rabble army. What's going to happen when such a large crowd of vermin descend on the imperial Threshold? And these two—Kapudan Murad Pasha and Defterdar Moralı Mustafa Pasha—how are we going to deal with those sacks of sedition?"

"Well you know," said the pasha, "when I was grand vizier and Ipşir Pasha was governor of Damascus, I sent a noble command with Dürzi Mustafa Agha, along with letters of counsel, warning him not to attack the Druzes lest he trample underfoot the honor of the vizierate. But he did not act in accordance with the imperial order. By his own ill judgment he attacked the Druzes. He got caught in the Bekaa Valley, his army was decimated by the Druzes, he lost a fortune in state funds, he himself was wounded in the thigh at the hands of a Druze wielding an *akva* dagger,[17] got away with a single horse and six servants, and returned half-dead to Damascus. Now he has been my mortal enemy ever since I sent those letters of counsel. Well, we'll see what happens when he comes." His mind was troubled with fears and fancies.

As we were discussing the vicissitudes of the world in this fashion, a Bektaşi dervish—the same who a moment ago cried "Allahu Hak"—burst inside, without fear or hesitation, crying "Allahu Hak! Dost! Illallah! Love to you, sincere and subtle lovers!" He raised his shepherd's trumpet of Moses and first of all blew twelve thunderous blasts for the love of the twelve *imams*. The pasha and myself were dumbstruck. How was this heart-wounded dervish able to penetrate into our cell, with so many gatekeepers guarding the gates of this deputy vizier's palace,

crowded with men, and the doorkeepers not allowing even a speck of dust—let alone a bird—to fly through. We put finger to mouth in astonishment.

Meanwhile I took a close look at this dervish.[18] He was barefoot and bareheaded and raggedy. But his face and his eyes gleamed with light, and his speech sparkled with pearls of wit. He was extremely eloquent and quick witted. On his head perched a "water-pot" headgear,[19] with the turban awry and adorned with twelve ruby-colored brands, like appliqué roses, standing for the twelve Pirs of the Bektaşi order, and signifying his love for the dynasty (of Ali) and his devotion to the twelve *imams*.

Now this love-intoxicated holy man again raised his trumpet and intoned a melody consisting of the Beautiful Names—including el-Kayyum, el-Vahid, el-Macid, el-Ehad, el-Ferd, es-Samad, el-Kadir, and el-Muktedir—after which he cried "Er Hak! Allah Dost Dost!" and fell silent.

I examined his person once again. On his shirtless and guileless pure and saintly chest were marks of flagellation he had received in Tebriz during the Aşura ceremonies marking the martyrdom of el-Hüseyn,[20] each gash the size of half a stirrup thong. He removed the "water-pot" from his head revealing, just above his forehead, a "brand of submission" the size of a piaster. His purpose in displaying it to us was to demonstrate that he was an adept in the holy law (*şeriat*), in the mystic path (*tarikat*), in the mystic truth (*hakikat*), and in the gnostic wisdom (*marifet*), and that he had submitted to the way of Truth (*tarik-i hak*). On both arms[21] were wounds and gashes of the four companions of the Prophet, and on his left arm were brands and lashes of the plain of Kerbela. He was mad, pure, wild, and radiant, but not exactly naked. He was shaven in the saintly "four strokes" manner to indicate that he was free of all forbidden things—thus there was no trace of hair, whether on his head, mustache, beard, brow, or eyelashes. But his face was shining. In short, the apron round his waist, the staff in his hand, the words "Oh Beloved of hearts" on his tongue, the sling of David in his waistband, the *palheng*-stone[22] of Moses, the pomp of Ali, the decorative plumes, bells, and other ornaments—(all these indicated that he was) a companion of the foot-travelers, they were the outfittings and instruments of poverty of the noble dervishes, and he himself was the perfect mystic.

I plucked up my courage to address him: "My padishah, whence do you bring greetings?" Then with humble attitude and lofty voice I recited the following sextain:

Ne gülzarıñ nesimidir hava-yı unsur-ı pakiñ
Ne şem'iñ şu'lesidir nar-ı ruhsar-ı araknakiñ
Ne nehriñ suyıdır abıñ ne yer toprağıdır hakiñ
Ne halkatsin ki kırsañ halkı yokdur kimseden bakiñ
Efendim saña kim derler ne yerdensin nedir adıñ
Cefayı kimden ögrendiñ a canım kimdir üstadıñ

The breeze of what rose garden is the breath of your pure
    essence?
The flame of what candle is the fire of your sweat-beaded
    cheek?
The water of what river is your water, the soil of what land
    is your soil?
What creature are you, that if you murder creatures, you
    have fear of no one?
My lord, what do they call you, where are you from, what
    is your name?
From whom did you learn cruelty, my soul, who was your
    master?

When I finished reciting these verses, the dervish said: "A master who though merciless is love to the soul, oh saint!"

"May it be a divine lesson to your love, may God succor you," said I.

Hearing such lovely mystical replies, the heart-wounded dervish was fairly lifted off his feet with joy, and in response to my verses he intoned this Arabic poem:

Yakūlūne Leylā bi'l-'Irāķi merīżatün
Fe-yā leytenī küntü ṭabīben müdāviye
'Aleyye iżā lāķaytü Leylā bi-Ḥulvetin
Ziyāretü beyti'llāhi riclāye ḥāfiye[23]

They say that Leyla is ill in Iraq.
Would that I were a healing physician.
I must, when I meet Leyla in Hulwa
Visit the house of God, my feet bare.

He recited the verses with the utmost eloquence, pronouncing every consonant exactly and correctly. I congratulated him fullsomely on his eloquence, and he said:

"With the verses of your sextain you inquired in mystical and poetical fashion about my wretched state and my identity. Here is the answer to those questions. First of all, I am a Bektaşi dervish in the path of Hoca Ahmed Yesevi.[24] My master was Derviş Ali Nadimi who resided in Hazret-i Imam Riza (i.e., Mashhad in Iran) for forty years, fasting by day and praying by night, and who never in his life tasted food of an animal slaughtered with a knife. This humble one is the spiritual son of that paragon.

"In one verse you inquired where I was from. And in my Arabic verse, bi'l-'Irāḳi merīżatün, I hinted that I, weak and sickly, reside in Iraq, that is to say, Iraq-ı Acem, which is Baghdad, the garden of paradise and the abode of the caliphs.

In another verse you inquired what they call me. This humble one's name is Derviş Sünneti. For I am a Sunni dervish, and I go by the name of Sünneti because I was circumcised by the Hand of Power.

"In one verse you inquired, 'What creation are you?' I am pure and unsullied, created according to the verse (Koran 17:70) 'And we ennobled the sons of Adam,' and clothed in the robe of honor of the outfittings of poverty.

"In another verse you asked about my river. It is the Tigris, otherwise the Shattularab, which rises in the Tercil mountains in the vicinity of Diyarbekir. And you asked about my soil. The fragrant soil of Baghdad, garden of paradise, is where my head fell to earth.

"You asked of what candle I was the flame. The flame of my clay is filled with the light of Faith. You asked about my sweat-beaded cheek. My cheeks are ruddy with the unity of Monotheism. You asked about the breath of my pure essence. My breath and my passion are for witnessing the beauty of the Lord of sublimity. And my pure essence was kneaded by the Hand of Power, so that I have become the greatest Name."

Thus he gave apt and Sufi-like replies to all of the questions in the verses of the sextain which I had recited. Love for this holy man sprang up in my heart, and I kissed his noble hand, crying, "Homage, my sultan!"

"Please honor me with your name," he said.

"They call your slave Evliya, son of Derviş Mehmed Zilli."

120   *The Intimate Life of an Ottoman Statesman*

"Now," he said, "you are truly a saint (*veli*, singular of *ev-liya*). Accept me as your brother and your intimate, one who shares your inner state, and your way-companion on the sea."

"I accept," said I, and recited this couplet:

> *Verdim beni benden saña*
> *Aldım seni senden baña*
> *Oldı temam beyᶜ ü şira*
> *Yok arada sim ü zeri*

> I have given you me from me
> I have taken you from you to me
> Buying and selling are finished
> There is no silver or gold between us.

We grasped each other's hands, and I recited the noble koranic verse from the *sure* of Victory (48:10): "Those who pay homage to you pay homage to God. God's hand is above their hands." Thus I renewed my homage through that holy man, and received new life.

Our lord the pasha saw what was going on and, since he was a Nakşbendi (*tarik-i hocaganda*),[25] decided that he would seize the opportunity to renew his homage as well, and made a bow.

"Oh lover,"[26] the dervish said, "are you not Melek Ahmed Pasha? You have conformed to the eternal homage. It is for your sake that I set foot in this country. For seven months I have been racing here, and now, praise God, I have been vouchsafed this meeting in good health. Listen, Melek Dede! Mübtecil Hoca Cafer and Derviş Angil Haydar, who are among the saints of Spain, pass there as Christians, but both are believers and monotheists, and secretly possessors of the prayer rug and sultans in the vanguard of the Nakşbendis.[27] They paid homage to this humble one and said, 'Go forth, Oh Derviş Sünneti, meet Melek Ahmed Pasha in Istanbul, and become acquainted with his companions. Convey to Melek Baba our greeting as a divine trust. And let him find solace in this verse from the *sure* of Yusuf (Koran, 12:31): "They said, this is not a human being (*be-şer*). This is nought but a noble angel (*melek*)." ' They sent you this verse along with their greeting, saying, 'Do not be afraid of Ipşir. God will be your protector.' "

The pasha leaped up. "Thank God and praise be to God, peace be upon you and God's mercy and blessing, may both the

sender and the deliverer be safe and sound! God be praised that
the dread of Ipşir is departed from my heart. I am delivered of
cares and fears, free of gloom and despair. As soon as I heard
this noble verse from their pearl-studded speech I found spiritual comfort. God be praised, I have attained my goal and my
desire."

He took Derviş Sünneti's hand in his and began to inquire
about whatever holy men there are in Spain and in other countries. "Mübtecil Baba Sadık in Cordoba greets you. Şeyh Mansur
in Tangiers greets you. Izzeddin Burnavi in Fez of Morocco
greets you."

The pasha rose to return the greetings. "I had sent them
letters with Cezayirli Ali Piçin-oğlu and had heard that they
received them." Once again the pasha and Derviş Sünneti
embraced and kissed, and for a period they were busy in a
corner with private conversation. Indeed, the two of them began to commune in a most mysterious fashion, such that I
understood not a single word of their pearl-studded speech,
and remained nonplussed. Only I understood that they were
in a very merry mood from their frequent exclamation of "God
be praised" or "Thanks be to God" or "This is of my Lord's
bounty." Eventually they returned to the point, and Derviş
Sünneti said:

"When sending you this noble koranic verse (they said):
'Give glad tidings to Melek Dede according to the interpretation
of the şeyhs based on the approximate readings of the şeyh of
the readers, his holiness Susi. In the verse ḳālū mā hāẕā beşer
("They said, this is not a human being") they elide the elif between hāẕā and beşer and read mā hāẕāʾ bşer; and the mā of
mā hāẕā is the mā of——(i.e., negation); so the meaning is:
"Ipşir is not, he is doomed." And "This is nought but a noble
angel" signifies: "You will stand firm, you are an angel (melek)
in life and possessor of nobility." '

"This does not mean, of course, that the Koran commenta-
tors understood this noble verse to refer only to you, Melek and
Ipşir. God forbid! The people of the şeriat would reject such an
interpretation. Only the esoteric şeyhs, being masters of all the
occult sciences, aware of symbols and hidden meanings, and
possessing the *Encompassing Onomancy*[28] in the science of Divine Presence (ledün), have extracted this sense out of the letters (huruf) of Ali and the words of Muhyiddin, and have sent
you this message of solace."

"I have derived peace of mind from this noble verse," the pasha replied. "This is a veiled utterance of the people of hearts. The glorious Koran contains myriads of divine mysteries, in each expression and word, in each letter and each jot, which those who know the science of Ali are able to extract. They are aware of these secrets, and can apply them until the end of time. It is an independent science." For Melek Ahmed Pasha was himself a Sufi adept and a heart-wounded dervish, and he always used to associate with the Upright of the Community.[29] This time he conversed intimately with Derviş Sünneti a full five hours.

When dinner arrived, Derviş Sünneti suddenly shook the pasha's hand, leaped up from his place and went out the door like lightning. "Hey Evliya," shouted the pasha, "catch up with the Dede, don't let him get away!" I chased after him, but saw no sign of him, nor did the gatekeepers or the people in the street. When I reported that he had disappeared, the pasha gave me 200 gold coins and two Kashmiri sashes and sent me after him, saying: "Make haste, my Evliya. Wherever you find that holy man, greet him from me, give him these things, and tell him to please visit me at any time."

I mounted my horse and went out the palace gate. "People of Muhammed," I exclaimed, "have you seen a wild radiant dervish of such-and-such a description?" As I was questioning people here and there, one man in front of the Bayram Pasha palace said: "There's a dervish going toward Ahır Kapı and playing a trumpet." Spurring on my horse, I emerged from Ahır Kapı and caught sight of him in a caique in the middle of the straight. I jumped into a caique with five pairs of oars, and we took off, rowing sharp, with oars and sail.

As we got to the middle of the straight, I waved a handkerchief at the Dede's oarsmen, who cut off rowing until we caught up. Jumping into the other caique, I kissed the holy man's noble hand and said: "Your son the pasha greets you. He entreats you to accept these 200 goldpieces as road money, to don these two Kashmir sashes, and to honor him from time to time with your visit."

" 'Gifts should be shared though held in common,' " he quoted. "May God requite him with the blessings of Abraham. The sashes belong to me, the gold belongs to the rowers and to you."

"Please my sultan," I insisted, "all of it belongs to you."

"Ah, but you see, that is impossible." He removed his "pocket-book of love"[30] from the collar of his sheepskin apron. "Permission granted," he said; "stick your hand into this ocean of grace."

I recklessly stuck my hand into the "pocket-book of love" and behold: it was filled with Venetian ducats—warm and fragrant and fresh from the oven—also rubies, diamonds, and Sudanese emeralds. "Now my sultan," I exclaimed in bewilderment, "you know better, this humble one submits to your will." He gestured to the sack, as if to say "Take, take!" So I took out a handful, which amounted to eighty-seven fine gold coins and seven precious jewels—a ruby, an emerald, a diamond, a red ruby, a garnet, a turquoise, and a chrysolite.

"My dear Evliya," he said, "if you spend one of these gold-pieces every year, you will enjoy the blessings of Abraham, sufficient to last you a lifetime." "Well," said I to myself, "it seems I am going to live for eighty-seven years." All sorts of wonderful fantasies rose in my head.

To this bounty he added 100 of the pasha's 200 goldpieces, and the remaining hundred he distributed evenly among our ten rowers. One of the sashes he wound around his cap, and the other he tied about his neck. "Give the pasha my greetings," he said. "I will not set foot in the country of Rum (i.e., Turkey) again. For I am charged with making my way past the ports of the Holy Land and directing my steps toward Mecca and Medinah. I hinted as much to your worthiness earlier in one of my Arabic verses: 'Visit the house of God, my feet bare.' Now I have directed the reins of intention in that direction. And when I asked you to accept me as your way-companion on the sea, I was alluding to this meeting, where we are companions on the sea. Do not forget me in your prayers."

As we were about to say farewell, he turned to the rowers and said: "I wish you to go to the pasha together with my brother Evliya Çelebi. Bear witness that I refused to accept the goldpieces and that I distributed them among you, so that the pasha will feel peace of mind, and his heart will be free of any evil suspicion regarding Evliya Çelebi." This made me very happy.

"Evliya," he said, "my prayers are with you. 'Go dance on the sand and don't let a straw get into your rump.'[31] On the road to Mecca, and in the land of Egypt, never grieve and never fear.[32] You are safeguarded from the calamities of fate. The transcendant God is your Helper and Protector. In all the lands where you sojourn you will be held in honor by the sultans and the viziers and the deputies and the grandees. And you will be secure from insidious plots. Do not forget to pray for me in the castle of Van. El-Fatiha!"

After the prayer I kissed his hand, he proceeded toward Üsküdar with sail unfurled, and I returned to Ahır Kapı in a cheerful mood. I went to the pasha with two of the rowers, conveyed the Dede's greeting, and told him what happened. The pasha, full of astonishment, said: "I have found a wonderful solace and contentment at this noble verse from the *sure* of Yusuf. That man was truly a saint." And afterwards we always took great joy in recounting his qualities.

This humble one was privileged to encounter such a holy man during the deputy vizierate of Melek Ahmed Pasha. I questioned the gatekeepers: "You were stationed at the door of the pasha's room with sticks in your hands. How did this dervish get into the pasha's cell? Didn't you see him?" They all swore that they had not seen him; "but we did hear a voice between the doors crying 'Allahu Hak,' and we did hear a dervish trumpet sounding near the pasha." It was simply a marvel.———

Having carried out the above-mentioned sultanic offices in five months according to the imperial command, and in return for what we surrendered to the imperial arsenal, our lord Melek Ahmed Pasha was awarded a sultanic robe of honor in the imperial *divan* and in the presence of the Padishah, and into our hands were delivered official documents and *şer'i* vouchers from Defterdar Moralı Mustafa Pasha and from the overseer of the arsenal. So we remained tranquil in Melek Ahmed Pasha's service.

But Ipşir Pasha still had not come from Aleppo. Gossips and rumors spread about in Istanbul and the people were all wondering if and when Ipşir would arrive. As for the officials, they hoped that Ipşir would not reach Istanbul but that, as he was a *celali*, he would be broken at Üsküdar and would run away, as happened to Nasuh-paşa-zade Hüseyn Pasha.[33] Meanwhile, Ipşir Pasha was moving this way like thunder with his sealike army.

By God's wisdom: One day, while I was conversing with Melek Ahmed Pasha, the oppressive topic of Ipşir Pasha came up, and our lord said: "Get ready, Evliya. I'm going to send you to my brother Ipşir Pasha with letters relating to certain important affairs of the Muslims. He was very fond of you, and used to call you 'Hafiz Evliya.' You're the one to go. There's no doubt that hypocrites have come between us and have poisoned Ipşir's mind against me. For he has not allowed any of my (provincial) appointees to assume their offices. Associate with him for a few days, sound him out, take note of all his activities and his conduct of affairs; then get letters from him and return to me."

"Your wish is my command," I replied, and prepared to depart, taking the seventy letters and the orders of courier (ulak). *Stages of the journey, and difficulties encountered, when going as courier to Ipşir Pasha in the year——on the——th day of the month——.* First of all I received road money and douceurs to assure my good word on their behalf from the pasha, Kapudan Kara Murad Pasha, Moralı Defterdar, the grand chancellor (koca nişancı), the şeyhülislam Ebu Said, the chief black eunuch, Kudde Kethüda, the customs inspector Şami-zade—in short, from seventy different officials—amounting to 2,073 goldpieces, which I deposited with my sister. Then with my three gulams, each outfitted with a sword, a quiver, and a whip, I acquired mounts in Üsküdar from the post-horse master, whose name was Acem; and that day, taking refuge in God, and beating the leather strap, we reached the station of the town of Gebze.

That day and night we pressed on, undergoing hardships at Kırk-geçid the likes of which God should not visit upon the Malta infidels. The merciful rain of winter was for us that night a merciless downpour. The post-horses fell head over heels, and my head was split. Thus wounded, we reached the stage of Iznik, where we acquired fresh mounts and passed Lefke to the stage of Söğüt. There again we acquired fresh mounts, passed Eskişehir with great difficulty, and arrived at the stage of Seydi-gazi. From there we skirted the caravansaray of Husrev Pasha and the village of Bayındır,[34] and after much suffering reached the stage of Akşehir. Exhausted, we stayed that night in the inn. Then we passed Ilgın to the town of Ladik and thence, on the sixth day, arrived at *the plain of Konya.*

As this broad valley came into view, it was covered end to end with tents, set up in dense formation, tentrope to tentrope, and adorned with grand and varicolored royal pavilions. An army was camped there whose number and extent only God knows. It took me a good four hours to make my way through this great throng. I went straight to my clansman Kara Abaza

Hasan Pasha. He rose, pressed me to his chest, and without removing my weapons from my waistband, immediately ushered me to Ipşir Pasha's pavilion.

But what a grand and varicolored royal pavilion, as though it were the tent of Afrasiyab![35] By the time I went through the door and reached the pasha's quarters, I was exhausted. Nevertheless I stepped briskly into Ipşir Pasha's presence, reciting these verses:[36]

> *Afakı begim madeletiñ nur pür etsin*
> *Hurşid gibi encümen-i dehre çirağ ol*
> *Geh nafe gibi eyle diri deşt-i muattar*
> *Geh gonca-sıfat gülşene gül zinet-i bağ ol*
> *Dadar-ı cihan eylemesin alemi sensiz*
> *Her kanda iseñ Asaf-ı şah dünyada sağ ol*[36]

May your justice, my Beg, fill the horizons with light.
Be like the sun a lamp to the council of time.
Now liven like the musk-pod the perfumed plain.
Now smile like the bud in the rose-garden and be the
      garden's ornament.
May the Ruler of the World not deprive the world of you.
Wherever you are in the world, oh royal vizier, may you
      be well!

And I kissed his noble hand.

"Welcome Evliya," he cried. "I haven't seen you since the year of Varvar Ali Pasha.[37] How many days since you left Istanbul?"

"Five days, my sultan. But the weather was awful."

"And what's new in the capital?"

"Rich and poor alike, old and young, nobles and commoners, all are in expectation of being honored by your arrival. Especially your brother Melek Ahmed Pasha is anxiously awaiting you, saying, 'Ah, if only my brother, my lord Sultan Murad's protégé and favorite, would come!' He sent my sultan these letters." I handed over the seventy letters in their satin pouches, kissed the ground, and stepped back.

Turning to his treasurer he said: "Evliya is your guest. Look after him well. Give him a sable fur, a suit of clothes, and a purse of piasters for bath money." So I repaired to the treasury tent, ate a meal, and fell asleep from exhaustion.

To make a long story short, I conversed with Ipşir Pasha for seven days in the plain of Konya. "Words bring forth words." If I were to record in detail our consultations and conversations over these seven days, it would be a very long scroll. The jist was this:

One day Ipşir Pasha addressed me thus: "Tell me the truth, my Evliya. Do Murad Pasha and the janissary corps want me?"

I swore that they did. "The fact is that all of the Padishah's *kuls*, including viziers and deputies, are hoping for my sultan's arrival. 'Ah,' they are saying, 'if only he came to the capital, and the Ottoman state were restored to order!' And all the *ulema* and the notables and grandees are saying, 'He is the protégé of Sultan Murad, and has the character of Husrev Pasha.[38] If only he came, and saw to the important affairs of state; if only he took vengeance upon the Venetians, and secured the sea lanes to Egypt against the infidels!' "

"Now tell me the truth, Evliya. Did Moralı Defterdar really pay 2,000 purses for the seal?"

"Yes, he did seek the vizierial seal when the late Bıyıklı Derviş Mehmed Pasha was paralyzed. But the felicitous Padishah refused. He thought the best idea was to bestow the seal on your brother Melek Ahmed Pasha. But your brother the pasha said: 'I have already possessed the seal once, and have savored its sweetness. I really think that the Padishah ought to give it to his *lala*, Ipşir Pasha. He has an army, and he is a wise and brave statesman. He deserves the seal a thousand times over. And he is your old vizier.' He sang your praises for an hour; and the *şeyhülislam* Ebu Said, and the chief eunuch, and——— —— all of them concurred, saying, 'My Padishah, your *lala* Ipşir Pasha deserves the seal.' A Fatiha was recited, and the noble seal was sent to my sultan, while the deputy vizierate was bestowed upon your brother Melek Pasha. He took matters in hand, mustered his resources, and seven days later brought out the salaries for the entire (janissary) corps."

There was a great deal more conversation, which it is impossible to record here. Finally, eight days later, he gave me three purses, two horses, 300 goldpieces, one quiver, one suit of armor, one suit of clothes, plus 50 goldpieces for each of my *gulams*; and entrusted me with ninety-five letters. He also arranged the post-horses. After kissing his hand, I bade farewell to the various grandees, and received gifts of road money which, along with Ipşir Pasha's gifts, I deposited as a divine trust with his holiness Mevlana-zade———Çelebi. I visited the shrines of the holy Sultan-el-ulema[39] and the holy Celaleddin Rumi, then bade farewell to the Çelebi Efendi, and set off from the well-guarded city of Konya.

Proceeding north, we passed the town of Ladik and stopped at the town of Ilgın. Thence, skirting Akşehir, we exchanged post-horses at Bayındır, and proceeded without stopping to the stage of the inn of Husrev Pasha. Next we passed Seydi-gazi and Eskişehir and alighted at the town of Söğüt. Thence, while skirting the town of Lefke, I crossed paths with Ayşe Sultan's Mercan Agha who was on his way to Ipşir Pasha. We halted at the city of Iznik, passed Kafir Derbendi and Hersek Dili by boat, halted at Gebze, then passed Üsküdar and entered Istanbul on the————th of the month of————.

I found the pasha at the arsenal equipping the fleet for the Crete campaign. I kissed his noble hand and delivered all the letters, and as the Pasha began to peruse them, I dozed off.

If I were to enumerate all the events and discussions that occurred at this juncture until Ipşir Pasha's arrival, it would take an entire volume. Suffice it to say that those to whom I brought conciliatory letters from Ipşir Pasha, Kara Hasan Pasha, Tayyar-zade Ahmed Pasha, Can Imirza Pasha, and the other notables were greatly relieved and, in their joy, bestowed generous gifts on this humble servant. Defterdar Moralı, on the other hand, was greatly upset, since he received letters from no one. He kept asking me, "What did Ipşir Pasha say about me?" And I gave him answers calculated to put his mind at rest, following the prophetic dictum, "He who makes peace between two peoples deserves the reward of a martyr." So the *defterdar* was quite cheerful. Kudde Kethüda and Mevkufati Mehmed Efendi, however, were not at all happy, in fact, they had grave misgivings.[40]

From the arsenal we made our way to the pasha's palace in Istanbul. When we were alone, I gave the pasha a full account of all the conversations I had had with Ipşir Pasha. "Will Ipşir definitely come to the capital, then?" he inquired.

"He will. But he will be accompanied by a huge and unruly army. And he will station himself in Üsküdar. If he isn't given the men he demands, he will return to Anatolia. And while he is in Üsküdar he won't go to see the felicitous Padishah without detaining as hostages the men who come out to receive him. Then, if he goes and is settled in his palace, he won't dismiss his troops that are in Üsküdar."

"Of course," said the pasha, "he will have to do that."

To make a long story short: Ipşir Pasha came on apace, cutting stages and rolling stations. At Eskişehir he was greeted by the first reception party which included, from the janissary corps, the court usher Kuyumcu Süleyman Agha, also Sarı Cavuş-başı, Sami-zade Reis, the seven corps commanders (bölük ağaları), and other courtiers whom the pasha had given leave to go. Ipşir Pasha proceeded apace. At Izmid he received countless gifts sent by the terrified Istanbul notables.

Now Melek Ahmed Pasha took counsel with the admiral of the fleet, Murad Pasha. "My brother," he ordered, "convey the imperial barge, by the sultan's leave and as a gesture of love, to our brother Ipşir Pasha. So, if he decides to come by sea, he may board the Throne of the Sultan of the Sea and proceed to Saray Burnu. And if he decides to come by land, you will have performed him a service."

"But my sultan," replied Murad Pasha, "the sea is treacherous. Possibly a northeaster or a southeaster will blow up and some harm will befall the imperial barge. How will I answer to the Padishah in that case?" He made all sorts of excuses, and the pasha realized that Murad Pasha did not relish the idea of going to greet Ipşir Pasha.

Finally he outfitted the bostancı-başı's caique and sent it to Izmid with the treasurer, Ahmed Agha, along with gifts totalling 40,000 or 50,000 piasters. Ipşir Pasha was very pleased with all of the gifts that arrived by land and by sea. He loaded them on boats and sent them off to Istanbul. Then he proceeded in state, like Alexander the Great, stage by stage, until he halted at the bostancı-başı's bridge.

When news of this reached our lord Melek Ahmed Pasha, he immediately ordered all the troops of both the janissary and the sipahi corps to cross over to Üsküdar to receive Ipşir Pasha. Thousands of boats in Istanbul harbor—skiffs, caiques, and lighters—were pressed into service to transport the sealike troops to Üsküdar. Several thousand soldiers set up their tents on the plain of Üsküdar, while the troops of the janissary corps all stationed themselves within the town.

That same day Murad Pasha was ordered to cross to Üsküdar with the imperial barge. As soon as Murad Pasha had gone across with the imperial barge and seven galleys, he began to harangue the janissary corps: "Do you realize what he will do? Don't you know that Abaza Pasha had Kör Hazinedar and

this Ipşir Pasha massacre the janissaries in Erzurum?[41] Now, in the same manner, he will have his 40,000 Segbans and Sarıcas and his 50,000 mounted troops massacre *you*, and thus he will take revenge for the blood of Sultan Ibrahim. You are a band of homeless janissary foot soldiers. What will you do here on Üsküdar plain? When Ipşir comes to Istanbul and settles in his palace, *then* go out (to greet him) in procession."

When he stirred up the janissary corps with this sort of troublemaking speech, all hell broke loose in Üsküdar. A caïque could hardly be found for a goldpiece. The entire janissary corps fled back to Istanbul in terror.

Seeing the effect of his rabble-rousing, Murad Pasha praised God and sent the royal barge straight back to the imperial arsenal. He himself rushed panting into the presence of our lord Melek Ahmed Pasha and said: "Do you see, my sultan? It seems that Ipşir Pasha planned to have his Segbans and Sarıcas massacre the janissaries in Üsküdar, then to kill off all the ones now holding office, and put Prince Ahmed on the throne. But the Segbans and Sarıcas refused, saying, 'We are Hacı Bektaş Veli's dancing-boys, we cannot draw the sword against the janissaries of our own fraternity.'[42] The corps got word of this, and they all fled back to Istanbul, fearing for their lives. Several thousand of them even got drowned in the crossing because of the crowd. Does this suit the law of God? And does my sultan acquiesce in this behavior? For my part, I took the imperial barge and returned to Istanbul, as you see!"

By informing our lord Melek Ahmed Pasha of this sorry turn of events, Murad Pasha wished to appear statesmanlike, but his actual intent was to stir up strife. In fact, Murad Pasha was always known as a troublemaker. The pillaging of Deli Hüseyn Pasha's treasury on the island of Crete; the hippodrome battle in Istanbul; the murder of Hezar-pare Ahmed Pasha; the martyrdom of Sultan Ibrahim—these and a hundred other seditious acts were due to Murad Pasha's advice and encouragement.

Because our lord Melek Ahmed Pasha knew all this, he addressed Murad Pasha thus: "Well my good man, when Ipşir Pasha hears about these sorry events he is bound to take offense and to run back to Anatolia."

"How nice," replied Murad Pasha. "Then the fact of his being a *celali* rebel will be blatantly clear. Then you can order this slave of yours, Murad, to march against him with a great army under the Prophet's banner, just as Kuyucu Murad Pasha did,[43] and God willing I will wipe Ipşir and his inauspicious (*na-beşir*) cronies from the world's slate."

He blustered a lot, but the pasha knew that this was just another example of Murad Pasha's ugly tendency to stir up trouble. "God help us," he said, and hurried out to explain the situation to the felicitous Padishah.

Melek Ahmed Pasha was obliged by imperial command to go and receive Ipşir Pasha. Taking his leave of the imperious Padishah, he proceeded to his palace where he decked in arms his 2,000 aghas of the exterior service, also his 410 aghas of the interior service, and crossed that night to Üsküdar while all the council viziers and the other official grandees lit torches.

At noon, just as he was about to enter Ipşir Pasha's camp, we heard the departure trumpet sound once. The fact was that Ipşir Pasha had taken fright and decided to turn back, and the first trumpet had been sounded. The pasha rushed ahead and arrived at Ipşir's tent an hour before the other viziers. The two men clasped each other to their breasts, and wept so much, it seemed that both were having epileptic seizures.

"Brother," said our lord Melek Ahmed Pasha, "Why did you delay coming from Aleppo to the Felicitous Threshold for the past six months?"

"Well, brother," Ipşir replied, "now we regret coming at all. We got a message from the janissary corps saying, 'They proposed to massacre you in Üsküdar, but we refused, and now we have crossed back to Istanbul.' I sent spies seven times and it was confirmed that all the janissaries had indeed crossed over to Istanbul. So that is what happened. Now I too am going back. And while I have the (vizierial) seal I will do what I think right: I'll go to Iran; with God's command, I'll conquer Revan, Gence, Şirvan, Tiflis, Tumanis, Şamahi, and Demir Kapı (Derbend); and having subjugated those regions, I'll rule there for the rest of my days."

Melek Ahmed Pasha withdrew his noble breviary[44] from his bosom, struck it seven times with his hand, and swore seven times—enunciating *bi'llāhi* and *ta'llāhi* with *i* after the *h*—evoking the spirit of Sultan Murad. "Beware, my brother," he said, "this is a trick. Since you arrived in Istanbul, all kinds of vicious rumors have been propagated by those scoundrels. Beware, my brother. Do not be taken in by these schemes and machinations, do not rebel against the Ottoman state. If you are wondering why the janissaries crossed to Istanbul, it was in accordance with the statutes of their corps. When Hafız Ahmed Pasha and Husrev Pasha and Civan Kapıcı-başı Mehmed Pasha came to the capital with the seal,[45] the *sipahi* troops paraded in Üsküdar, and on the next day the janissaries paraded through the Edirne Gate. And don't you remember the procession when Husrev Pasha came with Abaza Pasha?[46] You ought to be informed about this." He won Ipşir over with 70,000 such consoling words, and managed to get him mounted.

Processions were arranged. When they arrived at the *bostancı-başı's* bridge, Ipşir Pasha performed a prayer of two prostrations and was about to remount, when our Melek Ahmed Pasha presented him a grey steed outfitted with jewelled harness and saddle and a golden chain. "God be praised, a horse fit for the Padishah!" remarked Ipşir Pasha, as he mounted with a *besmele* without a stirrup. As they proceeded neck and neck, directing their reins toward Üsküdar, a host of greeters appeared. The seven *divan* viziers[47] beat their drums in seven places, and each one, with his decked-out troops mounted in a row, rose to greet him. The gleaming armor of the soldiers ranked right and left dazzled the eyes of the beholders.

As for Ipşir Pasha's troops, they were all seasoned warriors, fully armed and accoutred, from the lands of the Arabs and the Turks and the Kurds, each one a walking armory, uppity Segban and Sarıca vermin, clad in mail and armor and helmets and link-mail neckbands and shields and felts, each one having ready in his hands and at his waist five or six double-barreled lead-shot muskets with double wick, like so many salamanders amidst Nimrod's fire, marching in close formation and brandishing their weapons as though they were entering a skirmish. Aside from Ipşir's regiment, large contingents of troops and old-style military bands paraded in eighteen places. When the Istanbul troops saw this huge procession, they shook like autumn leaves.

As Ipşir Pasha and our lord Melek Ahmed Pasha were approaching neck and neck with such pomp and ceremony, the seven council viziers started to come forward according to imperial statute. Our pasha served as grand chamberlain to the viziers, introducing them and characterizing them one by one.

First the grand chancellor (Koca Nişancı Pasha) and Dellak Mustafa Pasha approached. Ipşir Pasha and our Melek Pasha

dismounted. The two viziers were introduced to Ipşir Pasha.
They kissed, and the pasha showed them great honor and respect.————

Seventh, Defterdar Moralı Mustafa Pasha appeared. Ipşir
Pasha mounted his steed without using a stirrup. Our Melek
Ahmed Pasha tried to represent the *defterdar's* good offices, but
Ipşir would not listen. The *defterdar* kissed Ipşir's stirrup, but
Ipşir would not look at him or even ask his welfare. Then he
gave him a very haughty look and began to upbraid him severely. Melek Ahmed Pasha did all he could to plead the *defterdar's* cause. Finally Ipşir Pasha said: "Brother, is this the one
who wanted to get the seal away from me for 2,000 purses? Remove that catamite!" He spurred his horse ahead a good distance, and the poor *defterdar* had to go quite a ways on foot.

Next the Istanbul notables approached, group by group and
guild by guild. Our Pasha introduced some of them, and several
thousand of them were introduced by the *çavuş-başı*.

Marching thus in grand procession, Ipşir Pasha dismounted at Ayşe Sultan's palace opposite the quay known as Salacak in Üsküdar. Animals were sacrificed. Then 40,000 of
Ipşir's troops were dispersed in Üsküdar town, while another
40,000 or 50,000 camped with their tents and pavilions in
Üsküdar plain. The army, row on row, encircled the palace where
Ipşir had alighted. Then Ayşe Sultan treated Ipşir Pasha and all
of the viziers and deputies and other statesmen who had come
out to receive him to a grand banquet, like a feast of Hatem
Tay.[48]

Now the chief eunuch————Agha and the *şeyhülislam* Ebu
Said Efendi arrived with the *bostancı-başı's* caique and invited
Ipşir Pasha to the presence of the Padishah. "God willing, tomorrow in grand procession I will rub my face at the foot of my Padishah's throne." But all present pleaded that it was impossible
not to go, and insisted that he answer the sultan's summons.

Finally Ipşir Pasha, on the pretext of performing ablutions,
went into his private chamber to consult with Kara Abaza Hasan
Pasha, Can Mirza Pasha, Kürd Mehmed Agha,————, and other
vermin of that sort. *Ipşir Pasha's ill counsel and evil consultation:* "First of all, when I leave this palace and go off to the Padishah, you will detain here as hostages the viziers and deputies
and *ulema*, keeping them under close surveillance. If I suffer
any harm on the part of the Padishah, you will put to the sword
all of those here as hostages, and our 70,000 or 80,000 soldiers

will pillage Üsküdar, plunder the sultan's palace, take his slave
boys and slave girls, set fire to the city, and depart."

Kara Hasan Pasha and the other vermin swore to this
abominable pact, placing their hands on the ancient writ (i.e., a
Koran). Then Ipşir Pasha, pretending that he had gone to freshen
his ablution, came out and addressed Melek Ahmed Pasha, Nişancı Pasha, Dellak Mustafa Pasha, Moralı Pasha,———; and of
the *ulema*,——— -zade and Sami-zade, and the other grandees:
"You sit here. I have to consult with you when I return from the
Padishah. I commend you to God."

"Since you have commended us to God," replied Melek
Ahmed Pasha, "our Helper is that most glorious God. We too
give you to God as a pledge. Go, may the Lord of glory be your
Aid and Protector!"

(So Ipşir Pasha) went off in the *bostancı-başı's* caique with
the chief black eunuch and the *müfti* (i.e., *şeyhülislam*), while
those who remained behind were completely surrounded by Segbans and Sarıcas. Now all the notables, realizing that they were
being detained as hostages in place of Ipşir, began to pray fer-
vently that the Padishah be slow to upbraid Ipşir and not say:
"Damn you! Why did you take seven months to come from
Aleppo and then bring with you so many thousand soldiers?"

We could see that Ipşir Pasha had reached the Sinan Pasha
pavilion at Saray Burnu. But then nothing happened for two
hours. *Melek Pasha's bravery:* At noon our lord Melek Ahmed
Pasha rolled up his sleeves and started to leave the room in order to perform the ritual ablution. One of the guards was a brig-
and named Cehennem Bölük-başı—as ugly and frightful as his
name (*cehennem* = "hell"), a real dragon out of hell, and one of
those walking armories, with an iron helmet on his head, chain-
mail armor on his shoulders, six cocked muskets at his waist,
and an Aleppan shield on his back—this devil, in the presence of
so many government officials, blocked the door and said: "Grand
Melek Pasha, my raging lion! Where do you think you're going
before Ipşir Pasha returns safe and sound from the sultan?"

"It's prayer time," answered the pasha mildly, "I'm going to
take my ablutions and perform the prayer."

"My Ipşir went to your sultan. If he doesn't return safe and
sound, I'll give you some ablutions that'll make you say your
prayers in the tomb."

The pasha smiled and again started to leave the room. "Hey
Pasha! Sit down!" At this, the vizierial zeal was aroused and the

pasha's fury was fired up. He gathered all his strength in his arm and gave that Cehennem Bölük-başı such an angelic blow (*tabanca-ı melek*) that the cocked (*tabancalı*) muskets dropped from his waist, and the iron helmet fell off his head. The pasha bared his dagger and, in the presence of so many scoundrels, struck the head of the head of the regiment heads (*bölük-başı*) in five or six places with the butt of the dagger, and the blood gushed out of the gashes in his head and out of his nose as though blood had been shot from his muskets.

As Cehennem Bölük-başı fell on his face and seemed to be having an epileptic seizure, the Segbans and Sarıcas all shouted: "Hey, our leader has been struck!" and they rushed against the pasha. But Ipşir's Abkhazian and Circassian retinue came to the pasha's rescue and, with some difficulty, took him under their wing. Consigning Cehennem Bölük-başı to the flames of hell, they took him by the arms and lugged him outside. All the onlookers stood amazed at Melek Pasha's bravery in the face of that crowd of Sarıca vermin. As for Melek Pasha, not for a moment did he lost his composure. He directed me to serve as *imam* for the congregation and we performed the noon prayer.

No sooner had we finished than a caique appeared off Saray Burnu and shot like lightening toward Kurşumlu Mahzen.[49] From within the caique waved a white flag stuck on a spear. When Ipşir's retinue saw this they cried: "Praise be to God! Our lord is safe and sound. Look, they've raised the white flag. And the caique is going up (the Bosphorous) and coming this way. If it had gone down from Saray Burnu, and they had unfurled a red flag, it would have signified that the Padishah had killed the pasha. That was the signal agreed upon when the pasha went from here to the sultan. Thank God, the pasha is safe and Üsküdar has escaped burning." Each member of the retinue collared one of the viziers or the other notables to tell him about these signals. Şami-zade and our own Kudde Kethüda and Moralı Defterdar regained their ruddy complexions and their lost wits.

By now the *bostancı-başı's* caique had set off from Saray Burnu and was coming like thunder, rowing sharp against the current. Everyone was watching the caique, whether with a spyglass or the naked eye, and crying joyfully: "Praise be to God, the pasha is safe and sound!" As the caique approached the Salacak quay, they all went to greet (Ipşir Pasha), taking him by the arm and conducting him to the palace. Melek Ahmed Pasha was standing still in his place. As soon as Ipşir set foot in the palace, Melek Pasha stepped forward. Ipşir donned a rose-pink sable fur. Our pasha embraced him and said: "Congratulations, brother. God be praised, it turned out just as planned. Welcome."

"What is this man lying here?" asked Ipşir upon entering the room with the pool.

"My sultan," came the reply, "your brother Melek Ahmed Pasha struck your slave Cehennem Bölük-başı and wounded him."

"He was a hellion; remove his corpse and let his soul rot in hell."

A friendly interview with our pasha ensued. "Brother," he said, "if you had not come out to greet me, those malicious Istanbulites would have forced me to rebellion (lit., would have made me a *celali*). God forbid, I would never agree to such wickedness. But still, my reputation would have suffered. May God be pleased with you. The felicitous Padishah honored me even more than your good advice and counsel (led me to expect). He took a solemn oath that I was safe at his hands, and he presented me with this jewelled dagger. Now I am going to give it to you—please accept it, brother." And he gave the pasha the dagger.

Now all the other courtiers took their leave from Ipşir and went home, leaving the pasha with him alone. The two of them conferred wonderfully together, now laughing, now crying. Their intimate conversation went on until sunset, when Ipşir ordered a hundred sheep and fifty camels to be sacrificed and given as alms to the poor.

That evening Kapudan Murad Pasha came with great pomp to confer with Ipşir Pasha. They treated each other with such loving concern, you would have thought they had lain together in a single womb. When Murad Pasha had gone, our lord Melek Ahmed Pasha, alone again with Ipşir, regaled him with warnings and counsels. Ipşir Pasha was pleased. "You are my dear brother," he said. "You were my vizierial deputy for seven months. We don't have to worry about money matters. I'll settle accounts with your steward, Kudde Kethüda. My only request is that you protect me tomorrow morning when I march in grand procession from Eyub Sultan to my palace in Istanbul."

The Far-Sighted Counsel of Melek Ahmed Pasha for the Short-Sighted Vizier Abaza Ipşir Pasha

"If you wish to be protected in this world and the next," replied Melek Pasha, "then do not be led astray by these hundred thousand brigands and scoundrels you brought from Aleppo. Do not harbor enmity, or shed blood out of covetousness for anyone's wealth and property. Be on friendly terms with everyone, and reconcile hearts.

"Take your brother as an example. During the time of my grand vizierate, there were seventeen great viziers. First there was Bektaş Agha and his Ömer Çelebi. Second there was Çelebi Kethüda and his Halil Bazcı. Third there was the janissary agha. There was Kara Cavuş and his secretary Yusuf Çelebi. There was Alahoz Mehmed Efendi and Sarı Katib and his Mimar Mustafa. There was the *valide-sultan*. And there was the chief architect. Aside from these there were several hundred men in the line[50] of the viziers, and I was sick of them all. But I made a virtue of necessity, and I got through my sixteen-month stint as grand vizier unscathed.[51]

"After me, my brother Siyavuş Pasha was grand vizier. Motivated by greed and base desires he killed off all of these I just mentioned who were at the vizierial rank, including his master's mother, Kösem Valide. Just when he thought the state was totally in his grasp, after fifty-four days in office, the Lord of glory dealt his comeuppance from a completely unsuspected source: such an ugly boor as the chief eunuch, Div Süleyman Agha, delivered him a mighty blow, took the seal from his hands, and gave it to Gürcü Mehmed Pasha.[52]

"Therefore, my brother, be forbearing. Don't kill people. Drive away this crowd of vermin, and take the side of the state. My brother, you arrived with 80,000 or 90,000 soldiers. They all remained behind in Üsküdar when you went to the Padishah. You entered his presence with only your own head and holding on to your two sleeves. What use to you was that pack of ruffians in Üsküdar?

"Furthermore, my brother, first and last you were raised and nurtured in this dynasty. In the Revan campaign you were Sultan Murad IV's chief stable master, and I was his swordbearer. Praise be to God, after thirty-one years you have returned to this Threshold and have attained the seal. Now muster your forces. Inquire after the Clear Religion from disinterested individuals. Together you will gird your loins; muster sealike armies on land and on sea; clear the sealanes to Egypt of the Venetian and Maltese infidels; conquer, God willing, by land and by sea, the islands of Crete, Misina, Malta, Corfu, and Istendil, and the fortresses of Kotur, Şibenik, and Zadra; and so earn a name for yourself, like the conqueror of Yemen, Sinan Pasha, or Kılıç Ali Pasha, or the conqueror of Cyprus, Kara Mustafa Pasha,[53] and be remembered with benedictions until the end of days."

Having completed this peroration to Ipşir Pasha, Melek Ahmed Pasha continued:

"Now, my dear brother, in the morning, God willing, I will serve as your marshal during the grand procession from Eyub Sultan to Istanbul. We'll conduct you there with more pomp and ceremony than were seen even when Hafız Ahmed Pasha or Husrev Şir Pasha had their parades. Right now draw up a white order (beyaz buyurdı) to the captain of the guard and the chief of police to clear all the streets. Order the admiral (Kapudan Pasha) to have several thousand caiques and skiffs and lighters go to Üsküdar and convey all the Muslim soldiery to Beşiktaş. You yourself will board the imperial barge with the admiral in the morning, fill up all the galleys with your troops, and come to Ya-vedud Sultan quay. Farther than that the water (in the Golden Horn) is too shallow and you have to proceed with the admiral's caique. You'll disembark at Kurban quay in Eyub where you'll find horses waiting. First you'll pay your respects at the shrine of his holiness Ebu Eyub-ı Ansari where you'll pray for succor from his spiritual grace for an auspicious end, and you'll have quite a lot of animals sacrificed and given as alms to several thousands of the poor. Then you'll proceed in slow and stately fashion, mounted majestically on the zephyr-swift steed, until you come to Edirne Gate. I shall be there ready to greet you for the grand procession. May God ease your way!"

Ipşir Pasha gave Melek Ahmed Pasha a sable robe of honor and three purses of pure gold. They kissed, and Melek Pasha took his leave from Ipşir Pasha at Üsküdar to visit the sultan. We came via caique to Saray Burnu, and the pasha's meeting with the felicitous Padishah took place at the Sinan Pasha pavilion.

"My Padishah," he began, "tomorrow morning your lala Ipşir Pasha will enter the capital in grand procession. It is for my Padishah to command."

"Oh Melek lala! When my lala Ipşir visited me today, were you and the other viziers held hostage in Üsküdar?"

"No, my Padishah. We had to have some consultations when he returned from my Padishah. It was for that reason that we remained in Üsküdar and could not be present at your interview."

Thus Melek Pasha tried to put a good construction on it, but the Cemşid-like Padishah said knowingly: "The case is clear."

"*Lala,*" he continued, "tomorrow convey my *lala* in grand procession to his palace. I'll watch the parade from a certain spot. Take account of my *lala's* dignity, and arrange a procession such as no vizier before him has witnessed."

Melek Pasha bowed to the ground and preceeded to his palace. Orders on white (*beyaz üzre buyurdılar*) were sent to the aghas of all the (janissary) corps and the (other) military groups.

In the morning he clad all of his interior and exterior aghas in cloth-of-gold and arranged the grand procession of the seven *divan* viziers and 4,000 picked troops. The viziers proceeded to Eyub Sultan, each one playing his military band, then each took up position in the midst of his entourage and stood ready to receive the greeting.

Eulogy of the Grand Procession of Ipşir Pasha, May God Facilitate What He Wishes

First of all the chief of police, Tahir Subaşı, marching through with his troops, cleared the public thoroughfares. The captain of the guard and the chief of police then cleared a path through the crowd of onlookers lining the royal roads to the right and the left, marching through with all his guardsmen and executioners.

Leading the parade was Ipşir Pasha's Tatar soldiery; the conscripts and irregulars (*delis* and *gönüllüs*); the *muteferrikas* and other regiments worthy of consideration; the marshals of the palace guard; the agha of the stable masters and all 390 aghas with their spare mounts—a stupendous sight!

Then passed the troops of Hasan Pasha, Kürd Kara Mehmed Agha, and Can Mirza Pasha, each consisting of 5,000 or 6,000 men. Following them came Ipşir Pasha's banners and the spare mounts clad in cloth-of-gold and jewel-encrusted saddles. But his steward, official secretary, treasurer and *imam* were behind his personal retinue.

Now began the Ottoman troops. First the *divan çavuşes* paraded past, fully armed, clearing the roads. Next came the *muteferrikas* of the Sublime Porte, authoritative figures, like so many *begler-begs.* Then the guild of the noble tasters; the troops of the imperial arsenal; the gunners; the armorers; the janissaries of the Porte. That broad Divan Yolu was packed for three whole hours as the janissaries, clad in felt and fully

armed, flowed by like a sea of men. All of the old veterans remarked that they had never seen such a sealike parade of janissaries. Truly, it was an awesome array.

After them came the *sipahis*, following Ipşir Pasha's order.
Just as the *sipahis* fight cheek-by-jowl with the janissaries on
the battlefield, so in the parade they had to march right on their
heels. For the *sipahis* were his—Ipşir's—partisans. Next came
the *sipahis* of the six regiments (i.e., *sipahis* of the Porte) and
—glory be!—they too were decked out in armor and mail, and it
took a full five hours for them to march past. No such *sipahi*
corps had been seen in living memory, except perhaps for the
cavalry troops that went on the Chotin campaign with Sultan
Osman (II in 1621).

Following them came the companies of the privileged (*ge-
dikli*) fief holders, who also passed with their spare mounts in
the manner of *begler-begs*; the privileged youths (*fetayan*) of the
fief holders, without spare mounts but with their clothed and
armed servants and outfitted with superb robes of honor; the
imams and *hatibs*, walking with great majesty and dignity;
from the pious of the community, 6,000 *şeyhs* passing on horseback two by two, their woolen scarfs round their necks, accompanied by all their Sufi adepts; the *kadis* and *ulema*,
numbering 10,000, fully outfitted but without weapons, (led by)
the *kadi* of Istanbul and the two *kaziaskers*; the noble *seyyids*,
descendants of the Prophet, with their majestic garments and—
glory to God!—their green turbans of Hasan and Hüseyn, passing
on horseback two by two, and (led by) the *nakibüleşraf*———
Efendi and the noble banner of the Prophet—none of the onlookers who saw this noble company failed to burst out weeping
and to cry blessings upon them, saying: "God bless Muhammed
and his family and his descendants!"

Next the marshals of the palace guards of the Sublime
Porte passed by, accompanied by their underlings clad in felt,
while they themselves rode on Arab horses with jewel-encrusted
saddles.

Now came the companies of the seven council viziers.[54]
They were so richly appareled and marched with such lordly
grace that each one appeared to be Rüstem-i Sam-ı Akran.[55]
Their soldiers passed by first, fully armed, with their stewards;
only then came the viziers themselves, two by two, each one accompanied by his swordbearer and footmen, twenty interior
aghas of rank, canteen-bearers and musketeers. The most

sumptuously outfitted of these viziers were the admiral of the fleet, Murad Pasha, and the deputy vizier, Melek Ahmed Pasha. These two, having once served as grand vizier themselves, sauntered by with extraordinary pomp, as though each one were Alexander the Great.

Finally (the company of Ipşir Pasha himself. First,) 4,000 janissaries, with leopard-skins, silver-threaded headdresses, felts worked with gold thread, jeweled muskets, aigrettes on their heads, fully armed and accoutred. Just in front of the grand vizier Ipşir Pasha strolled twelve janissary minstrels with guitars (*çögür*), performing all sorts of jests, and crying: "Sultan Murad's protégé, your *lala*, Ipşir Pasha, is the hero!" In the midst of the company rode Ipşir himself, neck-and-neck with the *şeyhülislam* Ebu Said Efendi. Behind them came Ipşir's 500 aghas of the interior, clad in cloth-of-gold and armor and mail, the tips of their mustaches wound round their ears, their livers branded,[56] like so many lions, mounted two by two on their fleet Arab thoroughbreds, each outfitted with six pieces of flank armor and osprey plumes. Following them were the Pasha's steward, Salih Agha, the treasurer, and Ayşe Sultan's chief agha——— Agha, along with Ipşir's banner, then the nine-tiered military band and the thundering kettledrums. At the end were about a thousand of the interior aghas' saddlers and water carriers, completing Ipşir Pasha's parade.

But this is an abbreviated account. If we were to record this procession in all the detail which we observed, and according to the protocol of the House of Osman, it would require a long scroll. In summary, then, this grand procession entered (Istanbul) through Edirne Gate at noon and was hardly finished an hour after the time of the late afternoon prayer. People rented shops at the rate of ten piasters to view Ipşir Pasha's parade.

When Ipşir Pasha finally reached his palace, he had sacrifices performed and, having entered his gracious abode, liberally awarded and feasted the forty-six companies of Muslim soldiery who had conveyed him thither in procession. He gave out 40 purses to the janissary corps, 30 to the *sipahis*, 5 to the gunners, 5 to the armorers, 5 to the marines of the arsenal—a total of 110 purses to all the Muslim troops. Then he rested in his palace.

Such a marvelous procession had not been witnessed since the time of Cemşid and Feridun and Zahhak of the serpents.[57] But although Ipşir was brought to his house amidst eulogies and benedictions, certain learned astrologers stated that he had entered Istanbul at an inauspicious hour.———

Ipşir Pasha came from Aleppo to the felicitous Threshold with the seal after a full seven months, and discussed the affairs of the Muslims with our lord Melek Ahmed Pasha in the *divan*. The two of them became as close as brothers. For three days and nights they conferred intimately and uninterruptedly, Ipşir Pasha carrying out affairs of state with Melek Ahmed Pasha's counsel.

On the morning of the fourth night, after he had performed the dawn prayer and I had recited the noble Yasin (Koran, *sure* 36), Melek Ahmed Pasha said: "My Evliya, this night I had a strange dream, may it be auspicious!"

"May it be auspicious indeed," said I, "a dream such as the prophet Joseph saw and interpreted."

A Marvel: A Genuine Dream

"This night in my sleep I saw the late Sultan Murad, may he rest in peace. He held a loaf of fine white Tophane bread[58] in his hand and said: 'Ahmed, do you see this bread? It is very tasty. A man in Kurdistan bakes it. Ipşir once asked that Kurd for this bread, but the man would not give it to him. But it is very fine bread. I once gave you a piece of bread like this in the inner fortress at Van. Take it now, it is bread like that. Eat it with peace of mind and assurance of victory.'

"With these words he put the bread in my hand. I kissed his hand and said: 'My Padishah, this bread is smeared with blood, how can I eat it?'

"'Send some of that bloody part to my daughter, Ismehan Kaya, your wife,' he said: 'let her wash it and eat it. And give one part to the khan of Bitlis. The rest eat yourself.'

"It was a strange dream, may it be auspicious."

I too found it strange and I said: "It will be for good, God willing!"

Verification of the Pasha's Dream

Then the pasha said: "I am not a dream interpreter, Evliya; but divine suggestion has led me to recall that during the Revan campaign (in 1045/1635) I was Sultan Murad's personal companion and his valet. Returning from Revan after the conquest, we laid waste to the province of Nahşivan and the towns of Serav and Tebriz and a hundred other Iranian towns and villages; then crossed the Mahmudi region via Kotur fortress and entered Van. The sultan climbed the fortress to survey it, had a meal there, and fell asleep. At that time my master Koca Nişancı Pasha was the royal sword-bearer. The sultan's bedclothes accidentally caught fire. He awoke and raised a cry. I entered to see the bedclothes burning and the sparks lighting up the room. I immediately put out the fire with my hand and perfumed the room with incense. The sultan asked who had been on duty, and they informed him it was the sword-bearer. 'Have the infidel thrown down from the fortress immediately,' he commanded. The former sword-bearer Mustafa Pasha and the other companions begged for his release, and he was banished to the outer service with the office of *nişancı*. While the sultan was eating breakfast he lifted a jeweled dish with a piece of bread from the golden tray and said: 'Melek Ahmed, from now on you be my personal sword-bearer and guard me well. Take this blessed bread, eat it, and continually pray for my welfare.' He placed a sable fur on my shoulders, wrapped a Muhammedan turban on my head, and I became independent sword-bearer and personal companion to the sultan."

Interpretation of the Dream

"Now Evliya, the interpretation of this dream according to divine suggestion is as follows—but God and His Prophet know best! His telling me tonight in my dream, 'A Kurdish man in Kurdistan bakes this bread; it is the tasty piece of white bread I gave you in the inner fortress at Van' means that the Padishah will give me the province of Van.

"His saying, 'Ipşir once asked for that bread, but the Kurd who bakes it would not give it to him' means that during the sultanate of Ibrahim, Ipşir was given the province of Van, but the Kurds of Van would not let him 'eat the bread'—they kept him with cannons from entering the city, and he returned frustrated and disappointed.

"The bloody part of the bread is Judgment Day. His saying, 'Let her wash it and eat it' means that Kaya Sultan, my wife, will somehow suffer a bloody death. And his saying, 'Give some of the bloody bread to the khan of Bitlis to eat as well' means that he too will die at my hands. For the late Sultan Murad once said to me: 'Ahmed, I have given you Diyarbekir, haply you will take my vengeance upon the khan of Bitlis; for when I was returning from the Revan campaign I stayed in his palace, showered him with 100 purses and his seventeen sons with *zeamets*, and gave him outright and in perpetuity the *harac* of Muş that pertains to the Van garrison by way of stipend (*ocaklık.*) But on my way to and from the Baghdad campaign (in 1048/1638), he did not come to offer his greetings and good wishes for the holy war. Ahmed, you must certainly take my vengeance upon the khan of Bitlis.' This is what he said; so his saying in my dream tonight 'Give some of the bloody bread to the khan of Bitlis' must mean that the khan will die at my hands. Finally, his saying, 'You too eat of that bread' indicates that I, too, will be martyred on my appointed day."

Melek Pasha saw this dream and interpreted it himself. "My sultan," said I, "you told me this dream, so the interpretation— be it objective or subjective, whether by divine suggestion or according to the dream book of Ibn Sirin[59]—ought to have fallen to me. But you gave me no chance and interpreted it yourself."

I went on to try and put a favorable construction on it, but he said: "No, my Evliya, this dream of mine will not bear a favorable construction. Also, I interpreted it by divine suggestion. I shall be appointed governor of Van, or else Erzurum or Diyarbekir, and I shall certainly reprimand the khan of Bitlis. Kaya Sultan will also eat of the bloody bread. She will die, and I too shall die. This is the only intrepretation the dream will bear. What will be will be." And he recited this couplet:

Edemez def⁺ sakınmakla kazayı kimse
Biñ sakınsân yine öñ soñ olacak olsa gerek

No one by wariness can ward off destiny.
Though you be wary a thousand times,
      Sooner or later what will be will be.

"By God, my sultan," I cried. "The other day, after the Bektaşi Dede came to visit you, and I caught up with him by caique off Ahır Kapı, he would not accept my sultan's gold. And when we were bidding farewell, the Dede said to me: 'Evliya Dede, do not forget to pray for me with the Pasha in the castle of Van. We, too, will not forget to pray for your welfare in Mecca the noble.'

Now in your interpretation of this dream, you also predicted that you would be awarded the governorship of Van. May it be auspicious—a strange and marvelous dream!"

"My Evliya," said the pasha, "my brother Ipşir Pasha delayed coming with the seal from Aleppo to wipe his face at the imperial stirrup for seven months. He still has many enemies, and no real friends." And he cited the verse, *Görelim ayine-i devran ne suret gösterir* ("We shall see what face the mirror of Fate displays").

This was the manner in which he interpreted the above dream. *The effect of the interpretation of the genuine dream— wondrous to relate!* And indeed—God is sufficient as my witness, and Muhammed is His Prophet—it turned out precisely thus. The very morning after he had interpreted the dream in this way, one of Ipşir Pasha's majestic aghas arrived bearing a noble rescript and imperial *ferman.* He barged into the pasha's private chamber and handed over the document. The pasha rose to his feet, kissed the noble rescript and raised it to his head, then perused it. "It is for my Padishah to command," he said. "Have the horsetails brought out immediately to our council hall!"

He presented the agha with a purse of gold and a sable pelisse. "I am not authorized to receive these gifts," said the agha. "Rather, I am charged to convey my sultan all the way to Van castle. Such is the imperial command and vizierial decree."

"My Agha," replied the Pasha gently, "please do me a small favor. Go to my brother Ipşir Pasha. Convey my greetings, and ask him to give me a respite of one week in order to make preparations for the journey. I am prepared at his command to go not only to Van but to Isfahan and half the world!"

The prudent agha took the purse and the fur and proceeded to Ipşir Pasha's presence where he repeated point by point all that Melek Ahmed Pasha had said, including his humble "It is for my Padishah to command."

Ipşir Pasha now turned to Kara Hasan Pasha and Kürd Kara Mehmed Agha. "God damn you," he said. "It was you who told me to send such a gentle vizier to such a worthless province as Van. And out of courtesy to us he gave our agha, the one who conveyed the Van appointment, a sable pelisse worth the entire income of Van province! He served as our deputy for seven months. It really was unworthy of us in return to banish him to Van. In the future, God willing, I will give him either Baghdad or Diyarbekir."

"Hey my sultan," retorted Abaza Hasan Pasha, "he must surely be a clansman of ours. When he was grand vizier he took the aghaship of the Turcomans from my hands, with the evil urgings of his janissary corps chiefs and his steward Kudde Kethüda, and gave my aghaship to Ak Ali Agha. Seventy purses of mine were left in the inter-porte treasury. Still he tried to have me killed for no good reason in Üsküdar, and sent the *sipahi* corps chiefs and his Zühdi Efendi to do the job. I barely managed to get out of Üsküdar alive and join my sultan below Aleppo.[60] For Melek Pasha, even Kars of Maraş would be too much, let alone Van."

"Well," said Ipşir Pasha, "what is past is past. May it be for nought but good." And he fell silent.

Meanwhile the Pasha, thinking of the hardships he would suffer traversing the eighty or ninety stages (to Van) in the middle of winter, called for a horse and proceeded to the sultan's presence without prior notice. This humble one was with him.

The felicitous Padishah happened to be at the place called Çemen Soffa. Our pasha bounded in saying "*Es-selâm aleyküm* my Padishah" and, without kissing the ground, merely uttered a prayer and kissed his hem.

"Look here, Melek *lala*," said the sultan, "I have given you Van. It's a big province with an income of 800 purses. It has thirty-six *sancaks*, four independent *khanlıks*, seventy janissary *begliks*, and seventy-six castles. Why won't you go?"

"Yes my Padishah, that is correct. All of those *sancaks* are there. But because it is Kurdistan, its pashas' authority does not extend beyond the territory below the cannons of Van castle. It is the farthest frontier (of the empire), a merciless place, where the governors manage only by dissimulation. My Padishah! They're casting me out to that frontier post on purpose. The income isn't even 80 purses, let alone 800. It's an isolated outpost.

"In fact, during the reign of your father Sultan Ibrahim, may his dust be sweet, your *lala* Ipşir Pasha was awarded the province of Van. He arrived there after much hardship and wished to enter the castle in a grand procession. But they closed the gates and held him off with 200 balaramada-guns, saying: 'Are you going to ruin the city with 400 men?' Certain that he would ravage the countryside if he got control of the province, they didn't even let him near the castle. They drove him away."

Just at that moment, Ipşir Pasha himself, who apparently had gotten word that the pasha was in the sultan's presence, came hobbling in on his lame leg. "Look," said the felicitous Padishah, "my *lala* Ipşir is coming."

The Debate of Melek Ahmed Pasha and Ipşir Pasha in the Presence of Sultan Mehmed IV

Ipşir approached, kissed the ground three times, and stood in a line with our pasha, as though they were pleading in a şe-riat court.

"Look here, lala. You came from the mountain a few days ago, and are you driving out my old lalas who are in the orchard,[61] casting them all out under some pretext or other to some God-forsaken frontier post? When my lala Melek was grand vizier, whom did he banish, and whom did he kill? You said that Van provides an income of 800 purses. My lala Melek says that its legitimate revenues do not amount to eighty purses. And one time during my father's reign you were given Van, but the Vanites, fearing your tyranny, bombarded you with cannons and would not let you in the castle. Is that true?"

"It is true that they did not let me in. But, my Padishah, at that time the people were all rebellious. But now it has become a nice province. There's no doubt that, including gifts, it will amount to 800 purses."

Melek Ahmed Pasha broke in: "Once my Padishah has bestowed it, I'll go even to Kadıköy. However, lying is forbidden in all the religions. The Prophet said in a Hadith, 'The liar is not of my community.' Telling a lie in the imperial presence is worse than being an infidel. My Padishah, according to imperial statute, Van has an imperial stipend providing an annual income of 540,345 aspers.[62] Along with other perquisites that makes forty-eight purses a year; and adding the penalties and fines it comes to sixty purses.[63]

"In fact, when this slave of yours Melek was grand vizier, I appointed your slave Şemsi-paşa-zade Mehmed Emin Pasha as governor of Van. He was very greedy, and imagined that he would get sixty purses out of Van province. But then the entire garrison (kul) revolted. Şemsi-paşa-zade was ensconced in the castle, supported by your janissaries (kapı kullarıñ). The battle raged for forty days and nights; thousands of cannon were fired from the citadel; so many houses and mansions in the walled town below were demolished; thousands of quintals of black gunpowder were expended from the treasury; the pasha's palace and Hüseyn Agha's palace and hundreds of other grand houses were ground to dust by the pounding of the cannonballs. My Padishah will recall that by your noble rescript, the governor of

Diyarbekir, your *lala* Haydar Agha-zade Mehmed Pasha, was appointed commander-in-chief and sent against Van in order to free Mehmed Emin Pasha from the castle. Your *lala* Mehmed Pasha marched on Van and laid siege to the castle, and one night Mehmed Emin Pasha, in disguise, let himself down with lassoes and escaped. He took refuge with the janissary corps in the capital, and the janissary aghas requested my Padishah to spare him. My Padishah accepted their request, and bestowed upon Mehmed Emin Pasha the *sancak* of Köstendil in Rumeli province. He (subsequently) died in Crete, as you know.

"The purpose of this long speech is merely to indicate to my Padishah what a God-forsaken outpost Van province is. It is for the Padishah of the world to command."

"My Padishah," interjected Ipşir Pasha, "all that your *lala* Melek says is correct. But now it has become a very nice province, loyal and secure. However, when I was in Aleppo and received the seal, a tribe of Mahmudi Kurds in Van province known as Pinyanişi Kurds—they are 60,000 brave warriors, and have an enormous quantity of cattle in their summer pastures, and they border on the ignoble clean-shaven Safavids (*Kızılbaş-ı bed-meaş-ı rış-tıraş*)—were raided by those nasty Kızılbaş, who made an incursion into Kurdistan, dragging guns and drawing troops, killing Muslims, sounding their brass trumpets and beating their Afrasiyab kettledrums. They drove away 1 million sheep to the valleys of Salmos and the walled towns of Dumdumi, Dumbuli, and Urmia, and all the Kızılbaş became rich with this booty. Because they perpetrated such an act, contrary to the truce,[64] during the felicitous reign of my Padishah, the frontier aghas of Kurdistan all came to me in Aleppo to seek redress. I was monitoring the situation to see what other acts contrary to the truce were occurring in the Van region. That is the real reason why I delayed coming to the capital from Aleppo for seven months—otherwise I would most certainly have come with the seal from Aleppo in ten days and rubbed my face and eyes on the imperial stirrup. But then *fermans* kept arriving from my Padishah, insisting that I come right away; so I gave up my intelligence efforts in Kurdistan. But when I got as far as the Konya region, petitions were forwarded to me from the governor of Van, your *lala*———Pasha, and from your *lalas* the khans of Bitlis, Hakkari, and Mahmudi. Their cries and moans rise up to heaven, and their plaints from Persia are inscribed with blood."

He displayed the petitions to the sultan, and continued: "So you see, my Padishah, we need to appoint an experienced statesman and an enlightened vizier as commander-in-chief to deal with the disturbances in that region. We considered that Melek Ahmed Pasha was worthy of that office, and therefore we appointed him to that province. It is for my Padishah to command." And he fell silent.

"The case is clear," said the felicitous Padishah, smiling. "Quickly," he ordered, "a pen and pen-case!" The private secretary immediately produced a pen-case and a jewel-scattering pen, and (the sultan) wrote a noble rescript with his own hand (as follows):

> I have made you, my *lala* Melek Ahmed Pasha, commander-in-chief, having power of appointment and dismissal over all high posts in the Anatolian empire with the exclusion of Egypt and Baghdad, and I have bestowed upon you the province of Van by way of stipend (*arpalık*).

He placed the noble rescript in Melek Ahmed Pasha's hands, inserted into his turban a jeweled aigrette marking him as commander, presented him with five purses of gold, one Solomonic tent pavilion, one "stork" tent with poles, 100 files of camels, and 100 files of mules. The felicitous Padishah uttered a benediction upon Melek Ahmed Pasha. "March forth," he said, "may your aid and protector be God."

Turning to Ipşir Pasha he said: "Let my *lala* Melek Pasha and the admiral Kara Murad Pasha enter my presence on audience days. And let them attend my *divan* until my *lala* Melek departs. And whatever requisites and perquisites are afforded other commanders according to the ancient statute of my predecessors, give also to my *lala* Melek. In the spring, God willing, we will set out with an innumerable army from my felicitous threshold in campaign against Persia, and very soon we will march against the castle of Revan that was conquered by my uncle Sultan Murad."

When the felicitous Padishah gave Melek Ahmed Pasha the noble rescript appointing him commander-in-chief, Ipşir Pasha's face turned ashen grey.

After so much consultation and disputation, in the third hour Melek Pasha bowed, uttered a benediction upon the majestic Padishah, and took his leave. Boarding the *bostancı-başı's* caique at Saray Burnu, we uttered a *besmele—first stage, the great city of Eski Dar ("ancient abode"), that is to say, Üsküdar*—and halted at our gracious home, the *yalı* of Kaya Sultan.

That very hour, ten plumed *çavuşes* arrived with orders in their hands, insisting quite unreasonably that the pasha depart immediately and proceed to Van by forced marches. The pasha flew into a rage. He gave the *çavuşes* ten piasters each, loaded them all onto a caique, and sent them off without rowers down current toward Istanbul. Being oarless, they twirled on the waves like Mevlevi dervishes, until they finally came to Ahır Kapı. When they reported the matter to Ipşir, he sent ten more boorish and brazen-faced *çavuşes* who tried to get the pasha to set out, but the pasha beat them off with a stick and they ran away.

By God's wisdom: when our lord the pasha crossed over to Üsküdar, and the *çavuşes* were charged to follow at his heels, some hypocrites told Kaya Sultan that the *bostancı-başı* and the *çavuşes* were appointed to murder the pasha. Kaya Sultan was at her wit's end. She called for her coach, rushed to Bağçe Kapı, and, exhausted, boarded a caique and headed for Üsküdar. The pasha, also in a caique, came out to meet her.

By God's wisdom: Just after Kaya Sultan and the pasha entered the harem, a hue and cry broke out within. The pasha emerged bathed in sweat, and immediately distributed 10,000 goldpieces of Kaya Sultan's money to his 410 retainers and ordered them to recite a thousand times each the noble Ihlas (Koran, *sure* 112) to ease Kaya Sultan's giving birth and to assure her delivery (*halas*). He put me at the head of the party, awarding me with 500 goldpieces from the deputy's purse.

"See here, my Evliya," he said, "you are my son, my flesh and blood. Only let this secret remain with you. Three nights ago I saw Sultan Murad in my dream. 'Take this bread and eat it, Ahmed,' he said. 'But my Padishah,' said I, 'there is blood on this piece of bread. How can I eat it?' 'Give that bloody part to my daughter Kaya,' he said, 'let her wash it and eat it.' Now—but God knows best—Kaya Sultan won't give birth, she is on the verge of death." He was quite distraught.

After he had returned to the harem, some *çavuşes* came from Ipşir Pasha. When they saw the commotion going on within, the sensible *çavuşes* stood to one side and did not press the case. But some of them did keep up the pressure and insisted that the pasha depart right away. The pasha's Abkhazian and Circassian and Georgian braves surrounded them with clubs crying "Take that!" and gave them such a drubbing, they were lucky to escape to the latrines.

As it turned out, Kaya Sultan was seven months pregnant and not ready to give birth. But, frightened that they were killing the pasha, she had leapt into her carriage, and her delicate body was seized with tremors, so that when she arrived in Üsküdar she suffered a miscarriage. The foetus emerged—a little prince—like a piece of her liver.

Cries and laments rose up from the slave girls and the female companions in the palace. Then what should I see but the pasha, emerging from the harem, and in his hands a box containing the foetus. When he displayed the light-filled coffin of the little prince to his retainers and servants, they, too, began to wail and moan. And the viziers and deputies, who had just arrived to congratulate the pasha on his appointment to Van, also broke out crying when they saw this pathetic scene. Everyone tried to comfort the pasha.

"Look, aghas," the pasha cried, "what a fine lad he would have been. Look at his brow and his doelike eyes. Look at his height and stature. Alas for my son, my prince, who will not get his fill of heroic glory! Alas for my son who will not get his fill of mounting horses and girding swords!"

He came over to me and showed me the prince's body inside the box. What should I see? A piece of red liver! True, the brows and eyes were recognizable; but otherwise it was an unformed piece of liver.[65]

"Hey my sultan," said I, "what brow and eyes, what height and stature are you talking about? This prince fell out unformed, without life and spirit. Did he break enemy lines? Did he overcome infidels? Did he cut off heads? Did he even come into the world alive? What kind of prince is this who won't get his fill of heroic glory? It is only a piece of flesh. Even had he been born alive he would need forty years to become a hero. This is a piece of liver, hardly seven months old. But here you are wailing forty years in advance over a piece of blood born prematurely. Judgment belongs to God! May your lordship and our lady Kaya Sultan live long."

I tried to console the pasha in this fashion. "Oh my Evliya," he said, "I am not crying over this piece of liver. The other night when I saw Sultan Murad in my dream he gave me a piece of bread in Van; and now I have been appointed to Van. He told me,

'Give the bloody bread to Kaya, let her wash it and eat it;' now I
am afraid that this part of the dream will also come true. That
is why I am crying."

"His saying in the dream, 'Let her wash the bloody bread
and eat it' referred to this little prince," I replied. "You will wash
off the blood and bury him in the ground, and you and Kaya
Sultan will once again eat bread and salt. Also, you always used
to be in terror of Ipşir; but with this, that terror has gone. A
Fatiha on this intention!" Thus I consoled the pasha as best I
could. But the fact was that lovely Kaya Sultan was suffering a
great deal and would not stop bleeding.

From the felicitous Padishah came a noble rescript offering
condolences to Kaya Sultan and our pasha, as well as a robe of
honor for each of them and some sable furs, plus a note to the
Pasha saying: "My *lala*, as soon as my cousin Kaya Sultan recov-
ers, set out for Van without delay."

They washed the foetus of the stillborn prince and buried it
in the———quarter of Üsküdar. No sooner was this done than
twenty *çavuşes* arrived like ravening dogs and insisted that the
pasha depart right away. The pasha beat them all off, and they
fled with their tails between their legs.

In short: The pasha had made all the provisions for his
journey and was ready to set out, when he summoned me for a
private interview.

"My Evliya," he said, "you are my son. Let your servants
camp with your tent in my own quarters and eat and drink with
my personal retinue. Put your *gulams* Küçük Ibrahim, Rum Ali,
and Gürcü Mustafa in charge of your slaves and let them take
care of all your clothing and other effects. Let your horses stay in
the stable master's stable. When they are saddled they will be
brought to your *gulams* to mount. I will stand guarantor and
surety for all of your property.

"I want you to stay behind in Istanbul for a few days. Attach
yourself to Ipşir and Kara Hasan. Find out what you can about
our Kudde Mehmed Kethüda, and Mevkufati Mehmed Efendi,
and Moralı Defterdar Pasha, and the other notables and servants
from among our retinues; also about Ipşir the infelicitous (*bi-
beşir*) and his false dealings with the people. Whatever events
may occur, get letters from Kaya Sultan and from our protégé,
the customs inspector Hasan Çelebi. When you are certain no
one is aware, follow us speedily with your own horses and come
by forced marches until you catch up with me."

He gave me 500 Venetian gold ducats, and uttered a benediction. He also blessed Arganalı Ahmed Agha and sent him off to Van as his deputy. I handed over my five *gulams* to the treasurer, and four sacks of clothing and five of my horses to the stable master, and remained behind with Kaya Sultan in Üsküdar with three of my slaves and five horses.

In the year———in the month of———the pasha bid Kaya Sultan farewell and set out for Van. First, with a *besmele, the stage of Kadıköy* near Üsküdar. Kaya Sultan gave me forty purses to give the pasha as road money. I crossed to Kadıköy by caique and handed over the forty purses to the pasha.

The pasha halted here in Kadıköy for three days to spite Ipşir Pasha. On the fourth day, as he was setting out for Van in the depths of winter, I kissed his hand. "Be cautious, my Evliya," he said, and we parted with a benediction, he toward Van, I returning to Istanbul.

The next day I went to see Ipşir Pasha's steward, my dear friend (lit., brother) Salih Agha. "Well, my Evliya, didn't you go off to Van with the pasha?"

"I'm tired of traveling, my sultan. Especially in this awful season, how could I undertake a ninety-stage journey to Van?"

"Call the disbursement clerk right away!" He consigned me twenty loaves of bread, five *okkas* of meat, three *okkas* of rice, one *okka* of unalloyed oil, and one candle apiece, and attached me to Ipşir Pasha's suite.

When the assembly was dispersed and the council chamber was empty, I intoned a melody in the Segah mode. Just as I came to the end, I heard a voice from outside the window saying: "Evliya! Evliya! Is this the due of bread and salt, that you are oblivious of me?!" As soon as I heard this I realized that Ipşir Pasha had wheedled our pasha's steward, Kudde Kethüda, away from the pasha by promising to make him agha of the swordbearers, and had straightway clapped him in prison.

"Evliya," said Ipşir Pasha's steward Salih Agha, "your Kudde Kethüda heard you singing and is calling you."

"It would be a favor, my sultan, if you invited him also into your presence and introduced him into the council."

"My Evliya, he is a prisoner, he cannot come here."

Just then a chamberlain came and said to the steward: "My sultan, our lord the pasha wants you."

"My Evliya," said the steward, "sit here and don't go away. The pasha will be summoning you shortly."

A minute later another chamberlain appeared and said: "There is supposed to be a *kadı* here named Evliya Efendi. The pasha wants him."

Seeing that I was clean shaven, the poor *gulam* could not imagine that I was a *kadı* and a *gazi*. "Boy," I said, "I'm the one he wants."

"No, my brave, he wants a much older man named Evliya Efendi."

Eventually, I was introduced into the pasha's presence. I uttered a benediction and kissed his hand. "*Hafız* Evliya, welcome! I knew you were sensible. I see you haven't gone off to Van in this winter season with that traitor Melek."

"God be praised," I said, "that after forty-one years I have managed to see my sultan as head of state. Even during the holy war against the *celali* Varvar Ali Pahsa we went through some hard times together![66] I thank God that He has let me witness these days. Why should I go off elsewhere?"

"Evliya," said Ipşir Pasha, "just now Kudde Kethüda cried out. What did he say?"

"My sultan, he addressed me in his Kurdish dialect: 'Evliyacıh! Evliyacıh![67] It is clear that you are oblivious of my condition. Where are the dues for past favors?' It seems he's in prison."

"Go now Evliya, I give you leave. Talk to Kudde and the *defterdar* and Mevkufati Mehmed Efendi. Kudde has been your pasha's steward for twenty years. They own the wealth of Croesus. If he wants to rescue the bird of his soul, 'The white asper is for a black day,' let Kudde give 3,000 purses to the public treasury, and the *defterdar* 5,000, and Mevkufati 1,000. Then I'll set them free. Go tell them."

So I went off with Ipşir's steward. They opened a door, and it turned out to be the dressing room of the bath. *The distressing situation of Kudde Mehmed, steward of Melek Ahmed Pasha.* As I went inside, what should I see but 200 Segban and Sarıca executioners stationed on the benches of this dressing room with their muskets ready. The big pool in (the middle of) the room was full of water and in the pool, on that bitter wintry day, there were the three of them—Kudde Kethüda, Moralı Defterdar, and Mehmed Efendi—stark naked, with chain collars on their necks, moaning and groaning. It seems they had been there for two days and nights, without food and clothing. Aside from that, every night they received a thousand lashes each from the executioners. They had suffered all sorts of torments.

When I saw Kudde Kethüda in this distressing state I nearly fainted. I rushed over and kissed the hands of all three of them—for they were my patrons, after all. "My Evliya," said Kudde Kethüda, "what is happening?"

"I was just with the head of state. He said: 'If Kudde wishes to go free he must give 3,000 purses, and the pasha (i.e., *defterdar*) 5,000, and Mehmed Efendi 1,000. Otherwise I'll kill all three of them.' And he took an oath to that effect."

Kudde was prepared to give 1,000 purses, the *defterdar* 2,000, and Mevkufati 500 plus 500 volumes of valuable books. This time Ipşir Pasha's steward, Salih Agha, spoke up:

"Mehmed Kethüda! What about the 40,000 sheep in Kırşehir? And the 1,000 purses of piasters in Çermik in Diyarbekir province? And the 500 purses of gold with your partner Mallı Kaya Çelebi in Van? And the 2,000 purses with the Armenian infidel Anton, brother of the customs inspector Hasan Agha?"

"Evliya will confirm," said Kudde Kethüda, "That those 40,000 sheep in the Sahra farm in Kırşehir all belong to Melek Pasha; and in Çermik I have no property, it all belongs to my brother Hacı Musa Agha; and all the money in Van belongs to Kaya Sultan—she is in partnership there with Kaya Çelebi, they've put their rocks together;[68] I don't have a single asper or a single grain tied up in that gold." He took an oath to that effect.

They took poor naked Kudde and the *defterdar* out of the pool, gave them 300 lashes apiece, and put them back in the pool, bleeding and wailing, in that bitter winter. They they resumed their groans and sighs.

"Hey Mehmed Kethüda," I said, "send word to all your friends, borrow a few hundred more purses and rescue the birds of your souls!"

"Who is going to entrust us with a single red copper while we are held prisoner? They should set us free first. Then we'll dig up as much money as the head of state desires."

I returned to Ipşir Pasha and reported what they said. "They're good men," he said. "They can come up with that much money even while they're in prison. Otherwise I'll kill them right now." I went back and told them exactly what Ipşir Pasha had said.

After two more days they squeezed 3,800 purses out of the *defterdar*. They also took all the property and goods in his palace, confined all of his retinue who were on duty, and extracted another 2,040 purses out of them. From Kudde Kethüda they got 2,000 purses; and imperial guards were sent to Diyarbekir with orders for the governor, Firari Mustafa Pasha, to arrest Bakkal-oğlu, Mehmed Çelebi, Kudde's brother Haci Musa, and his son Ibrahim Beg, and to confiscate all of their wealth. They could not get any money out of Mevkufati Mehmed Efendi, but they did sequester all his real property and farms and estates. And they continued their daily application of various tortures to all three.

Seeing them I thanked my lucky stars for my own impoverished condition, and humbly prayed to almighty God: "My Lord, do not demean this lowly slave in such fashion for the sake of a crust of bread; keep me in good health, and maintain me in abstinence and renunciation until the end of my appointed term." But as I observed these horrible events, I kept monitoring the situation, wondering what the outcome would be and what other calamities would befall Istanbul.

As for the Istanbul notables, they were all playthings in the hands of the Segbans and Sarıcas and other rogues. So the head of chancellery Şami-zade Mehmed Efendi had to cough up seventy sable furs, and the customs inspector Hasan Çelebi and the other grandees were subject to similar exactions, with no apparent limits.

If we were to set down all that we know of the events of that period, the recording of our *Book of Travels* would be hindered. Suffice it to say that while all these mishaps and misfortunes were occurring, I kept my horses and my servants on the alert and well concealed in Üsküdar. Every evening I reported to our lady Kaya Sultan and consulted with her from behind the lattice. And every day I consorted with Ipşir Pasha's steward, who gave me three purses[69] and dressed me in a sable robe.

In the year——on the——th day of the month of—— they released our Kudde Kethüda and——from prison. Condemning them to permanent exile, they sent Kudde Kethüda and——in the charge of some marshals of the palace guard and *sipahi* corps *çavuşes* by caique to Dil Herseki. Just outside Hersek, south of the town, both of them were executed. They were buried there, may God have mercy on their souls.—— And they committed thousands of other atrocities of this sort, shedding the blood of innocent Muslims, and rivaling Haccac ibn Yusuf[70] in tyranny.

That very day Kaya Sultan gave me ten letters and 500 goldpieces as road money. "Hurry, my Evliya, catch up with my pasha, tell him not to tarry but get to Kurdistan as quickly as possible. They have killed his steward Kudde Kethüda, his *defterdar* Moralı Mustafa Pasha, his head of chancellery Mevkufati Mehmed Efendi, and several other of his retinue, and they will certainly kill many more of my pasha's followers. They even requested a noble rescript three times from the felicitous Padishah ordering the execution of my pasha himself; but the Padishah (refused), and the *ulema* and *şeyhs* and viziers and deputies and the *valide-sultan* and the *sipahi* and janissary corps all objected when they got wind of it, saying 'Melek Ahmed Pasha is an upright and pious and faithful and mild and honorable and brave vizier. What crime has he committed, that you are requested a noble rescript condemning him to death? Do not grant it, my Padishah! Melek Pasha is still a man who is useful to this state. He served once as grand vizier and three times as deputy grand vizier, and he was on good terms with all the *kuls.*' All the *kuls* put their foot down, and so Ipşir could not obtain the noble rescript from the Padishah.

"But who knows, my Evliya? This Ipşir Mustafa Pasha is my husband Melek Pasha's kinsman (*akraba*) but he is also his scorpion ('*akraba*). Perhaps he'll manage to obtain secretly a noble rescript condemning my dear pasha to death. So hurry, my Evliya, catch up with the pasha, have him proceed to Kurdistan and his post in Van with all haste. After that, if he wishes, he can mount a campaign against Gence and Iran and Nahşivan and Revan."

Kaya Sultan, weeping, put the letters in my hand, and also gave me a jeweled watch. "You will have great need for a watch on your journey. Do not tarry!" Finally she presented me with a sable fur and sent me that evening to the customs inspector, Hasan Agha.

(This) Hasan Çelebi happened to be consulting that evening with Mahmud-agha-zade Bekir Agha at Baltacı Mahmud Agha's *yalı* in Ortaköy. When he saw me he got to his feet and said: "Welcome, my Evliya. I'm going to send you back to Istanbul tonight on an errand. But first come with me and let's have a chat." He took me by the hand and led me out of the crowded room into a private chamber, where he handed me three letters.

"Catch up with the pasha without delay. Here are 200 goldpieces for you. Did you get letters from Kaya Sultan?"

"Yes I did."

"Get going then. But until you get to Izmid stay away from the main roads, both night and day. Don't stop at the post stations for horses, but use your own horses and ride on the double. Here's another hundred goldpieces."

He put me on a caique, and just as we were about to set off, he (addressed me aloud): "Evliya Çelebi! Stop in at our customshouse in Istanbul and say hello to the cashier. Tell him I'll be in Istanbul tomorrow." Thus he pretended to be sending me that night to Istanbul.

"Very good, my sultan," I answered.

At 8:00 P.M. (*iki yatsı zamanı*) I set out by caique from Ortaköy and, floating down current, arrived back in Üsküdar in no time. I went immediately to the appointed spot where I kept my five thoroughbreds. My light-armed mounted party consisted of seven, including my three fully-armed *gulams* and my three Abkhazians, Abaza Merşan Yusuf, Abaza Kamış Mehmed, and Abaza Cembeli Ali.

At midnight, in that pitch darkness, murmuring "I put my trust in God," we mounted Çamlıca hill, where I performed two prostrations and begged succor from the spiritual natures of the saints buried in Üsküdar and in Istanbul. I then recited the noble Yasin (Koran, *sure* 36), granting the spiritual merit of these verses, as a freewill offering and for the divine pleasure, to all the Prophets and the Saints, the Pole of Poles, the Trustworthies, the Pegs, the Nobles, the Deans, the Substitutes, the Obsessed, the Reproached, the Men of the Unknown, the Ones, the Threes, the Sevens, the Forties, the Hundreds, the Thousands, the Thousand-and-ones, and all the noble Spirits.[71] And I passed my hands over my face. God knowns that this humble slave felt as though I had donned armor of Nahşivan steel. Uttering a *besmele*, we turned the reins of our zephyr-swift steeds in the direction of Van—may God the Absolute ease our way!

[End of Book III]

[Evliya departs Üsküdar on 1 Cümaziülula 1065/9 March 1655 (IV 191b.5) and catches up with Melek at Beg-bazarı. He warns Melek that Ipşir has a grudge against him, and Melek begins to gather a force of irregular troops. By the time they reach Sivas he has gathered twenty regiments of Segbans and Sarıcas (192a.22). "The pasha's soldiery grew day by day, and his fear of Ipşir Pasha subsided" (198a.36).]

Notes

1. A *yük* is 100,000; forty *yüks* = 4 million, probably the effective yield as opposed to the book value.

2. A virtual catalogue of pleasure spots along the Bosphorus and elsewhere in Istanbul. Sarıyar is presentday Sarıyer.

3. 15 Şevval 1061/27 September 1651–13 Receb 1062/20 June 1652.

4. 13 Receb 1062/20 June 1652–21 Rebiülahir 1063/21 March 1653.

5. A farrago of magical and pious phrases, adjuring by God, by the "lord of the fairies," by various prophets, and by the jinn.

6. Calling on angels and jinn with outlandish Arabic-sounding names and phrases. Cf. E. W. Lane, *Manners and Customs of the Modern Egyptians* (London, 1908), pp. 275–76.

7. The period of Derviş Mehmed Pasha's vizierate was 21 Rebiül-ahir 1063/21 March 1653 to 16 Zilhicce 1064/28 October 1654. Note the study by I. Metin Kunt, "Derviş Mehmed Paşa, Vezir and Entrepreneur . . . ," *Turcica* 9, no. 1 (1977): 197–214.

8. Note that Mehmed IV at this time was twelve years old.

9. A Rumi purse contained 500 piasters (*guruş* = large silver coins of European mintage) or 40,000 aspers (*akça* = small silver coins of Ottoman mintage).

10. *Tavayif-i müluk* for *müluk-i tavayif*; that is, anarchy.

11. According to Vecihi, 59v and Naima, vol 5, p. 447 the seal was sent to Ipşir on 18 Zilhicce 1064/30 October 1654. [Vecihi in Buğra Atsız, *Das osmanische Reich um die Mitte des 17. Jahrhunderts* (Munich, 1977).]

12. This is an error; she was the daughter of Sultan Ibrahim (see Alderson, Table XXXVII).

13. Lit. "Red Heads," a derogatory term for the tribal followers of the Safavids, the Shii rulers of Iran and rivals of the Ottomans.

14. The Ottoman-Safavid truce of Kasr-ı Şirin, established by Sultan Murad IV in 1049/1639. At IV 284a.9–25 (not in printed text), Evliya explains that Ipşir, while in Aleppo, was "afraid to go with the seal to such a confined place as Istanbul, and planning to mount a campaign in the direction of Iran," he urged the Kurdish emirs of Pinyanişi to break the truce and make a raid in Iranian territory. The Iranian emirs of Urmia, Dumbuli, and so on mounted a counterraid, in which they took 40,000 sheep. Cf. IV 293a.20–293b.11 (297–98), where Evliya states that Ipşir also wished to take revenge on the Iranians for wounding and laming him during the Revan campaign when he was Murad IV's stable master.

15. The reference is to the Revan campaign of 1045/1635.

16. "God is Truth;" the cry of a dervish.

17. A specialty of Egypt according to X 179b.2 (384–85): *kılıç kadar akva Arab hançeri . . . Rumda yokdur*. The *akva* dagger is also mentioned in Naima's account of this incident, vol. 5, p. 40.

18. A word here in the text (SLʾ?) is unintelligible. For the following description, cf. I 150b.4 (501; Hammer ii, 98), VI 44b.15f (Ch. 10), X 42b.1 (95), 202b.18–27 (430).

19. An additional phrase here in the text (*afitabe-i boz-doğan kisbeti üzre*) is unintelligible; perhaps the reference is to his "cap" (*külah*), mentioned below (176b.1).

20. Cf. Evliya's description of the Ashura ceremonies in Tebriz, II 300b.30–301a.16 (255–56; Hammer, 138) and in Dergüzin, IV 313a.5f. (355–57). On the tenth of the month of Muharrem (= *aşura*) the Shiis commemorate the martyrdom of Hüseyn, son of Ali, which took place on the plain of Kerbela in Iraq in 680.

21. Perhaps an error for "his right arm."

22. A carved stone the size of a hand with twelve flutings worn at the waist; see Birge, 235, [John Kingsley Birge, *The Bektashi Order of Dervishes* (London, 1937; repr. 1975)]

23. Evliya quotes this verse again at IX 347a.5 (755), attributing it to a certain poet who arrived ill at the Kaabe in Mecca and was cured upon drinking some water from the well of Zemzem

24. D. 562/1166. He was revered by the Turks of Central Asia, and the Bektaşis trace their spiritual ancestry to him as well; see EI [2], arts. "Ahmad Yasawī" (F.Iz), "Bektāshiyya" (R. Tschudi).

25. See Ch. 3, n. 6.

26. *Aşık*, a Sufi term meaning "lover of God." Dede and Baba (below) are Sufi titles.

27. Cf.I 19b.27 (73; not in Hammer), where Mübtecil in Spain is mentioned among the peoples (*kavm*) who accepted Islam at the time of the Prophet. (The word derives from Ar. *mudajjan* > Sp. *mudejar*, properly referring to Muslim subjects of Christian Spain following the Reconquista.) Angil is probably to be connected with Gk. *angili* "angel" (VIII 256b.32, 349b.29), cf. *melek* "angel." *Monotheists* means Muslims.

28. *Cefr-i cami*—that is, *Miftāḥ al-jafr al-jāmiʿ*, a book by Muḥyi'd-dīn Abū l-ʿAbbās al-Būnī (d. 622/1225) or else by Muḥyi'd-dīn Ibn ʿArabī (d. 638/1240), and a standard work of Islamic cabbalism, a science attributed to Ali; see EI², art. "djafr" (T. Fahd).

29. *Suleha-yı ümmet* —that is, the *şeyhs* of the Sufi brotherhoods.

30. *Cilbend-i mahabbet*; see Birge (ref. in n. 22 above), p. 247.

31. *Var kumda oyna götüñe çöp batmasın.* Cf. I 107b.23 (361; Hammer ii, 16: Gisudar-kapanı Mehmed Efendi's blessing of baby Evliya): *kumda oynayıp ayağına çöp batmasın.*

32. The reference is to Evliya's travels from 1082/1671 to 1094/1683 (Books IX and X). Evliya's last redaction of the *Seyahat-name* was twenty to thirty years after the incidents recorded in this chapter.

33. Refers to an incident in 1053/1643 when Nasuh-paşa-zade, one of the rebellious Anatolian governors, marched against Istanbul hoping to be appointed grand vizier but was lured away from his army in Üsküdar and eventually killed; see Danişmend, p. 390.

34. The text has Baydı, but Bayındır is correct; cf. 177b.20.

35. The king of Turan in the Iranian epic.

36. Evliya uses the same verses, with slight variations, to greet the sultan at V 164b.19–21 (539: omitted) and VIII 380a.29 (775). The same verses are also found at I 69a.34 (246; Hammer i,133: omitted), V 63b.30–32 (215), and X 43a.7–10 (96–97: Selim I, in disguise as a dervish, addressing Shah Ismail!).

37. That is 1058/1648. See II 365b (452; Hammer, 238).

38. He was grand vizier under Murad IV from 1037/1628 to 1041/1631 and associated with that sultan's policy of military action against rebel governors, notably Abaza Mehmed Pasha, and the Safavids. See EI², art. "Khosrew Pasha, Bosniak" (H. Inalcık and R. C. Repp).

39. That is, Hasan-ı Balkhi, Rumi's father; cf. III 14b.16 (24).

40. Lit., the blood left their hearts, *yüreklerinden kan giderdi*.

41. See Ch. 1, n. 12. Kör Hazinedar was Abaza Mehmed Pasha's protégé.

42. Hacı Bektaş, the seventh/thirteenth century eponym of the Bektaşi order (see n. 24 above), was the patron saint of the janissaries.

43. He was grand vizier under Ahmed I from 1015/1606 to 1020/1611 and carried out bloodthirsty campaigns against the Anatolian rebels.

44. "En'am": a collection of verses from the Koran, including the *sure-i en'am (sure 6)*.

45. The first and third of these were grand viziers under Sultan Ibrahim, Hafiz (~Hezar-pare) Ahmed in 1057–58/1647–48, Kapıcı Mehmed in 1053–55/1644–45. For Husrev Pasha see n. 38 above and the following note.

46. Husrev defeated Abaza Mehmed in Erzurum and conducted him to Istanbul, where the triumphal parade took place on 12 Rebiülahir 1038/9 December 1628.

47. See Ch. 1, n. 10.

48. A pre-Islamic poet, proverbial for generosity.

49. See Ch. 3, n. 5.

50. *Perese*—that is, retinue?

51. See Ch. 2, n. 43.

52. See III 117a (end of Ch. 2) for Evliya's account of this event.

53. The conqueror of Yemen was Hadım Süleyman (not Sinan) Pasha; see Ch. 10, n. 27. For Kılıç Ali Pahsa, see Ch. 1, n. 4. Lala (~Kara) Mustafa Pasha was commander of the Ottoman forces at the conquest of Cyprus in 978–79/1570–71.

54. See Ch. 1, n. 10.

55. The great hero of the Persian epic.

56. *Cigeri dağlı*—this phrase, generally used of distraught lovers (and, by Evliya, of captives and prisoners), is thrown in here merely for the sake of rhyme with the previous phrase (*bıyıkları düm-bina guşlarına bağlı*).

57. Ancient kings of Iran in the Persian epic.

58. See I 134a.3–7 (445; Hammer ii, 61) for Evliya's description of this bread.

59. An early Islamic dream interpreter; d. 110/728.

60. For this event, see III 98b.14f. (Ch. 2).

61. One who "comes from the mountain" is a boor; one who "comes from the mountain and drives out the ones in the orchard" is a disrespectful upstart.

62. The text has *yük akça*, but the *yük* is an error; cf. n. 1 above.

63. At IV 253b.17 (174) the annual income of Van is given as 1,132,000 aspers (cf. I 49b.29 [176; Hammer i, 89]: 1,132,200) plus 40,000 piasters for penalties and fines; but there Evliya is citing the Kanun-name of Sultan Süleyman.

64. That is, the truce of Kasr-ı Şirin; see above, n. 14.

65. "Piece of liver" (*ciger-pare*) is also a common idiom for one's own child.

66. See Ch. 1, n. 13.

67. "Little Evliya;" Eastern Anatolian dialect for Evliyacık.

68. ?—*taş kayasıyle*; evidently a play on words is intended.

69. A word here is illegible.

70. See Ch. 2, n. 30.

71. A catalogue of the Sufi hierarchy.

5

GOVERNOR OF DIYARBEKIR (1640)

[On their way to Van, Melek sends Evliya to Diyarbekir to collect some debts from Firari Mustafa Pasha. Evliya catches up with Firari in Sincar on 1 Receb 1065/7 May 1655 (IV 212a.17 [61]).]

Firari Mustafa Pasha had camped at the foot of Sincar castle with his sealike army. One side of Mt. Sincar is called Saçlı Dağı ("Mountain of the Hairy Ones") and on that merciless mountain live 44,000 or 45,000 Yezidis and Bapiris, dog worshippers, worse than infidels, a band of rebels and brigands and perverts, resembling ghouls of the desert, hairy heretic Yezidi Kurds.[1] These people felt not the slightest fear or awe toward the commander, Firari Mustafa Pasha, nor did they pay him the respect of even a token gift. The commander was extremely annoyed because of this. That day he said: "Evliya Çelebi, I have heard that when our father, your lord, Melek Ahmed Pasha was camped in this place as we are, these Saçlı Dağı infidels paid him no respect either, and so he punished them severely and got quite a lot of booty. Could you tell me something about that conquest?"

Story of the Conquest of Mt. Saçlı, that is Mt. Sincar, at the Hands of Melek Ahmed Pasha, the Serdar

"My lord," I began. "In the year————[2] when our lord Melek Ahmed Pasha was governor of Diyarbekir, these Saçlı Dağı Yezidis raided and plundered the villages of Mardin, swooping down from the mountain on the merchants and travelers and committing highway robbery. Finally the entire populace of the country came to the beneficent pasha to complain about the outrage.

The foresightful pasha outwardly dismissed their claim in the Diyarbekir council, and they returned to Mardin cursing and bitterly disappointed. Meanwhile the pasha was getting ready to wreak his vengeance on these Saçlı Kurds. But he revealed his plan to no one, according to the adage, 'The meaning is in the belly of the poet.'

"One day he sent a censuring letter to the khan of Bitlis, who sent a letter in turn, expressing his outrage and warning the pasha not to go too far. The pasha was furious. He announced an expedition against the khan of Bitlis, and set up his military tent pavilion and the horsetail banners in a place called Sadıköyü, across the Tigris. He also broadcast orders throughout the provinces of Van and Kurdistan, and a sea-like army made its way to Kara Amid (Diyarbekir province). In the city of Diyarbekir our lord Melek Pasha mustered seventy regiments of Segban and Sarıca troops, each regiment consisting of 100 warriors. It was a statute (*kanun*) for the banners to be unfurled, and it was a condition (*şart*) for the Sarıcas to be on foot, the Segbans on horse. In this fashion the army of Islam, including the pasha's troops and those from Diyarbekir and Van provinces, amounted to 87,000 armed men.

"After the pasha's horsetail banners had gone out, in the company of 3,000 soldiers, to Miyafarkin in Bitlis province, seventy famous champions and trustworthy individuals on the side of the khan of Bitlis, Abdal Khan—including Hakkari Molla Mehmed, Ziriki Molla Cibrayil, Mudiki Ali Agha, and Kanah-dereli Ali Agha—came to intermediate between the pasha and the khan of Bitlis, citing the Hadith: 'He who makes peace between two people deserves the reward of a martyr.' They gave the pasha eighty purses as 'travel expenses,' six strings of fine horses, ten virgin maidens, and ten moonfaced boys like the denizens of paradise. And they gave the pasha's officers and his personal staff so many gifts that they were all rich, and they joyously thanked God that they would not have to go on campaign after all.

"That night, however, when the pasha sent word to the billeting officers to give up the march against the khan of Bitlis, he simultaneously put Mehmed Emin Pasha, who was Şemsi Pasha's son, in charge of 10,000 soldiers and, adjuring by God, put some words in his ear like an earring. 'Go forth,' he said, 'may God be your Aid and Helper,' and he recited a Fatiha. So Mehmed Emin Pasha recrossed the Tigris to the Diyarbekir side and disappeared, with no one the wiser.

"Gınayi Efendi immediately drew up letters of love and affection to the khan of Bitlis and sent them off with Arganalı Ahmed Agha and the above-mentioned intermediaries. As the horsetail banners were withdrawn and the trumpets sounded for the march, the prudent pasha, with 70,000 soldiers, recrossed the Tigris to the Diyarbekir side, ordering the heavy baggage to be brought behind. He put Kudde Mehmed Kethüda and Receb Kethüda in charge of the army, while he himself, in a forced march, crossed the Zirzivan Gorge that very night. By noon the next day he halted below Mardin, camping in little tents, and went foraging. From there he made another forced march. An hour before dawn 40,000 of the light cavalry surrounded Saçlı Dağı, joining forces with those of Mehmed Emin Pasha, which had been sent from below Diyarbekir and which had already invested Mt. Saçlı on all four sides.

"The faithless Kurdish Yezidis who resided on that merciless mountain were exchanging musket fire with the aforementioned pasha (Mehmed Emin) when, an hour before dawn, the soldiers who arrived with the pasha (Melek Ahmed) immediately took cover in the trenches below the crags of Mt. Sincar. In fact, when dawn came, our regiment commander, Zipir Bölük-başı, with forty regiments of Sarıcas like yellow bees *(sarı arı)*, rather than sounding the call to prayer, began, in plain view, to spread *(saç-)* fire toward Mt. Saçlı, and to enter the trenches.

"In the morning the sealike army appeared, and the Sincar plain was decked out with tents and equipment like a tulip garden. The rest of the army arrived within three days, the Sincar plain was studded with tents and pavilions, and day by day the sealike army won sway over the Saçlı infidels."

When I reached this point in my narrative, Firari Mustafa Pasha cried out in amazement: "My dear Evliya Efendi! How did you gain entrance? How did you do battle? How did you take booty? How did you gain victory and take revenge on these Yezidi Kurds in this accursed mountain? I am in terrible straits because of these Yezidi devils. How many reproachful letters and noble orders have I received from the Padishah. I, too, kept secret my plan to march against this Saçlı, I revealed it to no one. I, too, pretended to march against the khan of Bitlis. I marched in his direction with a sealike army and, by God's command, I did give that infamous khan quite a few reprimands and did get from him quite a bit of money. Then I turned my reins in this direction. And here we are now besieging it. But my dear Evliya

Efendi, how did you manage to conquer it with our father Melek Ahmed Pasha? Tell me in detail."

Completion of the Adventure of the *Gaza* against Mt. Saçlı

"My lord," I replied, "you should know that at that period your lord the pasha disposed of seventy regiments of Segbans and Sarıcas; plus 10,000 of his own retinue—all of them Abkhazian and Circassian and Georgian braves—who shamed one another in battle, and never held back their reins, and who knew what Muhammedan honor meant. They invested Mt. Saçlı with one heart and mind, intent on avenging upon these Yezidi devils the blood of Imam Hüseyn and the martyrs of Kerbela,[3] and determined to shave off the heads of all the unshorn Yezidis with their keen swords and to win booty, virgin maids and splendid boys. As for the Sarıcas, they swore to avenge the blood of 7,000 of their number who had been martyred when their lord and patron Nasuh Pasha, Sultan Ahmed's vizier,[4] the one who had founded the Sarıca regiments, was defeated in battle on this very Saçlı Dağı. So all the musketeers took solemn oaths. And our lord Melek Ahmed Pasha won the loyalty of all the Muslim *gazis* and urged them on with his attentions and persuasions, gifts and promises and threats.

"At dawn the *gazis* began to go up the mountain in seventy or eighty places, as though ascending to heaven with a lasso. The battle between that race of satans and the people of Melek Pasha raged on all sides for seven full hours, so furiously that the heavenly cherubim put finger to mouth in astonishment. Seven hundred youths fell in that fray and quaffed the cup of death, and 3,060 Saçlı Yezidis were slain.

"The battle died down as evening approached, and the drums of repose were beaten here and there. Everyone stood armed and ready where he had done battle. Trenches were dug and sentries stationed. Of the Yezidi Kurds who came stealthily that night to attack the *gazis* lying in their ambushes, 800 lost their heads and 75 were taken alive—these, too, were turned into heads and trotters and their souls sent off to hell.

"The following morning the *gazis* invaded the vineyards all over Mt. Sincar and raided 300 villages. But they found not a single needle or thread, not a dove or a hen, not an item of furniture or food or drink, not even a nail or a mustard seed. By

the pasha's order they set fire to all the houses, which were covered with reed mats, and the black smoke filled the heavens. As
for the grapes in the vineyards, God is my witness that this
humble servant Evliya the dervish has never seen their like in
these forty-one years of travel. The people had abandoned all
this produce in the thousands of vineyards and all the grain in
the open fields, and had taken refuge in some underground
caves, each holding 1,000 or 2,000 faithless Kurdish Yezidis,
where they fortified themselves with all their children and families, valuable goods, food, and drink.

"According to some captive informants, when Mehmed
Emin Pasha came by surprise and laid siege to this mountain,
the people had not yet reaped the millet and other grain that
was ripe in the fields. Nevertheless 40,000 or 50,000 cursed
musketeers had entered the caves and, shooting from loopholes,
let no one approach. To take refuge in such caves was these people's last resort. In fact, during the reign of Sultan Ahmed, these
devils wrought such havoc upon vizier Nasuh Pasha on this
mountain that the heaps of Ottoman bones are still quite visible.

"Our lord Melek Ahmed Pasha, taking cognizance of this
sorry state of affairs, had the entire army of Islam remove camp
from the plain below to the top of Mt. Sincar. He quartered them
in the vineyards, where each man was given his plot or garden
and settled down in his hut-of-sorrows. Then he ordered the soldiers to gather the sheaves of grain, with the stalks, from the
fields, and to pile them up like mountains at the mouths of the
caves, to serve as a rampart. Countless sheaves of millet, with
the stalks, were put on top of the caves, and he set fire to them.
Skin upon skin of sharp vinegar was poured over the rock face,
making it crumble away. He had master miners break the rock
face with their Ferhadi picks, boring holes in the rock through
which he had thousands of flaming millet sheaves hurled into
the caves. Those devils within, young and old, began to cry and
wail. He also had artillery brought from Mardin on six camel-
drawn carts, and placing the cannons where possible against
the walled-up mouths of the caves, blew up the walls and massacred the devils within. The miners, meanwhile, pierced the
rock face with their chisels and picks and pokers and augers,
and they tossed hand grenades through the holes, which blew
up those cursed Saçlı Yezidis wherever they struck them inside
the caves.

"Some of the cave mouths being quite high, the soldiers and miners where possible channeled streams, which ran even higher, down into the caves inundating those within. When the devils, harried in this fashion, ran out crying for mercy, they all began to direct streams into the caves. And as the wind fanned the flames of the millet sheaves, piled at the mouths of the caves, which had been blown open by the cannons, a fire of Nimrod roasted the Yezidis inside. All the bottle hand grenades exploded. The cannonballs made heads roll. And people drowned in the flowing streams.

"In short, on the seventh day, all the people, harried in one fashion or another, sallied out crying, 'Mercy, mercy, O excellent Ottomans!' But the Muslim *gazis*, wondrous to relate, disregarding the fires of Nimrod that were still blazing, rushed into the caves seeking martyrdom or victory. So battle and truce alternated for three more days.

"Finally, on the———day of the month of———in the year———they dragged those Yezidis in Saçlı Dağı out by the hair, and the Muslim *gazis* shaved off their hairy *(saçlı)* heads with their trenchant swords like Selman Pak's dancing boys.[5] Some of the Yezidis, seeing that their wives and children were taken captive, gouged out their own eyes. Hundreds hurled themselves from the cliffs and were broken to pieces on the rocks below. Thousands killed their own wives and daughters and sons; or stabbed themselves with daggers; or fell on their swords, and died. Thousands bared their swords and rushed on their foes, to kill or be killed; or they embraced their children and leaped together from the cliffs.

"When the army of Islam saw this spectacle they too expended the utmost of their powers and smote with their swords. Blood of the Yezidis flowed down the mountainside. God willing, vengeance was exacted at the hand of Melek Ahmed Pasha for the blood of the martyrs of Kerbela.

"In short, such a mighty battle raged for ten days and nights that even Küçük Ahmed Pasha's battle on Jabal Druze with Ma'n-oğlu was not so fierce.[6] A total of 9,000 heads were taken; and 13,600 captives, women and men, girls and boys. And more gold and silver vessels and earrings and rings and caps and goblets and dishes and other booty was taken than tongue could say or pen could write. Also seven of their *bapirs*— which is to say, their governing officials and their sheiks—were captured.

"In fact, one *bapir* devil, even though he was in chains, managed to grab the dagger from the waist of the chief of the Sarıcas, Zipir Bölük-başı, while the latter was dozing, and before you knew it stabbed him in seven places. Zipir Bölük-başı, fearing for his life, wrenched the dagger from that cursed *bapir's* hand, and immediately dispatched him on the way of the *pir*-less ones.[7] He was such a cursed Yezidi Kurd. These are very brave and plucky infidels. They all worship black dogs. In their villages you never find a mosque. They know nothing of fasting and prayer, pilgrimage and alms, and the witness formula.[8] All of them are wine bibbers, since they raise juicy grapes in their vineyards.

"Also, these Yezidis were as wealthy as Croesus. All the multitudes of troops from the provinces of Van and Diyarbekir and Mardin who came to the aid of Melek Ahmed Pasha, all the Kurdistan soldiery who participated in plundering the money and food and drink and copper vessels and household furnishings and the like which emerged over ten days from the Saçlı Dağı caves, could not carry away more than a drop in the sea and a mote in the sun. For ever since the event of Kerbela these people have been rich, and no king had ever conquered them before.

"To conclude: Melek Ahmed Pasha got as his royal tithe of the booty 1,060 purses of silver, 11 purses of gold, 13,000 muskets, 300 bales of silk, several hundred bales of gunpowder, 300 mules, 1,800 captives young and old, and countless precious cloth items. Only God the Generous knows the amount that fell to the other emirs and nobles and officers and *gazis*. Certainly each tent got five or ten lovely lads and lasses and other captives. There were no sheep, horses, or water buffalo; but there were many mules and goats."

[Firari Mustafa Pasha has to lift the siege of Sincar in order to come to the rescue of Ali Faris of the desert Arabs (*çöl urbanı*). Evliya accompanies him back to Diyarbekir, where they arrive on 20 Receb 1065/26 May 1655 (IV 217b.11). Firari pays the debt, Evliya gives him a receipt, and he rejoins Melek Pasha between Hazzo and Kefender, south of Bitlis]

Notes

1. See J. S. Guest, *The Yezidis* (London and New York, 1987).

2. At IV 216b.3 (70) Evliya mentions that the conquest took place fifteen years earlier when Melek was governor of Diyarbekir (i.e., in 1050/1640–41).

3. See Ch. 4, n. 20. Yezid was the name of the Umayyad caliph deemed responsible for the martyrdom of Hüseyn. The Yezidi sect, in turn, is associated polemically with that Yezid, although the name of the sect probably has a quite different origin.

4. 1020–23/1611–14.

5. Selman Pak was a companion of the Prophet and is the patron saint of barbers.

6. The governor of Damascus, Küçük Ahmed Pasha, defeated the rebel Druze leader Fahreddin II (Maʿn-oğlu) in Mt. Lebanon in 1042/1633.

7. *Ba-pir* could be interpreted as "having a *pir* or a guide on the Sufi way." Evliya playfully alters it here to *bi-pir* meaning "without a *pir*."

8. These are the five "pillars" of Islam. For the witness formula, see Ch. 2, n. 24.

6

GOVERNOR OF VAN
(1655–56)

[The pasha halts for ten days in Bitlis, where he is royally entertained by Abdal Khan, the flamboyant quasi-independent Kurdish
(Rozhiki) ruler.[1] When the ten days are up, the pasha and the khan
meet privately.]

Melek Ahmed Pasha's Admonishment
to the Noble Khan

"My khan and brother," began the pasha, "when our lord
Sultan Murad Khan, the conqueror of Revan, came to your palace and stayed as your guest in the year 1045 (1635–36), I was
Murad Khan's sword-bearer and personal companion. At that
time too, this worthless slave, along with the Padishah, was a
recipient of your boundless and matchless bounty and favor.
And our lord Murad, pleased at your hospitality, granted you the
harac of Muş in perpetuity, and made you his protégé.

"But in 1048 (1638–39), when my lord Murad Khan was
returning from the conquest of Baghdad, you failed—a youthful
indiscretion!—to come from Bitlis to Diyarbekir and rub your
face on Gazi Murad Khan's stirrup, and to say, 'May your holy
war prosper!' Murad Khan was quite offended, and he said to
me: 'Ahmed, you must certainly take my vengeance upon Sultan
Yusuf Khan, the governor of Müzuri, and upon Abdal Khan, the
khan of Bitlis.'[2]

"After he had returned to Istanbul, and during my tenure
as governor of Diyarbekir, I gathered an army and with God's
help captured Yusuf Khan, the ruler of the Müzuri tribe, at
Imadiye. I killed 700 of his men and sent their heads to Murad
Khan at the Porte. But, as I am sure you know, I spared Yusuf

Khan, set him free from Diyarbekir castle, and confirmed him in his original governorship.

"After that, I gathered an army to go against you, according to my lord Murad Khan's command, and I had come from Diyarbekir as far as Miyafarkin castle, where intermediaries arranged that you would give me seventy purses and so much goods and merchandise. So I turned a blind eye, with the excuse that you were not in my province of Diyarbekir, but in Van province. I gave up the expedition against you, and instead used that great army to conquer the Saçlı Yezidi Kurds in Mount Sincar. I killed 10,000 of them, took a great number of captives and much wealth, and returned safely to Diyarbekir, the Ottoman soldiers enriched with booty.[3] All this is known to you.

"Also, my dear khan and brother, in the year———, during my tenure as governor of Erzurum,[4] you still did not sit quiet, but—another youthful indiscretion—you raided the Kurds who go up to the summer pastures of Bingöl, in Erzurum province, and took away 70,000 sheep, claiming this amount as a 'toll'.

"When the owners of the sheep came to me in Erzurum to complain, I sent you a letter with my marshal of the guards. You tore up the letter, and threatened to kill the man, saying, 'I am not in his province and jurisdiction. I am a noble khan. What have I to do with Melek Ahmed Pasha?' Mudiki Ali Agha intervened, and my officer managed to escape and return to Erzurum. Just as I was about to bring an army against you, Sultan Ibrahim removed me from office in Erzurum, so you again slipped from my hands.

"What is passed is passed. In those days you were young, and I too was young. But I warn you! True, God be praised, we were vouchsafed to meet again, and I am once again recipient of so much bounty and favor. But, my khan and brother, I do request that you keep this in mind: I am a grand vizier of the Ottoman sultans. In particular, I am the son-in-law of Sultan Murad IV. And now I am governor of the province of Van. You are an independent ruler under my jurisdiction, governing this subprovince as a perpetual inheritance (ocaklık). But do not be complacent, just because you have shown me so much hospitality. Do not let your Kurdish obstinacy get the better of you, and do not follow the counsel of your jugglers and mountebanks, or do anything irregular or improper. Stay on good terms with the tribal emirs who neighbor you on every side. And do not neglect your duties to the Padishah whom you serve. Your brother Melek's word is good: if you depart from the law one jot, if you so much as lift a single stone illegitimately, you will lose your head! So please act properly with everyone as long as I am in Van.

"You may well say, 'Ipşir Pasha banished this Melek Ahmed Pasha to Van. Why should I pay him any regard?' But keep in mind that I am now, by royal decree, a chief commander and an honored vizier, empowered to draw the imperial cipher. Therefore sit quiet, and do not depart from the path of right. This is my advice to you."

"Truly," said the khan, "it is the advice of a father and of a grandfather. Your wish is my command."

The khan and the pasha kissed again and were saying farewell, when the khan said, "My sultan, let your servant Evliya Çelebi stay with me a few more days. I'll send him after you to Van."

The pasha gave leave. "Evliya," he said, "stay with my brother the khan for a few days, then follow quickly." So the pasha rode off toward Van, and I returned with the khan to Bitlis, where he gave me a chamber in his own quarters among his personal retinue, and we spent several days and nights conversing and carousing.

One day, in the course of conversation, he said: "You see, my Evliya, your pasha informed me of his grudge in the tent at Rahva, and in the guise of 'advice' he threw in my face a record of my activity that he has kept for thirty years. It is better to be wary of this pasha of yours—though I hope for the best."

"The truth is," I replied, "the pasha is in awe of you. It is only out of his great affection that he has spoken to you in an advisory way. You should not be offended at his words. This is Kurdistan, and your subjects are the rebellious Rozhiki tribe. On the other hand are the people of Van. Your brother the pasha, out of affection, has given my khan some cautionary counsel to forestall any troublemaker who may wish to sow dissention between you. So you ought to be pleased at this counsel, my khan. For you know, the pasha is free of guile, pride, anger, or ill-feeling. He is the commander of the viziers, a generous and wise man."

Thus I praised the pasha quite a lot. The khan was pleased at my speech, and fell silent.

[Within a month of his arrival in Van, the pasha discovers a pretext for mounting an expedition against the khan of Bitlis.[5] On the eve of their departure from Van, the Pasha recalls to Evliya the incident twenty years before when he had put out a fire in Sultan Murad's bed-chamber in that very fortress. He then inquires of Evliya whether he had not told him a dream he had had before they left Istanbul. Evliya says he has forgotten, and so the pasha relates the dream and its inter-pretation, in nearly the same words as before (see Chapter 4). The cam-paign itself is full of incident. Here Evliya reflects on the pasha's reaction to bad news.]

Because this spy dressed as informant sang the khan's praises, the foresightful pasha learned the huge extent of the khan's army. But he betrayed no emotion, was not downcast or disheartened, revealed the matter to no one, but simply went about his business, and carried out the essential tasks. For old Melek Pasha had traveled through many a clime and killed many a foe, having fought at the Derne and Derteng frontiers during the Baghdad truce;[6] in the Saçlı mountains against the Sincar Kurds;[7] at Tenedos when the infidel fleet besieged the island; at Varna and at Özü when the cussed cossacks attacked the forts.[8] He was an intrepid vizier, not one to show fear at the great size of an enemy force.

As it turned out, however, that day was extremely hot, and the pasha became feverish and exhausted, and so distressed and out of temper that he could hardly speak. Even so, to keep up the spirits of the army he girded on the belt of resolution in two places, citing the proverb, "Noble ambition is of the Faith," and the verse:

Let us gird the sword of zeal in two places;
Let us enter the fray, though we be soiled with dust and dirt.

He never showed the slightest weariness, but continued to award those daring *gazis* who brought in heads and "tongues" (captive informants) and those who brought in "a thing,"[9] dis-pensing bounties from the pile of money in front of him, a mix-ture of goldpieces, piasters, and shiny silver coins. Sometimes he would mount his swift steed and ride out with 1,000 or 2,000 of his reckless braves. He would put the sentries in order, and hearten the men, inciting them to battle. He would show his own zeal by swooping down hawklike upon the khan's skir-mishing party; or, like a flock of eagles attacking a crow, he would enter at will a mass of enemy troops, scatter them left and right, seize his prey, and emerge safe and sound. He was a great champion and a courageous warrior.

On the————day of Ramazan the pasha consulted with all the emirs and notables, and they decided to postpone the fast. He gave a huge feast to the *gazis*, after which he addressed them as follows: "Emirs of the House of Osman, and nobles of the fortress of Van! We have come this far, and have rested here for some days. We told the Kurdish *begs* to come; but they have refused to come, and we have despaired of their coming. Now then, before the khan's army becomes too familiar with us and too sure of themselves, let us confront the khan. Throne or Fortune!"

All those present shouted, "Yours to command!" But they still hoped that the spies would return with news of the Diyarbekir reinforcements.

After this council, our lord the pasha put on his armor and retired with his personal retinue to the tent of Mehmed Beg, emir of Melazgird, for consultations. *A fearful adventure.* When the pasha had gone, I remained behind in the tent pavilion with a few chosen champions and menials, the key boy, the head pantryman, and a boy named Ikbal, and we were having our own private consultation. As I had been fasting, I was now enjoying my evening breakfast, cracking pistachios and munching almonds.

Suddenly a man appeared on a bay thoroughbred, with a steelyard pole in his hand and a shield on his shoulder. He slashed at the tent ropes with his sword, came bounding up to us on his horse, and demanded: *"Hani başa-yé té"*[10]—meaning Melek Ahmed Pasha. He was a huge Kurd, like a beast of the apocalypse.

"What do you want with the pasha?" I asked.

"I will stick this spear in the pasha's belly," he said, adding in Kurdish, *"Ey keran jini may gay paşa-yé té"*[11]—this was quite a juicy morsel aimed at the pasha.

The key boy, being an Abkhazian of limited mental powers, shouted, "Come on, let's kill that Kurd and take his horse!"

"What are you thinking?" I said, and held them back; then, turning to the Kurd: "O big one! There is the pasha"—and I pointed to the tent of Yusuf Kethüda.

Meanwhile the pasha's servants came swarming up with tent mallets and axes and spades, saying, "Was it this Kurd who slashed the tent ropes with his sword?" and they drove the fellow away, horse and all.

This time he took off like lightning to the tent of Yusuf Kethüda, thinking he was really the pasha as I had indicated. He charged right into the tent with his horse and gave the Kethüda such a joust with his spear, it was like a blow from Ipşir Pasha himself. Poor Yusuf Kethüda jumped up, fearing for his life, and cried, "Shoot this bastard!" The Kurd's spear was stuck fast in Yusuf Kethüda's pillow, so the doughty Kurd drew his sword and began slashing at those who now rushed upon him, tripping up one here and cutting down one there. Finally several hundred men managed to inflict a few mortal blows. The furious Kurd, like a rabid dog, still managed to keep them off with dog fights.

Suddenly twenty of his berserk Yezidi companions, who had been crouching behind the pasha's tent since he first approached it, now saw what was going on and came out with naked spears to save their friend, crying *"hov hov!"* At this, a few thousand men came rushing from their tents, and a battle royal ensued in the space between the Kethüda's marquee and the pasha's pavilion. The twenty Kurds wounded several hundred men, actually martyring seven of them. But they had fallen into a sea of soldiers, as though into a bottomless pit, so these twenty Kurdish braves—twenty-one if you count the one who first attacked the Kethüda—were like monkeys bombarded by cannonshot. The *gazis* cut them down wherever they tried to run, robbed them of their horses and appurtenances, deposited their heads in front of the tent pavilion, and buried their bodies next to the Husrev Pasha inn.

Heaven is my witness, that in all my travels I have never seen such courageous youths and pugnacious warriors as these. As it turns out, these fellows had been rewarded handsomely by the khan in advance, even contracting with the khan that their pay be continued to their children as a stipend *(ocaklık)* in case they were killed. So they had undertaken this berserk enterprise and come to martyr the pasha—indeed, should they not be considered martyrs on the pasha's behalf?

When the pasha, in Mehmed Beg's tent, heard about this affair, he gave up roving from tent to tent, and kept his armor on day and night.

[In the following episode, the pasha and his retainers are returning from an inspection of the Bitlis defenses.]

On the way back to camp, the pasha noticed a pleasant meadow and said, "Let us perform the noon prayer." We dismounted and I recited the call to prayer. After the canonical prostrations, the pasha faced the *kıble* and said: "I will offer up a prayer, and you say 'Amen.' " *Melek Ahmed Pasha's prayer.* He performed two additional prostrations of need, then bared his head, put his blessed and light-filled face to the ground, and said:

"My God, Yours are might and power, advantage and victory; Yours are succor and protection, guidance and glory. Out of zeal for the manifest Religion I have gathered round my head a band of Your servants of the community of Muhammed. Now, raising my hand to my face, I have come to beg at Your gate. This humble slave Ahmed is an old beggar of Yours. You never sent him away empty-handed; for kindness is Your custom. Again I beg You, Lord absolute. Again accept my plea. Do not cause this huge band to despair. And do not cause these Yezidi vermin to rejoice."

After these supplications his bloodstained tears flowed like the Red Sea. We all said, "Amen," and passed our hands over our faces.

"Good news to you my sons," the pasha said, "our prayer has hit the mark and victory will be ours, God willing." He smiled like a blessed rose, or like the angel *(melek)* he was; now flew hawklike upon his elephantine steed; uttered a prayer; then turned his reins toward Rahva plain, and rode neck and neck with his closest companions, all the while conversing with them and with the several hundred Van notables and the other valiant and experienced men.

As they approached the camp, a few of the Van aghas—Behlul-oğlu, Demirci-oğlu, and Deli Süleyman Beg, who was Husrev Pasha's nephew—said to cheer the pasha: "God willing, great vizier, by the blessing of your prayer, advantage and victory and booty will be ours." And they swore to fight body and soul on the pasha's behalf.

"I well know," he said, "that you are *gazis* and champions of the holy war, who will struggle for the sake of the Manifest Religion." And he uttered a benediction upon them all.

The Saintly Gestes of Melek Ahmed Pasha

As we were entering the camp, our lord Melek Ahmed Pasha turned to the Van aghas and said: "Now, my sons, you have sworn to die on my behalf and have made all sorts of valiant claims. Do you see that body of Kurdish soldiers coming out of our camp over there? What if they should prove hostile, and seeing us, should turn about, spur their horses, and attack us all at once. And if I should cry, 'Come on, *gazis!*' how would you react?"

"Noble vizier," they replied, "we would attack and strike on your behalf, we would take the enemy's heads even if it meant sacrificing our own."

At this the pasha suddenly cried out, as though he had a revelation: "Let us recite a Fatiha upon this intention of holy war!" We all passed our hands over our faces. The pasha then plucked his own spear from the hands of Süleyman Agha, his arms-bearer. Grasping it tightly, and passing his hands from node to node of its twelve nodes, for love of the twelve *imams*, he whirled it majestically about his noble head. After this, he spurred his elephantine steed onto the field. As we watched, his black fawnlike eyes turned to pools of blood, he pranced several times in a circle, and displayed his skill in various martial games and exercises.

Now 200 or so Kurdish horsemen had left our camp going toward Rahva plain. The pasha, instead of entering the camp, began to follow them at a distance. "My sultan," said the Van aghas when we had gone quite a ways, "the camp is behind us, this direction goes to the khan's side. What business do we have in that quarter?"

"We have just recited a Fatiha to pursue holy war," replied the pasha. "Has that Fatiha gone for nought? We're bound to have a battle very soon. Do you see those Kurdish soldiers who came out of our camp and are riding ahead of us? Do you know what clan they belong to, and where they are going?"

"By God, my sultan, there are men in our army now from the country of Kılbarak.[12] Perhaps they have left the camp to go foraging. Who knows?"

"You'll see soon," said the pasha.

During this conversation the Kurdish horsemen had gotten some distance from the camp. It seems that our emir of Pinya-nişi was ahead of them with a patrol party, just where the road forks toward the plain of Muş. The body of horsemen riding ahead of us who had come out of our camp, suddenly cried "Allah Allah!" and spurred their horses to attack our patrolers. They, however, thinking the others were our own soldiers, as they were coming from the direction of our camp, were slow to react. The two parties joined battle and there were several hundred musket shots.

"There!" cried Melek Ahmed Pasha, "the Fatiha was recited for them. Grab your weapons!

We came on at a jog-trot, neck and neck. Our patrol party, taken by surprise, gave way and began to flee in our direction, pursued by the 200 horsemen, who had passed their headbands around their throats and were brandishing their swords and spears and firing their muskets amidst cries of "Khan Khan!" But they were met by our pasha and the fleetest horsemen of the Van aghas. When the patrolers saw that the pasha and the Van aghas had come like Hızır[13] to their rescue, they got a lease on life, did an about-face, and rejoined the fray. The pasha meanwhile had come up with 700 or 800 horsemen. In a flash he knocked down three Kurds with his spear, as he let out his warcry, "Come on, my wolves!" which reverberated in the sky like thunder.

In short, only a few of the 200 Kurds were left alive or fled to the khan. When the pasha questioned the (two) captives, they said: "By God, the khan paid us well and challenged us to kill his arch enemy, the emir of Melazgird. We slipped out of Bitlis one by one and joined the sealike army in your camp. But we—all 200 horsemen—simply could not get word to Mehmed Beg. Finally, so that our effort would not be wholly in vain, (we decided to attack) this patrol body when we came upon them. We did notice you behind us, but could not make out who you were; we thought you were foragers, and finally we lost sight of you. But when we attacked the patrolers, there you were, attacking us. It is God's to command. God damn the khan! He destroyed us—may he die like a dog!" Because they cursed the khan, the pasha let them both go free. A few others had fled on foot. We took their 200 thoroughbreds as booty, stuck their 185 heads on spears, and marched victoriously into the camp just before sunset.

The Van aghas who were with us swore that the pasha had had a revelation, reporting how he had ordered us to recite a Fatiha, and how he had uttered such inspired phrases as, "Do you know who those are ahead of us?" and "You'll see soon." As for Demirci-oğlu, he kept on repeating how the pasha's words had come true, when he said, "If those men who just left our camp should prove hostile and attack us, how would you react?" Demirci-oğlu bruited this about among the troops as a revelation and a miracle. He himself was wounded in that battle, and had to return to Van. But the soldiers took up the notion, saying, "May we also participate in such a holy war as this, in the reign of such a vizier as Melek whose prayers are answered!" They incited one another to battle, and each man was busy preparing his weapons.

[It is the end of July, the night before the final assault.]

A Marvel: The True Dream of Melek Ahmed Pasha

Earlier that morning, following the dawn prayer and after reciting our litanies, our lord Melek Ahmed Pasha, in the company of quite a few of the aghas, said: "I had a dream this night."

"May it be auspicious, my sultan," they all replied.

"I saw in my dream an army of black ants marching and crowding round my foot. They did not bite me. But one of them—a large black ant with a thin waist—climbed up my shin, and I was quite upset. Suddenly an emaciated black ant, hopping over the dirt, came through a great crowd of men, climbed on my foot and bit me. It was very, very painful. Alarmed, I rolled up my pant-leg with my hands and all the ants that had climbed on my foot dropped to the ground dead. Then I saw that some were still alive. Taking pity on them I picked out a few and gave sixteen to Evliya, saying, 'Put these in their nest.' Some others I gave to Demirci-oğlu, the Van agha, saying, 'Put these in their hole, God willing they will recover.' Then I noticed that the sickly black ant which had bitten my foot was alive among the dead ants. 'I'll save you, too,' I said, and picked that ant up from the ground. I gave it to Yusuf Kethüda, saying, 'Look after this ant.' I picked out fifty or sixty more live ants from among the dead ones, but these I crushed with my shoe. May God cause it to come out well."

"May it be auspicious," they all cried as he finished relating the dream.

Molla Mehmed of Hakkari said: "God willing, because you killed the ants, you will make peace with the khan, and not even one black ant will be harmed by you."

Then I spoke up: "Because you presented me with several of the ants, when the khan's army is defeated you will give me several black-eyed and ant-waisted slave boys."

"These are both nice interpretations," said the Pasha, smiling; "knowledge is with God."

[The pasha's forces take the city, and Abdal Khan flees.]

God be praised, *on Tuesday 25 Ramazan 1065 (29 July 1655)* Bitlis castle was easily conquered. Yusuf Kethüda appointed the chief captain of the janissaries with 1,000 picked warriors as guards. He also took over the 300 chambers of the khan's palace, including the treasuries and storehouses, and they were sealed with the seal of this humble servant. Then he closed the castle gate from without. Next he sent ten Segban and Sarıca battalions to the khan's garden, along with ten chief door-keepers, 1,000 picked armed soldiers from the Van garrison troops, and the bureau chief Gınayi-zade Ali Efendi. They assumed control of the khan's 360 inner and outer chambers, plus the armories, treasuries, and storehouses. All these were sealed with the seal of the marshal of the guards, who then proceeded to the lower fortress of Bitlis.

When he arrived, Yusuf Kethüda clapped the castle commander, Kara Ali Agha, the one who shut himself in and insisted on battle, along with his warden and steward, and 700 other vermin, in chains. As they marched by in parade order they were weeping, and bleating like lambs, crying "O child" or "mother" or "father"—truly it was like a mothers' and fathers' day,[14] or like the gathering at the Day of Judgment. In this sorry state, 700 men were brought bound and chained before the pasha's tent and stood waiting for Mars's executioners.

The just pasha was seated on a stool underneath the canopy. "What are these?" he said.

"They are the ones who shut themselves in the citadel and defied the Padishah," answered Yusuf Kethüda.

"But I just set free 700 bound and miserable wretches who came out of the fortress. What happened to them?"

"My sultan," he replied, "those are the ones who raised the flag of surrender and came out with safe conduct. All are residents of the town, the ones whom you set free. But these 700 are the ones who deceived us after the grant of safe conduct and shut themselves in the khan's turret. All are slaves of the khan or Segbans and Sarıcas whose death was ordered three days ago in a noble rescript. It is my sultan's to command." Yusuf Kethüda fell silent.

By now a great crowd of onlookers had gathered around to see what the fate of these men would be, and the executioners stood ready, their hands on their sword hilts. "Which one is their wretched leader?" asked the pasha in a grave tone. The commander was dragged forward, a man named Kara Ali, a

black-faced, filthy brigand, gallows bound and good for nothing.
The pasha examined him carefully. "And what are these?" he
said.

"These are his retinue."

"Executioner!" he cried. At once the pasha's executioners and
personal retainers entered among the captives, cut down seventy of them in a twinkling, and piled their corpses in a heap.

One however, a certain Abaza Mihter Receb, though he
struck his captive seven times with his sword, could not make it
cut him in the slightest, although previously it had served well
enough for eight others. He struck the man one more blow, and
the fellow fell flat on his face, but then scrambled to his feet and
said: "Mercy, Pasha! I am innocent, a stranger to these parts. My
late father in Aleppo wrote a charm and put it in my hair inside
a leaden amulet. I am safe from every sort of accident or calam-
ity until I die. That is why the sword cannot cut me." The pasha
freed the man and made him his protégé, giving him a post that
was vacant with the Van garrison.

"Bring that black Arab here," ordered the Pasha, "that com-
mander of theirs who looks like black death." The miserable
Kara Ali Agha was forced to his knees in the arena of execution.
"Now call our Evliya Çelebi."

"Here I am, my sultan," said I.

"Look, Evliya. Didn't I tell you yesterday morning in the
council about a dream I had the night before, in which a black
ant bit my foot very painfully, but the other ants did not bite
me? Now you see, the ant that bit my foot is this infidel who
caused me so much anguish by shutting himself in the citadel.
Off with his head!"

I spoke up just as the executioner was baring his sword:
"Mercy, my sultan. You said then that in your dream you picked
out the black ant that bit you from among the dead ants and
gave it to Yusuf Kethüda, thus letting it go free. Now you just
said that that ant was this black wretch. 'God has fulfilled the
vision for His messenger in truth' (Koran, 48:27). This was my
sultan's genuine dream-vision. In your dream you let him go
free. Now let him go free in reality—by the head of the Beg, and
by your noble head, and by the soul of our lord, the late regretted
Gazi Sultan Murad." And I kissed the ground.

"Let the wretch stand up," said the Pasha.

Reprieved, Kara Ali Agha got to his feet with a sigh, and
began to weep. "Illustrious vizier," he said, "am I not your slave

Kara Ali, your stable master when you were governor of Diyarbekir the second time?"[15]

"What? Is it you, you old rascal? You fled from the field during the battle in the Saçlı mountains, and now during this battle I caught you. Off with his head!"

Knowing the pasha to be a gentle soul, I again kissed the ground at his foot and said: "My sultan, you told us that you freed the black ant that bit your foot from among the dead ants and that you gave it to Yusuf Kethüda. Here are the dead bodies strewn all about. You took this Kara Ali from among the corpses and set him free. He is the black ant, and this is the effect of your dream. Mercy, my sultan. Let him go."

"So be it," said the pasha. "But see here, you devil," he went on. "Why did you run away that time when you were my stable master in Diyarbekir?"

"That time you gave me fifty lashes, saying that I had jaded your white-blazed horse. I was publicly disgraced—it was a point of honor! So I fled in one night from Sincar to Mardin castle, from there to Hasan-keyf, and then to Bitlis, where I took service with the khan and became a family man. But I still feel the sting of those fifty lashes. I was innocent! Now it is up to you to redress the wrong."

"Well, then, coward, in exchange for those fifty lashes you got unjustly, I have now picked you out from among the corpses and let you go free." Kara Ali kissed the ground. "However," continued the pasha, "you were nourished with my bread and salt. Had you not heard my name mentioned, that you shut yourself defyingly in the citadel, and paid no regard to my previous claims?"

"I defied you to remove the sting of those fifty lashes," he replied.

"Hah! They do say that black Arabs are vindictive as camels. After twenty years you found an opportunity to defy me, you devil. I sent my steward to take the citadel, and gave safe conduct to all the Muslims. Why then did you shut yourself in?"

"This time I was eating the khan's bread and salt," he answered, "and was paying regard to his claims. I was devoted to his cause and was planning to bombard your soldiers who had stormed the trenches. But when I heard that my lord the khan had fled, and when I saw that so many thousand of our men had been put to the sword in the trenches, I did recall my due to you based on my eating your bread twenty years ago, and from fear of you I did surrender the citadel. But though I got safe conduct, when I came to this arena of chastisement you showed no mercy at all, but forced me to my knees before the executioner. It is my sultan's to command."

The pasha liked this man's fearless talk. "He's a brave fellow, the devil," he said with a laugh, "he tells the truth!" The pasha gave Kara Ali a robe of honor, charged Yusuf Kethüda with his upkeep, and let him go.

Before this exchange with Kara Ali, the pasha had killed 70 of those who had shut themselves in with him, and the other 630 still stood there bound and fettered. The world-conquering pasha announced: "Since a noble rescript has come from my felicitous Padishah, I will kill all of these. Let whoever will, execute the command, and they may take the victims' belongings."

Because no one else present knew the pasha's character, none dared to come forward and beg for these men's lives. So I once again, in that sea of men, fell at the felicitous Pasha's feet: "My sultan, you said that in your dream the other night you presented this humble servant with sixteen of the ants. 'When the generous man makes a promise he carries it out.' "

"God knows," said the pasha, "I did see that in my dream. Go now Evliya, take sixteen of those condemned men. But for each one you must recite a complete Koran on behalf of the soul of the Prophet."

"I will recite forty complete Korans and will freely bestow the merit accrued thereby upon the noble souls of the Prophet and his four companions and the martyrs of Kerbela and all the saints, if you gave me two men for each one and let eighty go free."

God be praised, he accepted my plea: "Go now Evliya, take some of these doomed men."

"God willing, not all of them are doomed," I said, then cried: "A Fatiha!" All the *gazis* present recited a Fatiha, as I began, with the help of my servants and some of the pasha's tasters, to pick out forty from among the fettered men about to be killed. We actually took fifty-three, and they were led away.

"Hey Evliya," said the pasha, "will you take away all of them because of a single Fatiha? That's enough!"

"My sultan," I replied, "this young man said 'I'm an emir;' this one, 'I'm a dervish of Abdulkadir Gilani;' this one, 'If God releases me from this bond I'll make the Pilgrimage;' this one, 'I'm a descendent of Halid bin Velid;' this one was my sultan's taster in Diyarbekir; this one said, 'I'm a Kurd and descended from the house of Abbas.' "[16]

"All the Kurds claim descent from the house of Abbas," said the pasha, "but there are Yezidis among them too. Enough now, take those and go."

In short, God be praised, for saying I would perform forty Koran recitals I was able to raise sixty men from the field of execution. I sent them all to my tent, where I loosed their hands and gave them food.

When I returned to the grand tent I saw that the pasha was quite incensed. He was standing on the stool in the imperial council, with a wooden beam in his hand, and shouting, "Let whoever will, kill these men!" At once, horrible to say, the Segban and Sarıca vermin, like butcher boys or yellow *(sarıca)* wasps, went in amongst the handcuffed and heart-stricken prisoners and began to cut them down with their swords. The field that was gay as a tulip-garden now turned ruby-colored with men's blood. Their moans were like the bleats of ewes separated from their lambs, their cries like the bleating of sheep in a slaughter house. The whole mournful scene seemed like Judgment Day.

At this juncture one of the Rozhiki braves managed to get his hands free. He grabbed the sword of one of those executioners, struck down seven men, and made havoc of the whole operation. "Stop, stop!" cried the pasha. He let the poor man go, and attached him to the Van garrison.

By now all the pasha's aghas and the Van notables were feeling pangs of compassion, as they watched the slaughter. "People of Muhammed," I shouted. "The pasha has a look in his eye as though he would like to see someone beg for these men's lives. But none of you is going and begging. Don't you see that he gave me sixty prisoners merely on the pretext of one Koran recital? Don't you see that this battlefield has turned into a river of blood for the past three days? Go, beg for men. The pasha's eye is hungry for men-beggars."

All our aghas and the Van aghas at once fell at the pasha's feet crying: "Enough, my sultan! The decree of the Padishah has been carried out. Free the remaining prisoners."

Their plea was accepted. Of the 700 men that came out of the citadel with Kara Ali, only 150 had been gobbled by the teeth of the sword; the remainder quaffed the sherbet of salvation.

[After the victory, the pasha inquires of Evliya whether he knows the true reason for this war. "No my sultan, I don't," replies Evliya (IV 272b.16 [235]), and the pasha once again, though more briefly, recounts the dream of the bloody bread.

The pasha appoints as puppet khan Abdal's lovable and compliant young son, Ziyaeddin. After returning to Van, Melek Pasha sends Evliya off on a mission to Iran. Evliya returns to Van at the beginning of book V after an absence of six months. A lightning trip to Istanbul, though probably apocryphal, does provide the stimulus for the subsequent narrative, since Evliya supposedly brings back from the grand vizier Siyavuş Pasha a warning for Melek Pasha to "take what he can get" (V 8a.2 [17]: alacağı kalmasın) because he will soon be recalled from office.

Melek Pasha immediately sends Evliya to Bitlis to help his other agents collect some arrears.[17] Shortly after he arrives, news reaches Bitlis that Melek Pasha has been removed from office, and the following day, 27 February, Abdal Khan himself returns. The situation becomes critical for Evliya, who manages to stay on the khan's good side by claiming that he has left the pasha's service and wishes to pass the rest of his days in Bitlis. The khan, apparently taken in by this, promises him slave girls, also a daughter for his wife, even appoints him tutor to his sons. But Evliya realizes that his position is precarious, and readies for an escape by each day training his horses in the snow.

In one gruesome incident the old wizard Molla Mehmed, after a playful display of his magical skills (he has some young lads ski up the slope as fast as they skied down), is ruthlessly cut down by one of the khan's goons, a giant named Altı Kulaç ("Six Fathoms"). When Evliya inquires what the mollah's crime was, the khan replies that the mollah had conspired to bring Melek Pasha's troops into Bitlis, even using charms and talismans to weaken the khan's soldiery.

In a dramatic scene the young Ziyaeddin is stabbed to death by his elder brother Nureddehir, and while the mayhem is proceeding Evliya makes his escape. When he reaches Melek Pasha near Adilcevaz, and he relates his adventures, the pasha inquires only about the arrears that Evliya was supposed to help collect. "Forget about that," says Evliya (V 14b.14 [38]). He persuades the pasha, who had intended to go through Bitlis and Diyarbekir on his way back to Istanbul, to alter his route and go through Erzurum. Their first halt is in Melazgird.]

A Remarkable Event: The Genuine Dream of
This Humble Dervish

One night, while I was asleep in my hut-of-sorrows in this town of Melazgird, I dreamed that I was in the Süleymaniye in

Istanbul and I saw Siyavuş Pasha's mother and Defterdar-zade Mehmed Pasha's mother weeping together.[18] "O matrons, my ladies," said I, "why are you weeping?"

"Evliya Efendi," they replied, "our two sons—Siyavuş and Mehmed—have drowned in the Istanbul sea. Please inform your Melek Ahmed Pasha in Erzurum. Tell him to provide a remedy for their pains. Tell him to revive them, although they are drowned."

At this I awoke. After performing my ablution, it being an hour before dawn, I entered the pasha's presence and we greeted each other.

"My Evliya," he said, "what did you dream in Erzurum?"

"Well, my sultan, let us go to Erzurum."

"Well, but tell me, what did you dream?"

So I recounted in detail the dream just related above.

"Praise be to God," cried the pasha. "I too just now saw you in *my* dream. You said: 'In Erzurum I'll tell you a strange dream, but do not weep.' That is why I said, 'What did you dream in Erzurum?' Now—may it be auspicious—those women weeping and saying 'Our sons have drowned in Istanbul' means that they have 'drowned' in the wealth of this world—but God knows best. And their saying 'Tell your pasha in Erzurum, have him revive our sons although they are drowned' means that we will 'revive' their protégés and their servants, we will shower them with gifts for the sake of their (masters') spirits, and they will gain new life—but God knows best. And in Erzurum we will get much news by your mouth—may it be auspicious."

He interpreted my dream in this manner and ended by reciting a Fatiha.

[After remaining another month in Melazgird they proceed to Erzurum.]

God be praised, after eleven years I was once again vouchsafed to enter (Erzurum) safe and sound, and to halt there. Our lord the pasha was lodged in the great palace, exclusive to viziers. The aghas, with their diplomas *(yafte)*, were housed in the city, because it was the dead of winter and because they were "our just pasha's aghas." Their baggage trains were lodged in Kânköyü, in the Erzurum plain, and their necessities were all provided by the city populace, so that none of our aghas had to worry about a frying pan or boiling coffee. For in the year——— our lord Melek Pasha served as governor of Erzurum; and because he was on such good terms with all the town notables, great and small, and because they did not lose a single thread (during his governorship), they now greeted him as "our mild and gentle lord the pasha," and they spared no pains on his behalf, showering him with gifts and with sweetmeats of every kind.

It so happened that the governor of the province was Zurnazan Mustafa Pasha. He had been master of the seal for one hour in the felicitous Threshold, but then was dismissed, and was now on his way to assume the governorship of Erzurum.[19] His deputy, a certain Abdullah Agha, was an excellent and prudent individual, a fine administrator and a charming person. As soon as the pasha set foot in the palace, he draped all the chambers and the council hall in cloth-of-gold, and laid out a banquet for the pasha's entire retinue, of such magnificence as to beggar praise and defy description. It seemed as though we had been dismissed from Van and were appointed to govern Erzurum.

It seems, however, that Topkapılı Mahmud Agha, who was the Erzurum customs inspector, owed 200 purses to the state treasury, and was being kept in confinement by a certain Iznikli Hüseyn Agha, who had been sent (to arrest him) by Defterdarzade Mehmed Pasha. Now when our pasha heard of this he summoned Hüseyn Agha, sat him at the deputy governor's banquet, and won his heart with all sorts of flatteries. After dinner the deputy governor presented the pasha with a sable fur, ten sacks of clothing, three Georgian *gulams*, three Arabian horses, three files of mules, and three files of camels; and the sagacious pasha gave one of the zephyr-swift steeds to Hüseyn Agha.

Then he said to him: "Hüseyn Agha, my son, is the customs inspector Mahmud Agha being held by you in chains?"

"Yes, my sultan, he is under surveillance."

"Now, I will stand surety for him. I pledge both my money and my life. Even if he owes 1,000 purses I will guarantee their payment. Free him from confinement this instant."

"Of course, my sultan," replied the prudent Hüseyn Agha. "Your wish is my command. Just have your marshal of guards attend me and I will surrender him immediately."

"That is clever," said the pasha. "I mean, now you will have an excuse, saying, 'I didn't free him (willingly), I was forced to free him and I surrendered him to such-and-such an agha.' "

"No, my sultan. I swear to you that such an idea never entered my head."

"Go quickly," said the pasha to his marshal of guards. "Hü-seyn Agha will surrender Mahmud Agha to you. Then you come here with Hüseyn Agha and let him surrender him to me. That will be proper according to the şeriat."

So Mahmud Agha was released from prison and brought to the pasha's presence, where he kissed the ground. "Now Mahmud Agha," said the pasha, "in the ten days that I am here you must pay your debt to the state treasury, otherwise you know the consequence." He also cried blessing on Hüseyn Agha, who retired to his quarters. As soon as he left, Mahmud Agha presented the pasha with eighteen purses of piasters in cash, plus fine stuffs worth twenty purses—brocades, silks, gold weaves, and other rarities—also seven Arabian horses and three splendid *gulams*. The pasha in return gave Mahmud Agha a sable-skin cloak and said: "Be sure to acquit yourself of your debt, otherwise I swear by God that I won't accept your gifts."

The next day Mahmud Agha arranged another banquet for the pasha in the "Pasha's Palace."[20] Had two noble Padishahs come together in this place they would not be put to shame. All the foods were dressed with sugar and musk. And all the notables were in attendance—Mahmud Agha even invited Hüseyn Agha, who had been sent to arrest him. After this sumptuous repast was consumed, and hands were washed, the pasha took a stroll about this charming pavilion and was admiring it fulsomely. Suddenly he caught sight of my own painting and inscription: "Drawn by the world-traveler, Evliya, a servant of Mehmed Pasha, in the year 1056 (1646)."

"Well, Evliya, was this pavilion built in that year, the year you went to Persia? Is that when you painted this?"

Hüseyn Agha, who had been sent to arrest Mahmud Agha, spoke up: "My sultan, 'get wisdom from Lokman'.[21] This pavilion was indeed built by our lord Mehmed Pasha, your son, while he was governor of the province. And all this lovely painting and blue and gold calligraphy is by the hand of your well-wisher Evliya Çelebi. The chronogram was composed by him as well; you can make it out here at the bottom of the inscription:'———for the year———' "

The pasha studied it very closely. "Yes, yes," he cried. "This perishing world! By God, it really is Evliya's composition, and his drawing. Praise be to God. So our son Defterdar-zade Mehmed Pasha left his mark in this pavilion as well! How many souls never leave such a mark. That is why they say, 'A man

dies, his name remains behind.' In short, one must erect several
such monuments in order to be remembered for good."

The pasha continued to wander about the pavilion, but he
seemed to ramble like a drunken man, and his eyes turned to
bowls of blood. "The pasha is in a rage again," said I to myself.
So I approached him and said: "My sultan, soon, God willing,
when we return to the felicitous Threshold, and when you meet
with Defterdar-zade who built this pavilion and who is himself now the Defterdar Pasha, God willing, you will get along
well together."

"May God postpone our meeting with him and with Siyavuş
Pasha," replied the pasha. "It is better to pray on the ground for
a day than to lie in the ground for a thousand years. God willing, Evliya, you and I will go together, safe and sound, to various
posts in Rumelia. Defterdar-zade and Siyavuş Pasha have gone
to a different post." And he fell silent.

I realized that these words of the pasha were ominous and
prophetic, but I was quiet about it, citing the adage, "The meaning is in the poet's belly."

What should I see next? Melek Pasha took up his prayer
beads and, gazing out over the plains of Erzurum, started to
count them: "Allah Allah, Kadir Allah, Baki Allah![22] Those who
build such pleasure domes and palaces in this perishing world!"
So I left the above-mentioned pavilion and went downstairs.

Learning that the customs-inspector Mahmud Agha's two
Tatar couriers had arrived, I immediately went back upstairs to
the pasha and said: "Good news, my sultan. The Tatar couriers
have arrived and have brought you some letters."

"There, my Evliya," said the pasha. "In your dream in
Melazgird castle, the mothers of Siyavuş Pasha and of Mehmed
Pasha said to you, 'Tell your pasha in Erzurum that our sons
have drowned,' and now here in Erzurum you have informed me
that the couriers have arrived. These couriers bear much news.
Quickly, summon the customs inspector Mahmud Agha, and the
orphaned Hüseyn Agha who was sent to arrest him, and the
deputy governor."

They were brought at once, along with the two couriers
who presented themselves before the pasha with their Tatar
bow-and-arrow cases, placed their Tatar caps on the floor,
kissed the pasha's hand, gave him the letters, and stood back.

First of all the pasha read the letter from Kaya Sultan.
"Judgment is God's." he said. " 'To God we belong and to Him we

return' (Koran 2:156)." And he broke out weeping. "Do you see, my Evliya? Just now you wished that when I meet Defterdar-zade in Istanbul we get along well together. And you were surprised when I said, 'May God postpone the meeting.' Well, Siyavuş Pasha has died while serving as grand vizier. The moment he died, the Padishah called for Defterdar-zade Mehmed Pasha and said: 'You had a noble En'am[23] recited for my *lala* Siyavuş Pasha. You must have murdered him!' So he was killed in the *bostancı-başı's* hut, and his corpse was left in front of Demir Kapı. At the very same moment Mehmed Pasha was being strangled, and he gave up the ghost, a son of his came into the world and was dubbed 'Orphan Mehmed.' "

When I heard this news my heart was in my throat, I broke out weeping and nearly fainted. For I had served that gracious vizier here in Erzurum as secretary of the customs and secretary of the treasury and as his boon companion.[24] And on the pretext of having painted this palace and composed the chronograms I received, in a year and a half, gifts from him amounting to seventeen purses, plus ten purses of piasters. May God drown him in mercy.

[Character sketch of Defterdar-zade Mehmed Pasha.]

The strange thing is that in Melazgird castle I dreamed that Siyavuş Pasha and Mehmed Pasha had drowned in the Istanbul sea, and that when Melek Ahmed Pasha interpreted the dream he said: "We'll have news of them in Erzurum; we won't be able to see them in the capital; now they are in a different post; you and I, Evliya, will go to various posts in Rumelia." So these prophetic utterances all came to pass! From this I realized that old Melek Ahmed Pasha was no ordinary person. He was a master of mysteries, a *şeyh* among the viziers, at the level of the saints. I loved him implicitly and never let his skirt from my hand.

After reading all of the letters, Melek Ahmed Pasha rewarded the couriers who had brought them to Erzurum. But Hüseyn Agha, who had been sent to arrest the customs inspector Mahmud Agha, was sobbing his heart out.

"Don't be upset," said the pasha. "If your lord Defterdar-zade had died, Melek is alive. Just now you performed a great kindness by releasing Mahmud Agha according to our request. In return, we will not leave you patronless.

"Call the steward!" *In praise of Melek Ahmed Pasha's generosity on behalf of Hüseyn Agha.* "Yusuf," said the pasha when the steward arrived, "this Hüseyn Agha has become our charge. He came from Istanbul as a courier with an accountant.[25] First of all let's give him a tent—but make sure it's a new and proper one, with a kitchen and five (subsidiary) tents. Also outfit him with one file of mules, five slaves, five horses with trappings, five quivers, a sword and a spear, and all the equipment needed for the road. And have the treasurer bring five purses."

He gave Hüseyn Agha the five purses. From his own back he removed his sable fur, which was worth 500 piasters, and put it on Hüseyn Agha's back. Then he got up and removed Mahmud Agha's sable fur from *his* back, saying: "Don't say that he came here to arrest you and that his patron died; you should be all the more solicitous," and he put it on Hüseyn Agha's back as well. So now Hüseyn Agha was wearing three fur pieces—his own, the pasha's, and Mahmud Agha's. The pasha also ordered Mahmud Agha to give him ten purses, which he did, plus three horses, two Georgian *gulams*, and one file of mules.

"Whoever loves me among the notables of Erzurum," announced the pasha, "let him be kind to my Hüseyn Agha." God is most great! In seven days the fellow was so inundated with wealth, he didn't know what hit him. The pasha also appointed his provisioning and attached him to the yeomen of the guards, ordering: "My Hüseyn Agha, pitch your tent side by side with your former fellow guards, march and camp with them." And that ended the matter.

[After a ten-day halt they leave Erzurum. The first stage is the village of Ilıca.]

Zurnazan Pasha, the governor of Erzurum, (having arrived at the same time) halted here, with his tents and pavilions, in the dead of winter. He laid out a grand feast for our pasha, and presented him with a sable fur, a horse with gem-studded saddle, a grand pavilion, twenty purses for "road expenses," five files of mules, five files of camels, and ten choice Georgian *gulams*. Melek Pasha was quite pleased.

In the presence of these two imperial viziers, the canny customs inspector Mahmud Agha turned over to Hüseyn Agha the 200 purses owed to the state treasury, and received *şer⁼i* vouchers, thus acquitting himself of his debt. Our pasha loaded the 200 purses on rented packhorses and appointed five regiments of Sarıcas and twenty chamberlains to guard this imperial property. Then the two brave viziers sat down to entertain each other.

In the course of their conversation Zurnazan Pasha said to our Melek Pasha: "My sultan, you musn't look at me as someone beneath your contempt. For I, too, was master of the seal, if only for half an hour. They took the seal from me and sent it to Deli Hüseyn Pasha on Crete. Then they took it from him and gave it back to Siyavuş Pasha. Well, at least I had the seal for half an hour. I have held it in my bosom, gazed upon it, and enjoyed its fragrance, legitimately, one time.[26] It was like a dream. Then they took it away and sent it to our crazy brother (i.e., Deli Hüseyn Pasha). But he did not even have the chance to hold the seal and savor its fragrance. Siyavuş Pasha was so greedy for it, he sniffed it so much, that it stung him, and he died from the poison. The savor of that seal also poisoned Defterdar-zade Mehmed Pasha—so I heard while I was journeying here."

"Now brother," replied Melek Pasha to these pleasantries, "because you were master of the seal for half an hour, you have risen to the top of the hierarchy and are now a grand vizier on a par with myself. But my brother, although I was grand vizier for a year and a half, I did not savor the seal as much as you did in half an hour. This sewer of a world is indeed like a dream!"

"Well, my sultan," said Zurnazan Mustafa Pasha, "I do wish I could have kept the seal for just a few days. Then I wouldn't be so sad. But I had just sniffed it once, and placed it in my bosom, and as I was taking my hand out of my bosom they ordered me to give it up. So they took it from me, and they cast me here to Erzurum. You'll see when you get there, they have now sent the seal to Boynu-egri ("Crooked Neck") in Aleppo—soon they will straighten his neck too with the seal!"[27] He was quite witty about it; but he concluded: "My friend, I would rather die a day earlier than see such days of confusion in the Ottoman state."

"Brother," Melek Ahmed Pasha replied, "don't be in such a hurry to die; you haven't even reached Erzurum yet!" His noble face turned red as a rose, his eyes glistened, and he sighed: "Praise be to God, praise be to God."

Zurnazan Pasha took our Pasha's remark as a joke. He spent the rest of that day carousing with the pasha in the village of Ilıca, and the following day he took his leave and went off to enter Erzurum in grand procession. We traveled south——— hours to the village of Cinis; thence to the village of Mama Hatun; thence to the village of Kötür, where we received the news that Zurnazan Pasha had passed away when he entered Erzurum. We recalled Melek Pasha's ominous expression—"Brother, don't be in such a hurry to die, you haven't even reached Erzurum yet!"—and were lost in astonishment. So we renewed our determination to serve Melek with all our might and to be a sacrifice on his path. He was a vizier worth knowing—may God be his guardian.

Notes

1. See Bitlis, Part I.

2. This is recounted more fully at IV 338a.30–338b.3,339a.25–32 (410,413).

3. See Ch. 5.

4. Erzurum is not among the governorships mentioned in the *Sicill-i Osmani* notice (see Introduction, "The Author and his Subject," at n. 10). It was some time during the reign of Ibrahim (1049–58/1640–48).

5. See Bitlis, Part II.

6. That is, after the conquest of Baghdad in 1048/1638; see VI 47b.29–31 (Ch. 10).

7. In 1050/1640; see Ch. 5.

8. In 1066/1656; see Ch. 7.

9. Evidently a euphemism for another part of the body.

10. Kurdish for "Where is your pasha?".

11. Kurdish for "Hey donkeys! he fucked our women, that pasha of yours!"

12. A mythical personage, proverbial for ruler of a distant land.

13. See Ch. 2, n. 41.

14. *Ana baba günü*, an idiom for a large crowd.

15. That is, in 1055/1645.

16. They claim to be Sufis in the Kadiri order, or to be descendents of the Umayyad or Abbasid caliphs.

17. See Bitlis, Part III.

18. Siyavuş became grand vizier (for the second time) on 9 Cümadilula 1066/5 March 1656 (see next note) and appointed Defterdarzade Mehmed, Evliya's old patron (see Introduction), as *defterdar.* Siyavuş had Mehmed put to death on 1 Receb/25 April. According to the chroniclers (see Naima, vol. 6, pp. 166–67; Danişmend, p. 586) Siyavuş himself died that same night, and the two were buried at the same hour the following day. Evliya's version below is slightly different.

19. His short tenure as grand vizier took place during a breathtaking rotation of the office on 9 Cümadilula 1066/5 March 1656. Most reports put it at four hours, others at three or six (Danişmend, pp. 421, 512).

20. At II 286b.20f. (209–10), listing the palaces of Erzurum, Evliya mentions the huge "Pasha's Palace," as well as "Defterdar-zade Mehmed's pavilion." From what follows it is clearly the latter that is intended here.

21. See Ch. 2, n. 11.

22. "God, Powerful, Everlasting."

23. A breviary containing *sure-i en'am* (*sure* 6); cf. above, III 178b (Ch. 4, n. 44). Cf. I 104a.8 (352: omitted; Hammer ii, 11: omitted) where having En'am recited is associated with preparing a charm *(vefk)* to bring about the death of Sultan Mehmed III; and IX 68a.16 (138), 102a.1 (209), where reciting En'am is associated with a curse on seven cities (but note 261b.2 [575]: *def'-i bela için biñ En'am-ı şerif tilavet etmek ferman oldu*). The political significance of *sure-i en'am* derives from the final verse (6:165): "It is He who has appointed you viceroys·*(halif)* on earth and has raised some of you in rank above others, to try you in what He has given you. Your Lord is swift in retribution; and he is forgiving, compassionate."

24. In 1056/1646; see II 276a f. (165; Hammer, 88).

25. ?—*rakamçı.*

26. In this context the pronoun could be rendered "her" instead of "it."

27. He was grand vizier for four months. His successor was Köprülü Mehmed Pasha who finally, if ruthlessly, put the confusion in order.

7

GOVERNOR OF ÖZÜ
(1656–57)

[Events in the summer of 1066/1656. Melek Pasha is on his way to
take up his new post as governor of Özü province. They halt in the
plain of Devne near Varna, the Black Sea port in present-day Bulgaria.]

In the morning, having completed the dawn prayer in the
pasha's presence, and after I had recited the noble Yasin (Koran,
sure 36), our lord the Pasha said: "Evliya Çelebi, God grant it be
auspicious, this night I had a dream."

"May it be auspicious," I replied, "a genuine dream such as
the veracious prophet Joseph interpreted—a Fatiha on this intention!" We all recited a Fatiha.

A Marvel: The Genuine Dream of Melek Ahmed Pasha

He began with a *besmele*, then went on: "Evliya, this was
my dream. I was squatting to relieve myself—excuse the expression—when someone poked me in the back. I leaped up and
what should I see but a bunch of cossacks, dressed in sheep-
skins. I got very angry and began to cleave their heads open
with my toothpick. Then you and our Rıdvan Halife and a few
other of our aghas started to lap up their blood. When Çerkes Ali
and the barley agent Mustafa Agha and Kürd Haydar and Elvend
Agha saw you drinking the cossacks' blood, they too started to
lap it up. So all of you were spitting blood!"

"This is a strange dream, my sultan, may it be auspicious."
We again recited a Fatiha.

By God's wisdom, as we were eating lunch, a man
mounted on a pack horse rode shouting into the pasha's tent
pavilion. He dismounted, kissed the ground, and said: "Mercy,

my sultan! Twenty-six cossack *şaykas* are ravaging the coast and have set fire to the villages between Varna and Balçık. God knows, they must be heading towards Varna. Come to the rescue, my sultan!"

The pasha immediately left off dining and called for a horse. As soon as he mounted his white-blazed horse, without using a stirrup, the seventy regiments of Segbans and Sarıcas; and the timariots and *zeamet* holders charged with the security of the *sancaks* of Silistre, Kırk-kilise, Nikebolu, Çirmen, Vidin and Vize; and the pasha's 7,000 aghas also mounted their zephyr-swift steeds (and set off). Dismounting, all the troops lay in ambush amidst the vineyards between the town of Varna and the village of Galata.

Those cursed infidel cossacks in twenty of the *şaykas* landed without fear or trepidation, while the six others stayed just off the coast. The cussed cossacks started pillaging the city. But there was no one left there except for the Greeks, the rest of the populace having taken to the hills with their valuables. Among the Greeks, however, there arose such a hue and a cry that it touched the hearts of all who heard.

Now the sagacious pasha, paying no heed to the cossacks who were plundering the city, rushed down from the vineyards with all his troops upon the boats on the shore and showered them with lead. The filthy infidels in the *şaykas*, taken by surprise and unable to withstand the volley of musket fire, weighed anchor and moved off shore, leaving the infidels who had gone up to pillage the town high and dry.

The latter, fearing for their lives, dropped their booty and ran about aimlessly, blasted by artillery from the Varna citadel and from the *şaykas* lying in the harbor. Those not struck by cannon shot headed for the hills but were turned back by bands of the country populace who attacked them from one side or the other. Fleeing to where they had left their *şaykas*, and seeing that they were off the shore, some threw down their arms and plunged into the sea, while others lunged desperately into the land. Our *gazis*, on horseback, caught the swimmers by the hair, fished them out, and struck them in chains. Those fleeing landward rushed into the grain storehouses along the dock, blocked the doors, punched out loopholes and began to do battle. They martyred quite a few men on our side. Finally the populace rummaged the town for wood and kindling, which they piled on the roofs of the storehouses and in front of the doors, and set aflame. All of them came running out, crying for mercy, and were taken captive.

When the cossacks in their boats saw this sorrowful spectacle, their chief Hetman raised the flag-cross and they began to row furiously in our direction, hoping to rescue their stranded boats. They stepped on shore firing their muskets. Just then our Segbans and Sarıcas, who were lying in ambush in the vineyards, showed their colors and rushed out to attack the infidels, crying "Allah!" with a single voice. Those boats that had not yet reached the shore pulled away again—their holds were filled with loot plundered in other countries, as well as hundreds of Muslim captives. But the homeless *gazi* braves leapt aboard the *şaykas* that had landed, took command, and rowing hard, pursued the *şaykas* moving off shore, capturing twelve of them. All that booty, and all those captives, were turned over to the pasha, and all the frigates that had been commandeered were sent to Varna harbor. Also the pasha wrote orders to the people in the hills, saying that the fleeing cossacks were theirs.

In this fashion he freed the town of Varna from the hand of the inauspicious Ukrainians *(Rus-ı menhus)*. Of the 700 infidels he took 500 captive, turned 200 into heads and trotters,[1] and gave 200 as gifts to his aghas. On our side only twenty-six men were martyred. This humble one, also the above-mentioned Rıdvan Halife and Çerkes Ali Agha, were wounded. Apparently our lapping the cossacks' blood in the pasha's dream simply portended that we would be wounded in battle. But we were *gazis* and we were all victorious happy and smiling; we got three captives (each?) and a good portion of the booty.

[Ten more cossack vessels are captured. Celebrations in Varna and bestowal of gifts. The pasha frees the Muslim captives, and he sends the infidel captives, including twenty-nine hetmans, overland to the capital. There the pasha's agent Zühdi Efendi presents them to the grand vizier, Boynu-eğri Mehmed Pasha, and they are paraded before the sultan. The sultan is so pleased that he sends the pasha valuable gifts and a noble rescript, confirming him in office and ordering him to use the wealth contained in the thirty-six captured *şaykas* to repair and reinforce the fortresses at Varna and at seven other Black Sea ports. The pasha proceeds to undertake the Varna repairs, setting an example by joining the work force clearing out the moat.]

*   *   *

[The pasha has been transferred to the (provisionally independent) province of Silistre and finds himself in the town of Mangalia.]

The following day, in the year 1067,[2] the courier of the Crimean sultan Mehmed Giray Khan, whose name was Çolaq Dedeş Agha, arrived from the felicitous Threshold on his way back to the Crimea, bearing letters for our lord the pasha.

"Amazing," cried the pasha when he read the letters. "My Evliya, have you heard?" he went on in his astonishment. "Boynu-egri Mehmed Pasha has been dismissed from the grand vizierate, and Köprülü Mehmed Pasha has been appointed in his place."

"Well, my sultan," piped up the sealkeeper, Osman Agha, "just see what an evil day the Ottoman state has reached, when we get as grand vizier a miserable wretch like Köprülü, who could not even give straw to a pair of oxen!"

At this the pasha flew into a rage. "You stupid boy," he cried, "how dare you speak so insolently about *begler-begs* and viziers!" He grabbed hold of the rattan staff and began pounding Osman Agha like powder. "Take this fool away," he cried. They removed Osman Agha from the premises and locked him up.

The pasha was still so upset, he could not discharge his wrath, but kept pacing about the house of the commander of Mangalia, Gedik-oğlu Dişlen Mehmed Agha, muttering "Ya Fettah, ya Rezzak, ya Kahhar."[3] As it turned out, Köprülü's message in his letters to the pasha was as follows:

It is true that we were raised together in the imperial harem, and are both protégés of Sultan Murad IV. Nevertheless, be informed that from this moment if the accursed cossacks pillage and burn any one of the villages and towns on the coast of Özü province, I swear by God the Almighty that I will give you no quarter and will pay no heed to your righteous character, but I will cut you into pieces, as a warning to the world. Be wary, therefore, and guard the coasts. And exact the tribute of grain from every district, according to the imperial command, in order that you may feed the army of Islam.

A Strange and Wonderful Story

That very day, as I was sitting alone with the pasha, I said: "My sultan, for your noble head's sake, please release your slave Osman Agha from confinement."

"My Evliya," replied the pasha, "a fool like that really needs to be taught a lesson. But I accept your plea. Have that idiot released." They let Osman free.

"My sultan," I continued, "council is a trust. God knows that there is a coolness between my sultan and Köprülü. The reason is that during your grand vizierate you gave him the province of Anatolia, but seventeen days later, instigated by Bektaş Agha and Çelebi Kethüda, you dismissed him from Kütahya, and for quite some time Köprülü went begging. Please, in your pearl-studded letters, always be submissive to Köprülü; and have the letters be drawn up full of respects and flatteries."

"Yes Evliya, I must do that," replied the pasha. "Whoever has the seal, he is Solomon. Also, this Köprülü is not like other grand viziers. He has seen much of the hot and cold of fate, he has suffered much of poverty and penury, distresses and vicissitudes, he has gained much experience from campaigning and he knows the ways of the world. For example, in the year——————^{4} when the late Husrev Pasha was made commander-in-chief over Baghdad, with the seal, this Köprülü was together with him below Baghdad as his treasurer, and it was by his judgment and planning that Husrev Pasha mounted a campaign against Iran, raiding and pillaging Hamadan, Dergüzin, Erdebil, Şehriban, and Mihriban and put their populace to captivity. God be praised, now he has become grand vizier. True, he is wrathful and contentious. But he acts according to the principle of 'love for the sake of God, hate for the sake of God.' If he can get rid of the Segban and Sarıca vermin in the Anatolian provinces, and if he can restore the currency and remove the arrears, and if he can undertake overland campaigns—then I am certain that he will bring order to the Ottoman state. For as you know, breaches have occurred here and there in this Ottoman state.

"My Evliya," he continued, "in the year 1051 (1641), when I was governor of Diyarbekir, I once saw the saintly *şeyh* of Urmia^5 in a dream and I addressed him thus: 'My sultan, this Ottoman empire is being carved away on one side by the Venetians. Tell me what is in store for this empire.' He answered: 'My Melek Ahmed, in the year 1067 (1656) Köprülü Mehmed Pasha will become grand vizier. He will decimate all the *celali* rebels in Anatolia and in Rumelia. And when he dies, his son will be grand vizier.^{6} For a total of——————years during the reign of Mehmed Khan IV the world will be set right, seventy conquests will be carried out, and marvelous monuments will be erected.'

"That night the şeyh of Urmia also said: 'My Melek Ahmed, listen to these miraculous words that were spoken concerning Köprülü Mehmed Pasha to his excellency Ali in the presence of the holy Prophet, listen and take note:

> Şān Ka'b ismuhu Cisrī
> Ve-beyne ḫalḳ ismuhu Küfrī
> Ve-min 'inde'llāh ḳuṭb aḳṭāb
> Velī ṣaḥīḥ

> Glory of Ka'b, his name is Cisri.[7]
> Among people his name is Küfri.[8]
> With God he is Pole of Poles,
> A true saint.

His intention by the word *Ka'b* was that in the *ebced* reckoning this is equivalent to 92; and the name *Mehmed* also amounts to 92; so as a witticism, rather than saying Mehmed, he said "Ka'b of the bridge," referring to Köprülü Mehmed Pasha.

" 'Then he hinted that his son Ahmed Pasha would become grand vizier. This was revealed first of all in the portentous language of the *Cefr-i cami*:[9]

> Ve-ba'd cā'e Kellec ve-illā ḥalīm ḥalūḳ şecī' fātiḫu'l- Ḳāf
> Ve-faḥīmu'ş-Şīn yuvālī bilā fikretin
> Ve-ba'dehu cā'e zemān esvedi'ş-ṣafā ve-bilā vefā ve fātiḥ
> bilād ṣul'āti'l-cefā

> Then will come Kellec, but one forebearing, worthy, brave,
> conqueror of Kaf.
> Black one of China, he will rule without thought.
> Then will come the time of the black one of purity and
> without faithfulness and conqueror of the country of
> the bald ones of cruelty.

Köprülü-oğlu Ahmed is equivalent to 53; and the name *Kelec* also amounts to 53. By "conqueror of Kaf" he refers to the fortress of Candia.[10] And by "black one of purity" he refers to Kara Mustafa Pasha who, when he is grand vizier, will cruelly conquer the country of the bald ones—that is, the land of the cossacks.'[11]

"These are the prophecies concerning Köprülü that the şeyh of Urmia told me in my dream in Diyarbekir. Didn't I relate this dream to you when we were in Diyarbekir, my Evliya?"

"To tell you the truth, my sultan, after so much traveling for the past twenty years, I quite forgot."

"Now, my Evliya, you'll see what works this Köprülü and his progeny will accomplish in this Ottoman workshop. I can still vividly recall these pearl-studded words, which the holy şeyh revealed in my dream in Diyarbekir. If you are still alive, old Evliya, or if I am, one of us will see them. For now, as you say, let us stay on good terms with Köprülü, and let us keep a good watch over our province." With this he went on to a different topic.

By God's wisdom, because the magnanimous pasha went bareheaded in the heat of the day during the battle of Varna and the repair of the fortress, his noble temper suffered impairment in the town of Mangalia and he became weaker day by day. A pustule broke out on the left side of his neck and in five or ten days his neck swelled up with red matter like a loaf of bread. Physicians and surgeons and phlebotomists were brought from the surrounding villages and towns, even as far away as Transylvania and Wallachia and Moldavia, and although each prescribed a different medicine, it was all to no effect. The pasha's condition grew steadily worse. Several hundred aghas slipped out and ran away by land or by sea. The pasha also lost his voice and could only hum like a bee.

One day, in the presence of the remaining aghas, the pasha made his last will known through sign language and directed that he be buried in the Muharrem-sultan park outside Mangalia. To make a long story short, we were all in a quandary over the pasha's health, and were striking our heads together out of grief and desperation. The pus and matter could not be drawn out from the boil on the pasha's neck; only the sores in his mouth and nose were draining. Because of my kinship with the pasha, I did not leave his bedside night or day for a single moment.

The Wondrous and True Dream of Melek Ahmed Pasha and Its Interpretation

One morning, by God's wisdom, I was sitting next to the pasha massaging his hand, and I was feeling very sad—on the verge of weeping. Suddenly he opened his eyes, turned toward me, and using signs and gestures asked: "My Evliya, what did you dream this night? Tell me."

"I did dream something," I replied, "but because of my sorrow I cannot recall it. It is as though I didn't dream at all."

The pasha became agitated. "By God," he swore, "you did have a tremendous dream; you must tell it to me immediately." But the pasha's voice was as faint as the buzzing of a fly.

"O my sultan," said I, "why did you swear that I had a dream? Did *you* have the dream or did *I*? What I recall of my dream is that you were the Sultan of Egypt and were enjoying great pomp and festivity; and while you were proceeding to the Transylvania campaign with the Egyptian soldiery, you stopped to perform the prayer, with all your troops, in a mosque that was like the Süleymaniye (in Istanbul). News of victory arrived from Transylvania, so you gave up the campaign and decided to repair the Süleymaniye mosque. Some people said to you: 'My lord, in the morning inquire from Evliya Çelebi about the repair of this Süleymaniye mosque; he knows all about it; act on his interpretation and restore the mosque.' This is all that I recall of my dream. And just now I arrived and you swore that I had a dream and you told me to tell it."

I could see that the pasha was apprehensive. "This dream has surely had an effect on you, Evliya," he said. "I too dreamed that I was told to ask Evliya about his dream in the morning. That is why I am being so insistent. Put the rest of your dream into words right away, and relate it in an orderly fashion. A Fatiha on this intention!"

He recited the Fatiha and puffed over me. As God is my witness, when he did this, a certain dull heaviness was lifted from me, and I seemed to acquire the wisdom of Aristotle. The entire dream, from beginning to end, flashed upon my memory and I cried: "God is great!" Rising to my knees, I recited a *besmele* and began to recount the dream:

"May it be auspicious, my sultan. This night in my dream we were in Cairo, you and all of your aghas and well-wishers. There in the citadel was a mosque called the Süleymaniye. Several thousand people, young and old, approached my sultan and said: 'The wall on the left of the *mihrab* (prayer-niche) of this Süleymaniye mosque has swollen and is jutting out, so that it is about to collapse. The administrator of the endowment, Şeyh Ahmed Agha, and the caretaker, Evliya Çelebi, have not reported to the governor that this mosque is falling to ruin. For God's sake, investigate the matter and do something about it. Repair and restore this Süleymaniye mosque. You are the governor of

Egypt until your appointed term. This matter is your responsibility. On the day of judgment you will be asked about this pious endowment.' Thus did the Egyptian populace inform my sultan of the matter."

"Boys," cried the pasha, "raise me up." The *gulams*, expressing thanks to God, rushed over and propped up the pasha with pillows and cushions. He sat up and listened closely as I recounted the dream. "Now go on, my Evliya."

"My sultan," I continued, "in my dream you mounted a roan horse and proceeded to the Süleymaniye mosque in the Cairo citadel, along with your aghas and the men who informed you of the mosque's condition. When you saw that the left side of the *mihrab* was jutting out and collapsing, you cried: 'Help, we must do something about this!' All the Egyptian notables assembled and consulted as to the various plans for restoring the mosque. Some said the minaret was top-heavy and had to be torn down. Others said the dome was too big and should be made smaller. Some suggested propping up the places that were awry with scaffolding poles. Others thought that the foundation should be excavated from the outside and a part of the wall torn down and rebuilt, or else another layer of wall be erected just next to it. There were all sorts of suggestions, but no one could come up with any definitive solution.

"Then amidst this great crowd I caught sight of my late father. In his hand was the backscratcher that Sultan Süleyman Khan once gave him. He seemed to be strolling about the mosque and was pointing out the delapidated parts as though he were an architect making repairs. 'My sultan,' said I, 'that man holding the backscratcher is my father. He is an expert surveyor and architect. Why don't you put the problem to him as well?' You instructed me to call my father, so I went and kissed his hand, and he came and greeted you. You returned the greeting and said: 'Father, what should we do about this mosque?'

" 'By God's command the solution is at hand,' he replied. 'This mosque is a strong building. It won't give way just because of one breach. It has suffered some damage on the *kible* side due to the passage of time and the effect of winter storms. These things happen. Here is what you must do. The mosque is bulging on the *kible* side. You must dig a rather deep ditch at the "nape," which is the back part of the *kible*. There put down a good foundation of two ells[12] until the water drains out. Feed and clothe the servants and the congregants who are in the mosque.

By God's command the mosque will settle into the ditch as the water goes out. Then the mosque will remain forever, or until the end of its life, as God decrees. This is the only solution. Also, here is my beloved son, the world traveler and boon companion of mankind, Evliya the unhypocritical. Send him to Istanbul right away so that he can fetch skilled physicians and all the gear and equipment required to repair the mosque.'

"My father imparted this therapeutic information, kissed your hand, and took his leave. So my lord, that is the dream I had this night."

When I finished my report the pasha cried "Yallah!" from the bottom of his heart. God be praised, his voice was stronger than before. *Interpretation of Melek Ahmed Pasha:* "Listen, my dear friend. What you called Cairo in this dream is the city of my body. The *kıble* side of the Süleymaniye mosque was collapsing, and the agha who administers the endowment and the caretaker Evliya Agha did not report it to the governor. That is, I was reared in the royal harem of Süleyman Khan of the House of Osman. The mosque of my body is their pious endowment. The *kıble* is my face, and the *mihrab* is my forehead. Now my face and eyes and forehead and neck are all swollen. The administrator of the endowment, Ahmed Agha, is myself, for *I* am the administrator of the mosque of my body; and the servant of my body is the caretaker Evliya Çelebi. Your saying that you did not impart to the governor the therapeutic information regarding the mosque of my body means that you did not inform *me*. That all the notables of Egypt consulted and could not reach a definitive solution means that my poor aghas are consulting together and are at a loss how to treat their master. The *kıble* wall bulging means that the *kıble* of my face has swollen up and I am bent over.

"Finally your father appeared. That is because I love you like my own son, Evliya, and also because your father and my father were brothers in this world and the next, having gone on campaign together with Öz-demir-oğlu Osman Pasha.[13] When he was asked about it he said: 'By God's command the solution is at hand; this mosque has suffered some damage on its *kıble* side; with the passage of time a breach appeared on the face of the *kıble*.' By that he meant that I have gotten old, my *kıble*— that is, my face—is awry, and I cannot stand up straight. 'Dig a ditch at the "nape" of the *kıble* and let the water drain out of the ditch'—this means that you should lance the back of my neck, next to the ear, and let the pus and the matter flow out. 'A foundation of two ells for two months'—this refers to your probing the wound for the past two months with setons. 'Feed and clothe the servants in the mosque'—this hints at the weakness of my spirit and lassitude of my soul, also the yellow and black bile and the phlegm and humors in the mosque of my body, and indicates that I should go on a careful diet and build up my strength. And 'By God's command the mosque will settle into that ditch and the mosque will right itself'—this means that the wound will be healed from the point where it is lanced. And 'The mosque will remain forever, as long as God wills' means that I will continue to live until my appointed term is complete."

As the dream was being interpreted in this fashion, all those present gaped in astonishment. "My dear," remarked the aghas, "while Evliya Çelebi was narrating this dream the pasha seemed to get new life, and as the sense of it became clear he started to talk. God is great! This is a wonderful and divine mystery." The people were amazed. And everyone was silly with joy, saying: "God be praised, the pasha has recovered somewhat."

Suddenly the pasha cried: "Let the interpretation of this dream come to pass. Bring me a surgeon immediately. I interpreted this dream by divine suggestion. So I will have this pustule lanced on the back of my neck. Call the surgeon!"

At this I became very frightened. "My sultan, that is not right," I said. "You have interpreted it subjectively, but dreams must be interpreted objectively. For your precious head's sake! I saw this dream, and you interpreted it, and now you are going to lance your neck. If your wound festers, you will get me in hot water. People will say: 'The pasha had his wound lanced because of Evliya's dream and he died; the pasha acted like this because of your dream, otherwise it would not have turned out this way.' Mercy, my sultan, do not bring a surgeon and do not lance the pustule, or there won't be any place for me in heaven or in hell or in purgatory or in the depths of perdition." I groveled at the pasha's feet.

Now the foresightful pasha had his secretary (divan efendisi) summoned. "Ali Efendi," he said, "draw up letters immediately to the grand vizier and to the chief black eunuch, also to Kaya Sultan and to my agent at court, Zühdi Efendi, informing them that I have recovered. And write an order for post-horses for six stages for my Evliya." The letters were written at once. I, too, armed myself and was ready to go.

What should I see next but that executioner of a surgeon coming and setting up his instruments and bedding next to the pasha. The pasha gave me the letters, plus 300 goldpieces for travel expenses, and I kissed his hand. Then that sawbones passed resolutely around to the back of the Pasha's neck and opened up a collar on the left side. As God is my witness, he drew off three gobletsful[14] of yellow pus and matter, evil-smelling as a corpse, along with lumps of rotted flesh. "Praise be to God," the pasha sighed, opening his eyes. He ordered ten purses to be distributed among the poor of Mangalia.

So I kissed his hand and—*stages of my journey by forced march from Mangalia to Istanbul*—setting out by forced march from Mangalia with post-horses and my three *gulams*, we traversed the villages of Sarıgül, Gelincikli, and Hasılcıklı. While we were changing horses at the walled town of Pravadi, rumors were flying that Melek Pasha had died, and I informed everyone that he was alive and well. We pressed on past the village of Çenge, Aydos castle, and the villages of Fakiler and Kovanlı. Again we changed horses at the city of Kırk-kilise, and there, too, announced that the pasha had recovered. We continued thence past the towns of Buñar-hisar, Uzun-haciler, Kösdemir, and Çatalca; and arrived in the district of Topçular on the third day after leaving Mangalia.

I presented the pasha's letters to Kaya Sultan and informed her that he was recovered. "Where is the pasha's own letter?" she asked.

"The pasha was too weak and out of sorts to write with his own hand," I replied. "He sent me here in three days to reassure you. And he has sent you seventy purses with the Wallachian and Moldavian treasury. God willing, your treasury will also arrive in eight days."

Kaya Sultan was pleased at this news. But her ladies-in-waiting insisted that the pasha had died. The rumor was abroad that the pasha was dead and that Kaya Sultan was being married off to Kara Murtaza Pasha. So it seems that I arrived, like Hızır, in the nick of time. "My lady," cried I, "the pasha is living. He requests from you a surgeon and a physician. Just take a look at these letters, and rest assured." But they did not believe me one jot.

Having remounted and ridden over with the Pasha's court agent to Köprülü Mehmed Pasha, I kissed his hand. "Evliya," he said, "are you coming from your pasha? How many days is it since the pasha died?"

"God forbid," I answered. "It is three days since I left the pasha. Here are his letters for my lord and for the chief eunuch."

He took the letter and read it. "God be praised, it seems he is alive. Those damned women! They started all sorts of rumors about poor Melek being dead so they could marry Kaya off to another husband." He sent me with the letters, attended by the memorandum writer Ramazan Agha, to the felicitous Padishah.

Arriving in the imperial presence at Yalı Köşkü,[15] I kissed the ground and conveyed the news. The wise Padishah was pleased to hear that the pasha was recovered, and gave me a present of 110 goldpieces. As I went out I also handed over the chief eunuch's letters, then returned to Kaya Sultan at her palace in Topçular. Conversing from behind the lattice, she asked me what words the felicitous Padishah had uttered, and then inquired into the pasha's lamentable condition.

By God's wisdom, while we were talking, Uzun Ömer Reis's boat arrived, having crossed the Black Sea in three days due to favorable winds, and among the letters was one in the pasha's own hand. But all he could write was: "God be praised, we are alive." Again he requested a surgeon and a physician, and he sent a shipload of grain and various other goods. This time Kaya Sultan believed me. She gave me 200 Şerifi goldpieces and a sable fur stole, and also the deeds and vouchers of a house that was attached to our house, which she had purchased for 87,000 aspers. That very day she summoned the infidel surgeon, Çipilyan-oğlu, and gave him all the provisions he needed, plus a purse of piasters for travel expenses.

Meanwhile I returned to Köprülü and got letters from all the grandees and notables. Köprülü Vizier said: "Evliya, tell the pasha to take special care in guarding the coasts (i.e., the Black Sea and Danubian frontiers). Otherwise, he has recovered from this illness, but he won't recover from *my* affliction so easily." And he presented me with seventy goldpieces.

When I returned to Kaya Sultan with the letters she gave me another 100 goldpieces for travel expenses, plus three loads[16] of electuaries and medicaments, foods and drinks and clothes. We loaded them on packhorses and—*stages of our journey to Silistre, setting out on the twentieth day of Safer 1067 (8 December 1656)*—passed through the towns of Çatalca and Kösdemir, the villages of Incıklar, Eregli, Karabınar, and Nadir, the walled town of Pravadi, Ortaköy, and the villages of Kırıçsa and Eflatar. I found the pasha in the walled town of Silistre, whither they had conveyed him in a litter from Mangalia, and rubbing my face at his foot, I gave him the letters.

Under Çipilyan-oğlu's treatment the pasha improved daily until, God be praised, in two months he was returned to health. He distributed twenty purses among the poor and he waived the stewardship accounts of all his aghas, then dismissed them, and they went off hunting or partying in the gardens and the vineyards. He had several hundred orphan boys circumcized, gave each of them into the custody of one or another agha or master craftsman or teacher and bestowed on each one a splendid suit. He also found Muslim homes for quite a few orphan girls, outfitting them as well and giving them a start in life. In Silistre he constructed a stone pavement over the main road, from the head of the bazaar all the way to the Istanbul gate, a distance of 3,000 yards; and in several of the roads he dug out gutters, thus relieving the town from a sea of mud. He built a harness shop and a luxurious coffeehouse and several houses, and established this property as an endowment for the upkeep of the pavement on the main road, appointing the deputy commander of the *sipahis*, Zankoç Hasan Agha, as administrator of these pious foundations.

In short, this lord of ours, Melek, was truly an angel *(melek)* in character. He spent all his time doing good deeds. Never, whether at home or abroad, did he miss one of the five daily prayers, but always performed them at the first moment. He was a pious Sunni and a protector of Islam. Most of his life he lived on the fast of David. He did not use to swear every minute, saying "Fuck this" and "Fuck that." When he became very angry he would say "Ho coward!" or "O shameless one!" He was endowed with a thousand virtues of this kind, a man who strove for justice, and who was content with his lot.

[1068/1657: The pasha, once again governor of Özü, has met with the Crimean khan following the Polish campaign.]

After the khan's departure, our lord Melek Ahmed Pasha was occupied with repairing the fortress of Ak-kirman. One night he had a dream. In the morning, after this humble one had led the dawn prayer and had recited the noble Yasin (Koran, *sure* 36), Melek Ahmed Pasha said: "My Evliya, God grant it be auspicious, this night I had a dream." And he began to recount his dream.

A Marvel: The Genuine Dream of Melek Ahmed Pasha

"Evliya, this blessed night I saw thousands of eagles landing on Özü fortress. Cawing and crying, they hurled down stones into the fortress with their claws and their beaks. At once a hue and a cry arose from within the fortress, the gates were opened, and all the Muhammedan community began to run out. Some of those who exited were gobbled up by the birds, whereas others caught several hundred birds by their legs and bound them or else tortured them to death. Then the eagles all flocked together, settled upon one tower of the fortress, and flying out to all sides brought back twigs and sticks and began to build a nest. Suddenly a fire broke out from within the fortress and all the eagles, singed in their wings, fell to the ground. They tried to lift themselves up, wingless and tailless as they were, but could no longer muster the strength to fly."

"May it be auspicious, my sultan," I said when he finished relating the dream. "God knows, the enemy birds wish to land on Özü fortress, but God willing their wings will be singed." And I recited a Fatiha.

[The pasha sends Yusuf Kethüda with men and materials to Özü (Ochakov) to repair the fortress. News arrives of Köprülü's victory at Bozca-ada (Tenedos).[17] The pasha sends Evliya with the victory announcement and letters to Özü. In the midst of the repairs and the victory celebrations the cossacks lay siege to Özü fortress. After five days of fighting, the sea-borne cossacks are reinforced by land troops.]

Ali Çelebi, who was Yusuf Kethüda's treasurer, said to me: "Come, Evliya Efendi, let's you and me climb up the minaret and take a look at the infidels over yonder. Let's see what they are up to. God knows, they must be tired after fighting for five days and they have lost heart. But these devils who came by land are frisky fighters, the swine. They don't care whether they live or die. They have absorbed thousands of cannonballs and have been decimated by 200 bombshells, but this hasn't deterred them in the least. These devils have been battling continuously for nine hours. Don't you see how they remove their dead, then freshen up and resume fighting? I'm really afraid of these infidels!"

"Nine days ago," I replied, "Melek Ahmed Pasha had a dream in which eagles brought twigs and sticks and tried to build a nest on Özü fortress. But a fire broke out from within the fortress, and the eagles all toppled to the ground with their tails and wings burned. Now that genuine dream of Melek Ahmed Pasha has come to pass: those black birds[18] are these very black-headed infidels who are trying to capture the fortress and take it over for their nest. The fire that broke out from within the fortress is the fires caused by these very bombshells that we have cast and that burned these infidels in the arms and the legs. Now the end of the matter is at hand and, God willing, this fortress will be saved from the hands of the infidels."

[Troops arrive from Ak-kirman and rescue Özü. Evliya returns to Ak-kirman to bring the news of victory.]

I kissed Melek Ahmed Pasha's hand and said: "Good news, my sultan. After a great battle lasting seven days, the 48,000 troops that my sultan sent arrived like Hızır.[19] Now all the infidels—those who came originally, and those who arrived later by land, even those who were on their way to the rescue yesterday—have been put to the sword. Only God knows the number of prisoners and heads and the amount of booty. A brief account is contained in these letters; God willing, a complete account will be sent along with the booty and the prisoners." I placed the letters in his noble hand and stood there.

The pasha, who was on his prayer rug, performed a genuflection of thanksgiving. "My Evliya," he said, "why don't you genuflect also."

"Do you think a man who has just arrived from a journey, and who has gone through the peril of the siege of Özü, is in a state of ritual purity, that I should genuflect?"

The pasha smiled broadly. "I'll give you a ritual purity!" So saying, he presented me with two purses of piasters, one Arabian horse with saddle, one Circassian *gulam*, one sable stole; and with his own hand stuck an aigrette on my turban. "May your great *gaza* be blessed, my Evliya," he said.

"My sultan," I replied, "you carried out the *gaza* where you were."

"Evliya," said the upright pasha, "I told you about the dream I had that night, when the eagles tried to land on Özü fortress. It was the fear inspired by that dream which impelled me to send Yusuf to Özü with five or six *sancak* regiments. God be praised, the fortress was delivered from the hands of the infidels without any disgrace."

[The pasha, making Evliya his deputy, sends gifts and congratulations to Özü. Evliya takes charge of the booty and the prisoners (who had been given the task of skinning and salting the heads). The Crimean khan arrives, and Evliya returns to Ak-kirman. The pasha has the 1200 carts of booty and munitions, 26 cannons, 70 hetmans, the prince of Cracow, 11,060 captives, and 6,000 heads sent off to the capital. Evliya, sent ahead with the victory news, meets with the deputy grand vizier, Kör Hasan Pasha, who conducts him into the sultan's presence to give a personal report.]

Then I went to Kaya Sultan and related to her all of our experiences and adventures, point by point.

"My Evliya," she said, "if, God forbid, Özü had fallen into the hands of the infidels, Köprülü would certainly have killed my dear pasha."

"My sultan," I cried, "how can you say this as long as you are still alive?"

"I assure you, Evliya, that not only I, but even the Padishah himself could not have saved him."

That day and night I conversed with Kaya Sultan from behind the lattice. God be praised, eight days later all the carts arrived with the heads and trotters[20] and the munitions. They were stowed in Kaya Sultan's palace at Topçular outside the Edirne gate. I immediately went with the pasha's court agent (Zühdi Efendi) to the deputy grand vizier to inform him.

"Well done," he said, out of affection for our pasha. "Now, how are you going to display these heads and 'tongues' and the captive generals and all of these munitions? Will you have a nice procession before the Padishah?"

"My sultan," I replied, "inform the captain of the guard and the chief of police. Round up 10,000 infidels—tavern keepers and grocers and Albanian boza-shop keepers[21]—and bring along a hundred Syrmian carriages; this will make a total of 1300 carriages. And tell the chief armorer and chief gunner to let some of their colonels join the parade with their men; we can hand over the munitions and the cannons to them after the procession. And have the chief of the admiralty and some of his commanders come with whips in their hands, also the Silistrian quarantine officers, to drag along the captive infidels; after the procession they can take them to the imperial arsenal."

"By God, Evliya, you've spoken well. Quickly," he ordered, "inform the captain of the guard, the chief of police and the viceroy of the arsenal. Have all the armorers and the gunners with their colonels go to Topçular, outside the Edirne gate, and proceed from there with the multitude of heads[22] and captives, parading them through Istanbul and before the felicitous Padishah below the parade pavilion. Afterward have them carry out whatever the imperial command may be."

I rushed back to Topçular with the pasha's court agent, and what should we see? Kaya Sultan had already arrived, with forty or fifty carts of hay and had ordered her gardeners and her halberdiers and all the poor people of Topçular quarter to stuff the salted heads with hay. The heads were piled up like mountains. Several thousand poles and pikes were commandeered from the lancers, or else removed from the pasha's treasury, and the heads were arranged on the poles. Halil Agha, who had been charged with conveying the heads, also had the captive generals and hetmans and the accursed prince put on their fine suits, which he had outfitted for them when they passed through Pravadi.

[Description of the procession. The sultan confirms Melek Pasha in office and sends him gifts. Evliya returns to Ak-kirman.]

Notes

1. Sheep heads and trotters were a favorite dish. Evliya means they cut off their heads.

2. Began 20 October 1656; the dismissal and appointment of the grand viziers, mentioned below, took place on 26 Zilkade 1066/15 September 1656.

3. That is, calling on some of God's names: Conqueror, Provider, Compeller.

4. 1038–39/1629–30. See Ch. 4, n. 38.

5. For the şeyh of Urmia (d. 1048/1639), see IV 208b.21f. (53; Diyarbekir, p. 191). "This humble author has recorded these episodes [of the şeyh's life] as he heard them from his lord Melek Ahmed Pasha. For the latter was Sultan Murad's sword-bearer in those years, and after

the conquest of Baghdad became the governor of Diyarbekir. He believed in the saint and used to visit his grave frequently" (209a.36–209b.1 [55]).

6. His son, Fazıl Ahmed Pasha, was grand vizier from 1072/1661 to 1087/1676.

7. "Of the bridge," a translation of Tk. *köprülü*.

8. An Arabic pronunciation of *köprü* (older: *köpri*, "bridge"); it could be interpreted as "infidel," or (reading *kefrī*) "of the village."

9. See Ch. 4, n. 28.

10. Candia on Crete was conquered in 1080/1669 (see Ch. 8, n. 6). Ḳāf in Muslim lore is the name of the mountain surrounding the habitable world; otherwise the Caucasus.

11. The reference is to the conquest of Czehryn in 1089/1678. Kara Mustafa Pasha was grand vizier from 1087/1676 to 1094/1683. Evidently Evliya composed this passage after 1678 but prior to the Ottoman defeat under the walls of Vienna in 1683.

12. Perhaps *eyi* should be amended to *iki ay* (as below, 33a.12) and the translation read: "a foundation of two ells for two months."

13. Cf. VI 46b (Ch. 10).

14. In the text the gobletsful are qualified as *yek-merdi*, a term of uncertain meaning.

15. One of the pleasure pavilions *(köşk)* in the Topkapı palace.

16. The loads are qualified by the term *segsane (? señsane?)*, of uncertain meaning.

17. The recapture of Tenedos from the Venetians occurred on 22 Zilkade 1067/1 September 1657.

18. *Kara kuş*, lit. "black bird," also means eagle. Evliya constantly remarks on the black headgear of the Christians.

19. See Ch. 2, n. 41.

20. See n. 1 above.

21. Boza, a type of millet beer, was a popular beverage.

22. The text has *kulle* ("towers") instead of *kelle* ("heads").

8

KAYA SULTAN (1659)

[Recalled to Istanbul, the pasha serves as deputy vizier for ten days, 10–20 Şaban 1068/13–23 May 1658. Upon his dismissal he is awarded the *sancak* of Afyon Karahisar as an imperial grant (*arpalık;* V 69a; cf. III 173a, beginning of Chapter 4).

Evliya characterizes the grand vizier Köprülü and his strict measures.]

He constantly consulted with our lord Melek Ahmed Pasha and with the court instructor Mehmed Efendi and with————. As for our lord Melek Ahmed Pasha, he was neither granted a provincial appointment nor did he attend the imperial *divan;* but he made do with the stipend from his *sancak* of Afyon Karahisar and spent his time conversing with Kaya Sultan in his palace.

During this period, by God's command, Kaya Sultan became pregnant. All of us retainers were overjoyed at this, because whenever Kaya Sultan gave birth she used to give twenty purses to the aghas as alms. So all the aghas merrily accompanied the pasha and the sultana in their pleasure excursions from park to park, from summer mansion to summer mansion, and to the Padishah's gardens.

The Marvelous Dream of Ismehan, Kaya Sultan, Daughter of Sultan Murad Khan, God's Mercy upon Him

One day at dawn our lady Kaya Sultan said to Melek Ahmed Pasha: "My dear pasha, you are very keen on interpeting dreams. My father, Gazi Murad Khan, asked you to interpret several of his. I too have had a dream this night. Please interpret it."

"Tell it, my sultan," he said. The sultana uttered a *besmele* and began:

"This night I was strolling in the gardens of paradise with my grandfather, Sultan Ahmed. He took me by the hand and showed me the lofty palaces in the gardens, and the houris and boys. 'Look, Ismehan,' he said as we strolled about, 'what blessings the Lord has bestowed upon me, how many gardens of paradise and palaces and houris and boys I have gotten. Once, when I was constructing the new mosque,[1] I set aside my regal dignity and entered among the workmen, carrying rocks and earth in the skirt of my robe. "O my lord," said I, weeping, "Behold the labor of your workman Ahmed. Accept it in your royal court." and I poured out the earth on the ground. God accepted this labor, and in return for this service He bestowed this paradise upon me. Now you come, too, my Ismehan, and enjoy yourself in my gardens of paradise.'

"Sultan Mustafa, who was on the left side, spoke up: 'Brother,' he said, 'that girl Kaya is Sultan Murad's daughter, but her wish is unfulfilled (*na-murad*). Let her have a thriving daughter of Melek Ahmed, that she may get her wish in this world, and the lineage not come to an end. After that she may come to our gardens for a pleasure stroll.'

"My grandfather Sultan Ahmed immediately cried: 'A Fatiha upon this intention!' and he passed his hand (in blessing) over my face. But as he did this, I noticed that my grandfather's hand was covered with blood. I, too, passed my hand over my face. My right hand was stained with the blood, and I awoke in terror.

"May it be auspicious, my dearest pasha. That is what I dreamed this night."

The pasha fetched such a sigh of anguish that the very rooftops trembled. "O my," he said, "what a pretty dream of paradise, may it be auspicious." He recited a Fatiha and began to interpret the dream, putting the best construction he could on it:

"My dear one, my khan, my life and my sultan! You speak of blood in the dream. Don't be frightened of that blood. God willing, from our common offspring will issue princesses and princes, each one thriving, and each of us, too, will live seventy years, and our final abode will be in paradise with Sultan Ahmed. Glad tidings to you, my sultan! But do give 1,000 goldpieces to the poor as alms; and 2,000 each to my interior aghas and my exterior aghas; and 300 to Evliya Çelebi; and 100 to his sister. And let Evliya's sister leave your harem; give her in marriage to a Muslim and set her up in life."

Acting on the pasha's interpretation, Kaya Sultan had her treasuress Şebtiz Bula bring 1,400 goldpieces as earnest. These were distributed in the proportions specified, so that I and my

sister and all the aghas of the interior and exterior services became rich.

Afterwards I accompanied the pasha to a place called Uzunca Ova. "These are divine mysteries, my Evliya," he said. "Let them be a divine trust with you, and don't reveal them to anyone." He made me swear to it, then added, weeping: "God knows, when our Kaya Sultan gives birth she will bleed to death."

Some time after this, letters arrived from Kırşehir informing us that 47,000 sheep, 300 mares, 370 Arvana camels, and
17 mule trains from our pasha's estate there had been confiscated by imperial agents, on the grounds that they were the
property of Hasan Pasha. Our pasha immediately went to Köprülü to protest. "My brother Melek," Köprülü replied, "you are a
good Muslim. Didn't those sheep belong to Hasan Pasha?"[2]

"It is true that when I was grand vizier in 1060 (1650–51) I
made Hasan Pasha agha of the Turcomans, and he twice gave
me 10,000 Şekaki and Beziki sheep as office dues.[3] But all the
rest are my own property, in fact I have owned them for the past
ten years."

"Everything returns to its origin," quoted Köprülü. "Apparently they *were* Hasan's property originally. So their confiscation was quite proper, and the Padishah has been informed.
Nothing can be done about it now, so don't fret about it."

The pasha knew that the fish stinks from the head, and he
resigned himself to the loss of 47,000 sheep and so much other
wealth. He left Köprülü and came straight to his palace. To console himself, he and the sultana removed the household to Beg-
koz park, near Akbaba Sultan above Anadolu Hisar.[4] They
vacationed there for a month.

One morning while they were there—*Kaya Sultan's strange
dream*—the sultana said: "My dear pasha, I had a dream this
night. Please be so kind as to interpet it, whether objectively or
subjectively."

"Tell it, my dear, may it be auspicious." "I dreamed that the
entire length of water (i.e., the Golden Horn) from Eyub Sultan
to Saray Burnu was covered with caiques, and every caique was
full of people. All the deputies and viziers, the nobles and *ulema*, the black eunuchs, the palace women and boys came crying and wailing. They disembarked at Eyub landing and said a
prayer in Eyub Sultan mosque. When the congregation came
out, they stormed the house of our *imam*, placed the *imam's*
wife in a white sack, tied the mouth of the sack, and put the
woman in a large caique. 'We'll take this woman all the way to
the Padishah,' they said; 'if he does not punish her, then we'll
leave her to the mercy of the Padishah of Padishahs, God.' All the
people proceeded with the *imam's* wife in the caique, some
weeping, some moaning and wailing.

"It seems that I, too, was in Eyub, in our summer palace
there, watching from the balcony. 'Help,' I cried, 'that is the wife

of our *imam*, Ahmed Efendi. By God, she is a chaste and upright woman. I'll give 10,000 goldpieces for that woman. Make them release her!' I gave my Cevher Agha 10,000 goldpieces and sent him off in a caique toward the mob of people who were carrying away Imam Ahmed Efendi's wife. But when he got there, no one would accept my plea for her life.

" 'This wife of Imam Ahmed has blood guilt,'[5] they told him, 'her case must be left to God. Your plea may be accepted There; it cannot be accepted here. Return our greeting to the sultana. Tell her to add another 10,000 goldpieces to that 10,000 and give them to her own orphans and servants.' This was the message they sent with Cevher Agha.

"From the window I watched them take the *imam's* wife all the way to Bağçe Kapı. At Saray Burnu I saw some men drag her away. They gave her to the trustee of Aya Sofya and ordered her to be confined there.

"After that, my dear pasha, I did not see that woman any more. But my heart ached with compassion and I said to myself: 'I wonder if they will kill her? O dear, she has a little daughter. If they kill that woman, and her daughter is left an orphan, God willing, I have a lot of money, I will raise that little girl.' Consoling myself with this thought, I woke up."

"May it be auspicious, my sultan," the pasha replied immediately. "This is the interpretation: In all the mosques just now people are praying for victory of our troops on Crete. So (in your dream) all the people and the deputies and viziers came to pray at the mosque of Ebu Eyub Ansari. Their prayer will be accepted. As for that wife of the *imam*, she represents hope of worldly success. The prayer will be accepted, and Lady World will be ours. As for their putting her in a white sack, it is a sign that, God willing, soon Candia will be conquered and will fall into the hands of the white-turbaned Muslims."[6]

Thus the pasha, with careworn expression, gave this brief and far-fetched interpretation. "But, my sultan," he continued, "set aside those 20,000 goldpieces from your funds and distribute them to the deserving needy. For God has commanded in the noble Koran (9:60): 'Alms are only for the needy and the poor.' "

"Great God, my pasha," cried the sultana. I was watching your face as you attempted to put a good construction on this dream, and you turned pale as a ghost. You and I both know what a frightful dream it was."

"My dear," the pasha replied, "you are a race given to fearful imaginings. Your father Murad Khan also had frightful fancies as a result of his dreams. He used to keep fretting about them, and there wasn't a man around whom he didn't tell them to. You are like that, too. But put aside these vain fancies. You told this dream to me first, and I interpreted it positively. Let it end there."

The pasha tried to console her in every way possible; but it was no use. The sultana grew more pious day by day. She gave 20,000 goldpieces in trust for Mecca and Medina, and another 20,000 for the benefit of everyone in her household, great and small, including those off campaigning, the cooks, the panters and butlers, the falconers, and her private staff. She provided in her will that 40,000 prayers be offered up for her soul nightly, stipulating 20,000 goldpieces to her trustee (for this purpose). She also made provision for her own household retainers, and for all of Melek Ahmed Pasha's aghas, granting her trustee another 20,000 each for these two purposes. She gave over the deeds of her seventy gardens and vineyards, her summer palaces and estates—in short, all of her real property—to her children and to her and Melek's servants, with provision in her will that if the lineage came to an end, all revenue from her properties should go to the Holy Cities. For among the sultanas of that period, none was wealthier than she.

Seven years previously she had renounced all partying and entertainments. She had taken orders from Hasan Efendi, the şeyh at Koca Mustafa Pasha, and had achieved stages (of asceticism and mystical illumination) the likes of Rabia-ı Adeviyye.[7] She never took pleasure in the company of women, preferring to withdraw to a corner of solitude and busy herself with devotions. In fact, she and the pasha used to perform the five daily prayers together.

A Marvel: The Genuine Dream of Melek Ahmed Pasha

One morning, in the palace at Eyub Sultan, our lord Melek Ahmed Pasha addressed me as follows: "God grant it be auspicious, my Evliya. I had a strange dream this night. It seems that our Kaya Sultan and I had a quarrel, and she said to me: 'Look here, pasha, from now on you cannot be my husband, and I am no longer your wife. Give me my dowry right away!'[8] We got into a huge argument again. 'Look here, my lady sultan,' said I, 'it is impossible for me to divorce you. Only death can part us. For how can I give you your dowry, which amounts to an Egyptian treasure?⁹ Beware, my sultan, do not answer me this way again or I will kill myself.'

" 'You won't die,' she retorted, 'but I will kill myself. My grandfather told me to come after I had my child. I will go to him. I don't want my dowry or anything else from you. I have your daughter in my womb. Take your daughter. I no longer want my daughter from you, and I acquit you of the dowry. Just divorce me and let my soul go free.'

"She cried aloud. I too wept and said: 'O my lady, why are you throwing this world to the winds? I won't leave you.'

" 'O Pasha,' she cried, 'divorce me. You won't lack for a sultana. Here is Fatma Sultan,¹⁰ marry her.'

" 'God forbid,' I said.

" 'My dear pasha,' she replied, 'you are men, there is no truth in you. I swear by God, you will marry Canpolad-oğlu's mother Fatma Sultan.'

" 'May God not bring it to pass, may God take my life (first),' I said. But, my Evliya, as I said this to the sultana, I trembled in my dream like a leaf.

" 'Now my dear pasha,' she answered, 'I will certainly be divorced, by peace or by force. If you still need me you may come in three years and marry me again; but for now you are a stranger, don't approach me.'

" 'My lady sultan,' I said, 'stop these whimsical jests and these melancholy replies.'

"Suddenly she flung open the wardrobe on the shore side of the room where I was sitting, went inside, and disappeared. While I was waiting to find out why she had entered the wardrobe, a voice cried from within it: 'My dear grandfather, Sultan Ahmed! My pasha does not want to divorce me. Talk to my pasha and tell him to divorce me.'

"The wardrobe door flew open and out walked Sultan Ahmed and Sultan Mustafa. 'Melek Ahmed,' they said, 'why are you distressing our Kaya Ismehan so much by not divorcing her? If you have any sense you, too, will be divorced in three years.'

" 'No, my Padishah, I will not divorce her. She is Sultan Murad's daughter and my wife. I would sooner die than divorce her.'

"Ahmed Khan said: 'Yes, you will die; but you will certainly divorce her. It is the command of God Eternal. Let the law of the Prophet decide the case. Seize that Melek and take him to court!'

"Then it seemed that all the nobles and *ulema* and the *şey-hülislam* were in Aya Sofya mosque, and all the palace viziers were also present. We kept arguing the case in the *şeriat* court, saying 'You will divorce Kaya' and 'I won't divorce her.' At last—I don't know how it slipped out of my mouth, but I uttered the divorce formula once, and then I sighed with such anguish that even now, Evliya, my whole body is trembling like an autumn leaf from that sigh. In my grief I said: 'God willing, I will remarry Kaya in a short time and we will stroll together in paradise.'

"But just then some men came and covered Kaya's head with a white cloth. Four men took her by the arms and were leading her away, when one of them said to me: 'Melek Pasha, why are you looking at Kaya? Henceforth she is divorced from you and a stranger to you.' And they led her away. I was left weeping inside Aya Sofya mosque.

" 'Don't grieve, martyr,' said Sun'i-zade Efendi. 'It is God's to command, for God has power over you as well.' He removed the white Kashmir shawl from his neck and draped it over my shoulders. Then he took my right hand in his left hand, and we performed a kind of prostration in Aya Sofya—in all my life I have never performed a prayer so awkwardly. But our *imam* Sun'i-zade was *şeyhülislam*. After the prayer service he led me to my palace, where he left me and departed. I awoke in terror, and found myself weeping.

"Well, my Evliya, and my lord *imam*, that was the terrifying dream I had."

Imam Mehmed Efendi and Gınayi-zade Ali Efendi spoke up: "A marvelous and subtle and joyous dream, my sultan; may it be auspicious. God willing, you and the sultana will both live long and will spend many years in mutual love. Her saying, 'Take your daughter who is in my womb and divorce me' signifies—But God knows best—that aside from that daughter you will have no more daughters, only sons; or else that the sultana will no longer conceive by you. And your weeping in the dream signifies laughing; just as the poet Vahdeti Efendi says in one of his ghazels:

If you desire the next world, weep in this, O heart,
For he who weeps in sleep must wake up laughing.

So, God willing, you will live very long, and will laugh very much."

This is what we said. But the pasha replied: "No, no. The interpretation of this dream was provided a few months ago in Tokat Park.[11] The sultana one time had a dream there in which she saw Sultan Ahmed in the gardens of paradise. When he told her, 'My Kaya, why don't you come to these gardens of mine?' Sultan Mustafa objected: 'No, brother, let her have a daughter of Melek and then she may come.' Now the sultana has become pregnant since she had that dream and—but God knows best—she will bear a daughter; may God make it easy for her.

"(In my dream) she was divorced from me, she wrapped herself in a white cloth, four men took her by the arms and led her away. That white cloth is a shroud. The four men bearing her away are the ones who will bear her coffin. Sultan Ahmed's saying, 'You must certainly divorce Kaya according to God's command; and if you have any sense, you too will be divorced in three years,' means that I will follow her (to the grave) in three years. My performing a prostration in an awkward manner with the şeyhülislam in Aya Sofya mosque points to the prayer service for my dead body, which the şeyhülislam will perform. For Sun'i-zade Efendi draped his shawl over my shoulders, not over my head, and this signifies that I have yet some time to live. Whereas Sun'i-zade's taking me by the hand and accompanying me to my palace means—but God knows best—that he will accompany me all the way to the grave. And Kaya Sultan will certainly die at this birth."

When he finished, I myself spoke up: "O my sultan, you both have the dream and interpret it; but they say that the dream turns out according to its interpreter, not its dreamer. God be praised, the *imam efendi* spoke up first and gave it a positive interpretation. God willing, the interpretation belongs to him, and your own interpretation will be without effect." In this way I tried to comfort him. But he was not consoled in the slightest.

The Death of Kaya Ismehan Sultan, Daughter of Gazi Murad Khan, God's Mercy upon Them Both

According to the definitive verse (Koran, 55:26) "Every one in it perishes," twenty-six days following this dream of our lord Melek Ahmed Pasha, on the——in the year——Kaya Sultan's months and days were fulfilled, and it was time for her delivery. All the sultanas and sisters and friends, and all the experienced women (*bula*) and skilled midwives of physicianlike disposition were present. God be praised, that blessed night 40 complete Koran recitals and 40,000 invocations of the Prophet were accomplished; and God the Creator brought forth from Kaya, just as He had brought forth Salih's she-camel,[12] a pure-starred daughter. There were joy and celebration that night in the summer palace of Eyub Sultan and in the town. By morning the pasha had given away ten purses as alms, plus forty purses of Kaya Sultan's money. He had also clothed 500 men in all sorts of garments, and they responded by showering him with benedictions.

But God did not answer their prayers. For the placenta, which is supposed to come down the uterus and exit the mother's womb as the afterbirth, in the case of Kaya, who was a very corpulent woman, remained stuck in the womb, attached to her heart. So that night and the next morning in the city of Eyub, joy and celebration turned to grief and woe, and the bliss of the pasha and of all the retainers and servants turned to torment. They placed the sultana in blankets and shook her mercilessly. Twice they suspended her upside down. They filled a honey barrel with orange-flower water and put her inside. To make a long story short, they tortured her so much for three days and nights that all the pleasures she ever enjoyed in this world were forced out her nose.

Finally the bloody midwives came with their arms smeared in almond oil and stuck their oily arms up into the sultana's uterus, all the way to their elbows. "There my dear, God be praised, the afterbirth has come out!"—and they brought out a piece of skin. "There is still some left in there," said another midwife, as she too stuck her hand up the vagina and brought out several items that looked like pieces of wet skin and liver and rennet.

At last, four days after giving birth, the sultana died.

Men had been stationed in the nearby palaces. They arrived on the scene immediately; locked the rooms where the sultana's body lay, and the other chambers, and the treasury; put the pasha and the rest of us in another room, and sealed off all the rooms; and sent word to Köprülü and the Padishah. In a twinkling, the chief black eunuch and the chief female and male treasurers and all the viziers came and confiscated all of the goods, leaving even the slave girls naked and wretched.

As they began to lay out Kaya Sultan's body, and as the poor pasha, distraught and bewildered, looked this way and that, a halberdier from Istanbul came to confiscate the goods in his Istanbul palace. They took 1,700 purses belonging to the pasha, 3,000 muskets and 200 swords, 800 harnesses and 300 scimitars, 800 complete suits of armor, including chain-mail, helmets, gauntlets, flank armor, and decorative plumes, plus three gold-on-gold tent pavilions, and——— —in short, the weapons and instruments of war that the pasha had accumulated in forty years of serving as vizier were confiscated on the grounds that "Kaya is dead."

"What has a woman to do with suits of armor and tent pavilions and muskets and leopard skins?" cried the pasha. "They belong to me."

"No, Kaya is dead, and they were found in Kaya's palace."

So the pasha lost 1,700 purses of cash, along with seventy purses of gold, and another ten that belonged to Kudde Kethüda. Deprived at once of both wealth and wife, he kept intoning: "Ya Sabbur" (O Patient One!), and he bowed to God's decree.

In Istanbul, meanwhile, the vizier Köprülü, thinking that Kaya Sultan's wealth was kept in the middle turret at Valide Hanı, went there himself and ransacked all four stories, but he only found a large porcelain bowl wrapped in an Egyptian reed mat. Frustrated and disappointed, he boarded his caique and proceeded to Eyub Sultan to attend Kaya's funeral. There he made an inventory of Kaya's goods and loaded them all into the *bostancı-başı's* caique, saying: "We'll take these to the Closet of the Holy Cities."

"O men!" cried Melek as they were hauling away this vast amount of wealth. "I am alive. And her daughter is alive. And when she was alive, she stipulated so much property for her trustee. And among these clothes are clothing of mine."

Köprülü was unmoved by all his protestations. "The Closet of the Holy Cities is a secure place," he replied. "We'll keep these goods there for her daughter. Let the funeral procession proceed."

They carried the dead sultana to the mosque of Ebu Eyub Ansari, where they performed a service amidst the cries and laments of a vast crowd of men; then put Kaya's bier on the *bostancı-başı's* caique at the Imam landing. All the nobles and *ulema*, the *şeyhs*, the deputies and viziers, boarded a thousand caiques, reciting the verse (Koran 11:41) "Embark on it; in the name of God be its sailing and its mooring," and they proceeded to bear Kaya with the caiques amidst the prayers of the *şeyhs* and the *ulema*.

As this flotilla was making its way, I recalled—*story*—that twenty years previously, when Melek Ahmed Pasha married Kaya, she would not let him approach her on the wedding night, and even struck him with a dagger. And another time she plucked out one side of the pasha's beard, so that he could not attend the imperial *divan* for five months until his beard grew back. The reason for all this was that her devilish boon companions had brought some astrologers and diviners who took the sultana's horoscope and warned her not to get pregnant by Melek, that she would suffer as a result, and that in the end she would die in childbirth. "When you bear his male children there will be no harm," they told her; "but when you bear a female child of Melek, you will die." They frightened the late sultana so much that she would not let the pasha approach her. This went on for seven years during which the pasha "paid dry penalty."

One day the Padishah's mother, Kösem Sultan, spoke to her: "My Kaya," she said. "You have no children. But your pasha is here at court, not away at some provincial post. Why don't you get pregnant?"

She had Melek summoned and asked him about it. "To tell you the truth, my sultan," he said, "for seven years now we have not entered the nuptial chamber."

The imperial mother handed the pasha a jewel-encrusted mace. "Strike Kaya," she commanded, "and kill her steward women and all her boon companions." With this she shut the door upon Kaya and Melek, and stood outside the room.

Melek, who was large and strong, took the mace by the handle and drew it over Kaya's "mount" (*kaya*) so delightfully that Kaya became pregnant, and the pasha showered the imperial mother with gifts. God be praised, a chronogram was composed on the occasion of this opening of the gate:"———/He who takes Kaya Sultan cuts the die in marble."[13]

Nine months and ten days later Kaya Sultan gave birth to a———, as a result of which she neither died nor lost the luster of her countenance. In the end she loved the pasha and, driving away all of the corrupting female companions from her company, spent all her time conversing with the pasha.

But now—"None knows the Unknown but God"—that dire prophecy of those necromancers, that she would finally become pregnant by Melek and die in childbirth, came back to me in the caique, and I hinted the matter to the pasha.

"Yes," he said, "it turned out that way. This is a divine mystery. Not every expert can divine these hidden mysteries. Here it is, seventeen years later, and she has died a noble martyr, just as they predicted. O my Kaya Sultan, my lady, my patroness, my soul, Kaya!"

As he wept we arrived at Bağçe Kapı. There several thousand men took the bier on their shoulders and carried it all the way to Aya Sofya, where they buried her in the tomb of Sultan Ibrahim and Sultan Mustafa, just inside the window overlooking the courtyard of the mosque.

At this juncture the pasha had a falling fit over the sultana's grave and was covered with dirt. "My good man," said Köprülü, "aren't you ashamed to act like this for the sake of a woman? Don't fret over it. I'll give you another sultana. That's a promise."

"May you not live to carry it out," said the pasha. Köprülü left in a huff, and all the viziers conducted the pasha back to his palace.

As for myself, I remained in Kaya Sultan's tomb for seven days and nights, and completed five Koran recitations. All the sultanas who came to visit the tomb gave me presents in exchange for benedictions, so that by the end of seven days I had accumulated 740 goldpieces, 20,000 shiny aspers for pocket money, seven pastilles of ambergris, and six *okkas* of aloes.

Every day, five times a day, Melek Ahmed Pasha came to perform the daily prayers, each time hiring someone to complete a Koran recitation. "O my Kaya," he would cry amidst his lamenting, "this was the dream I saw; now you are divorced from me indeed, separated by worlds and worlds."

It is a fact that, of the seventeen sultanas who were alive in those days, none got on with her husband so well as Kaya with Melek. She was, too, very clever and prudent in managing her household. She was a true daughter of Sultan Murad IV, a raging lioness, and a benefactress to all the other sultanas.——— But the late Kaya's wish was unfulfilled (*na-murad*). She had just entered her twenty-seventh year when she died.[14] She never saw any man's face except Melek's. Previously she had been engaged to Murad Khan's sword-bearer, Mustafa Pasha, but he did not marry her. Three years prior to her death she began to hear voices and see strange and wondrous visions, of a type that qualified her for sainthood.———In sum, if I were to compose an elegy of a thousand verses for this Kaya Sultan, I could not begin to describe her noble character and pleasant disposition.

Melek Ahmed Pasha assigned me a daily wage of twenty aspers for reciting prayers and Koran in her light-filled tomb. I received it from the trustee regularly on a monthly and yearly basis and was able to delegate the task to a deputy. Even now, Koran recitations are performed over her noble grave at each of the five daily prayers; incense is burned continually, and the dome of the tomb is filled with light and with the fragrance of raw ambergris; gilded candlestick holders as tall as a man stand at either end of the grave outfitted with all sorts of highly wrought and jewel-encrusted candles; and her cenotaph is adorned with a covering from the Kaaba.

Notes

1. That is, Sultan Ahmed or the "Blue Mosque." Cf. Evliya's account at I 59b.27f. (216; Hammer i, 112).

2. That is, Kara Hasan Pasha (formerly Agha, see Ch. 2), governor of Aleppo and leader of a *celali* rebellion that recently had been crushed (see Evliya's account, V 69a–75b [235–55]).

3. Cf. III 98b.19 (Ch. 2), where this office dues is put at seventy purses.

4. Present day Beykoz, a village on the Anatolian side of the Bosphorus; cf. Evliya's descriptions at I 139b.16, 146b.30 (464, 487; Hammer ii, 74, 89).

5. Lit., "she is bloody." Tk. *kanlı* means both "bloody" and "owing blood money, responsible for someone's death."

6. Candia was taken in 1080/1669 after a three-year siege, finally completing the conquest of Crete that had begun twenty-five years earlier; see Evliya's account at VIII 288a ff. (396f.).

7. The famous mystic of the second/eighth century; see Margaret Smith, *Rābi'a the Mystic A.D. 717–801 and Her Fellow Saints in Islam* (Cambridge, 1928; repr. San Francisco, 1977).

8. According to Bobovi, p. 69, the *nikâh* or dowry for sultanas was 20,000 to 30,000 piasters. It was probably a great deal larger in this case. The dowry (= *mahr* in Islamic law) was generally not paid at

the time of marriage, but it was part of the marriage contract, and served as a kind of insurance for the wife in case of divorce.

9. That is, the amount of tribute paid from Egypt into the Ottoman treasury each year; proverbial for "a fortune." At X 194a.16 (413) Evliya specifies the "treasury" (*hazine*) as 1,200 Egyptian purses (*kise*), each "purse" containing 846 piasters (*guruş*).

10. Kaya's aunt, the daughter of Sultan Ahmed I, whom Melek eventually marries.

11. In Beykoz (see above, N. 4; also I 139b.6—15 [464; Hammer ii, 74]); this had been a favorite hunting grounds of Murad IV, Kaya's father.

12. See Koran, 7:73, 11:64, 17:59, 26:155, 54:27.

13. As given in the text (*Kaya Sultanı alan sikkei mermerde kazır*) this adds up to 1234. At I 105b.18—19 (355: omitted; Hammer ii, 13: omitted), where the text has *yazar* instead of *kazır*, it adds up to 1145. Neither of these can be reconciled with the date of their marriage, 1054 (1644).

14. This would make her ten years old when she married if, as Melek stated above, they were married for seventeen years. According to Alderson, Table XXXVI, she was born in 1633, married in 1644, and died in 1652. The last date should be corrected to 1659. At I 105b.15—23 (cf. previous note) Evliya states that she died in childbirth at age twenty-seven, and gives the chronogram of the birth of her daughter, Fatma Hanım, as 1072 (1662; correct for *ola mahfuz*)—but this is the date of Melek's death; he also gives four further chronograms on Kaya's death (two of which correspond exactly to the ones given just after the text translated here)—but only one adds up to the correct figure of 1069; the others come to 1068, 1070, and 1072.

9

GOVERNOR OF BOSNIA
(1659–60)

On the twentieth day after Kaya Sultan's death, our lord Melek Ahmed Pasha was summoned to the presence of the felicitous Padishah together with Köprülü. "Please accept my condolences, Melek Lala," said the sultan. "Judgment belongs to God. This is the way of the world.

"Now, in order to dispel your grief over Kaya I have bestowed on you the province of Bosnia, free and clear. I recalled (its former governor) Seydi Ahmed Pasha because he committed so much oppression. But you will act justly. Also, do not give the Venetian infidels any respite in those regions. Carry out plundering expeditions against their countryside, and try to capture some of their fortresses. Put all of my noble rescripts into effect. Guard all of the frontiers well. Repair and restore all of my fortresses, and keep due watch over them. I in turn will watch over your daughter and her property and estates, and her wealth which has been placed in the Closet of the Holy Cities. As for those things pertaining to the armory that were brought there: I know they are your property, because Kaya Sultan never married any other vizier, so how could she have inherited tent pavilions and chainmail and helmets and muskets and shields and other such military paraphernalia? They are yours." And the sultan ordered them to be restored to him immediately.

"My Padishah," said the pasha, "1,700 of my purses, and 70 purses of gold collected over the past fifty years, have my seal. They are my portion and my due."

Köprülü Mehmed Pasha intervened: "Yes, they have your seal. But Kaya used to give you 100 or 200 purses whenever you went off to a provincial governorship, and you used to pay back these debts by sending her money with your seal from the provincial posts."

"My dear vizier," broke in the felicitous Padishah, "let's give my *lala* Melek 10 purses of gold and 100 purses of piasters from that money."

"My Padishah," Köprülü replied, "bestowing the post of Bosnia, and waving the office dues, and adding 10 purses of gold and 100 purses of piasters is a princely gift indeed! It is my Padishah's to command."

Thereupon the pasha was presented, in the imperial presence, with 10 purses of gold and 100 purses of piasters, along with all the above-mentioned instruments of war that had been formerly confiscated, including the nine-tiered tent pavilions. The felicitous world-refuge Padishah now dressed our lord in a sable fur. "You are my commander-in-chief over the Bosnian frontier," he said, as he stuck several royal jeweled aigrettes into the pasha's turban with his own blessed hand; and he uttered the benediction: "Go, may God the exalted be your Helper."

The pasha, as was his wont, merely replied: "Peace be upon you, my Padishah," and backed out. He and Köprülü rode abreast to the vizierial palace where, after dinner, Köprülü dressed the pasha in a sable robe of honor.

"May God bless your office," he said. *The argument between Melek Ahmed Pasha and Köprülü vizier.* "I have one favor to ask," he went on. "We have a certain Ismail Agha, a most prudent and productive and experienced man, who is also of Bosnian origin. Why don't you send him now to Bosnia as your deputy?"

"By God, my sultan," replied the pasha, "I value your request with my head and my soul. But someone under your protection who is serving as my deputy will converse with me in overly familiar terms and will behave in a high-handed fashion. And when I dismiss him he will come to you and make all sorts of complaints, thus sowing discord between us. Also, I have some homeless ones of my own, who have suffered my tribulations and whose character I can vouch for. They have been looking out for this day. To speak frankly, isn't it a more sensible plan for me to make one of them my deputy?"

"So," said Köprülü, "you don't accept my request to make him your deputy. God willing, I will make him a vizier equivalent to yourself, and give him Bosnia in your place!"

"God bless you, brother," Melek exclaimed. "If you like, you may give him not only Bosnia but the grand vizierate itself in *your* place."

At this Köprülü flew into a rage. "Leave for your post to-morrow," he cried. "You've become touched in the brain ever since Kaya died."

After sherbets and incense Melek Ahmed Pasha took his leave from Köprülü and went directly to the *şeyhülislam*, then to his palace. He immediately ordered his billeting officer, Ibrahim Agha, with 1,000 braves, to remove the standards outside the Edirne gate to the town of Topçular. And the next morning he marched in grand procession, with his fully armed and accoutred soldiery, below the parade pavilion and out of Istanbul.

How Our Lord Melek Pasha Went from Istanbul to Bosnia, Setting out on 20 Cümazilahir 1069 (15 March 1659)

First to the stage of Topçular where we halted for a full week. While seeing to the supplies for our journey, our lord sent this humble one perhaps twenty times to see Köprülü Mehmed Pasha. It was as though I was his marshal of the guards. Köprülü was fond of me. He had me recite the Koran several times and was so pleased that he said to our court agent Zühdi Effendi: "I would like your pasha to make this *hafız* Evliya his marshal of the guards. Write your pasha to that effect." Zühdi Efendi sent this message off to the pasha.

"All right," said the pasha, "if only Evliya accepts the post of marshal of the guards. He is first and last our confidant and our trusted kinsman." The rest of our gate companions overheard the pasha saying this, and some of the officers began to regard me with scornful looks. "Come here, Evliya," said the pasha, "I'm going to make you my marshal of the guards in accordance with Köprülü's request."

"Bless God," I replied, "albeit I am serving as my sultan's *imam* and his confidant, I do not want to enter affairs or be a servant, to put up with the tribulations of others or suffer the taunts of rivals." When I said this, the pasha gave up the notion.

Next day we proceeded to the stage of Küçük Çekmece, thence to Büyük Çekmece. *Adventure of the humble one, Evliya, the unhypocritical, the dervish.* From this stage the pasha sent me on certain business by forced march to Köprülü Mehmed Pasha. When I returned and gave him Köprülü's letter, which was of friendly disposition, the pasha was very pleased and presented me with a sable fur stole. Coming to our quarters in the great inn, I proceeded to carouse with the other aghas, when several of the pasha's officers showed up and started to pick a quarrel with me.

"Be off with you, gentlemen," said I. "Don't worry, I have no desire for your high offices. I am a world traveler and boon companion to mankind. Be off. You can purchase your honor from me."

"Pimp!" one of them exclaimed. "Now that Kaya Sultan is dead, what authority do you have? Soon we're going to kill you." I just jeered at them.

At this juncture, one of my *gulams* came up and said: "My sultan, come take a look at what happened to your clothes hampers." When I went outside I saw that the treasurer had torn open the hampers and thrown all my valuable effects out of the inn and into the mud. On top of that it was raining, and everything was getting soaked. Furthermore, one of my *gulams* had started to pick up my things, and was just lifting a copy of the Koran out of the mud, when he was struck with a sword. I nearly went crazy when I saw him lying there wounded.

"Hey, Mr. Treasurer," I shouted. "And you, marshal of the guards, Osman Agha! Aren't you ashamed to do such a thing?"

The treasurer leaped up, grabbed a javelin from one of the interior aghas, and shot it at me. I tried to dodge it but it struck me in the thigh; it even came out the other side, so I was impaled on the javelin like roasting meat on a skewer. All the onlookers began to cry out: "Hey, for shame, Mr. Treasurer!"

Meanwhile I extracted the javelin from my thigh. "Gentlemen," I said, "you are witnesses before God." But now the treasurer was heading toward me with his retinue, weapons drawn. My horse was at hand, since I had just returned from Köprülü, and my sword was at my waist; so I leaped on the horse crying, "Gentlemen, I commend you to God!"

In short, we had a huge brawl in the grounds of the Çekmece inn. I saw that they had shut the inn gate tight and had drawn a chain across it. While we were brawling and snarling, the pasha and his son and a few of our Abkhazian clansmen came in and broke it up. "What's going on here, my Evliya?" he asked.

"What do you think is going on? This all happened because of your overfondness. Just look at my clothes lying outside in the mud."

All the aghas who were present cried: "By God, my sultan, Evliya Çelebi is not the slightest bit at fault. It is all the fault of your treasurer. We are witnesses, we will bear witness."

"Yes," said the pasha, "it's all the fault of that ass, and of the marshal of the guards, and the steward Ibrahim Agha. In fact, one time in Van, when I sent Evliya as envoy to the Persian shah,[1] they slandered Evliya in my presence quite a lot. I told them to hold their tongues, that I had forgiven him, and that he was a dervish. Now you see that old business has turned up. Well, there's nothing for it, it's the way of the world. Such things happen when braves mount horses and gird on swords. Summon the kadi of Çekmece and his deputy immediately."

The kadi came to investigate. The witnesses all swore that the treasurer shot Evliya with a javelin first, and that Evliya struck him with a sword he had at hand. Their testimony was recorded in a şerᶜi voucher and a copy was placed in my hands. Surgeons flocked around the treasurer, and the pasha took me into his own quarters where surgeons treated my wounds.

In the morning the standards were advanced to Silivri. They were about to take the treasurer to Istanbul by boat when an agha arrived from Köprülü vizier with a letter for the pasha. "Send Evliya to me right away," it said. "You do not realize his value, and you do not allow him to serve you."

The pasha gave me 100 goldpieces as road money, a horse, and letters, and took all my slaves and my effects into his own treasury (for safekeeping). "Come to me in Bosnia when you can, my Evliya, after a few months or a few days." He pronounced a benediction, and we parted.

Outside Çekmece the court official made me get off my horse and mount a runty baggage-horse. He clapped a fetter on my feet beneath the horse's belly, and led me in chains into Köprülü's presence. They also brought the treasurer with his memorandum, and I handed over Melek's vouchers and letters.

"Don't worry, Evliya," he said after reading them. "If you die and the treasurer lives, I'll kill the treasurer; but if the treasurer dies, with this şerᶜi voucher you won't be put to death. Still, have Evliya confined in the janissary barracks until the whole affair is cleared up."

So they took me and the treasurer outside, and the usher sent me to our barracks where I lay confined for twenty days. God be praised, when the treasurer was released I was again brought to Köprülü and kissed his hand.

"Were you aware," he said, "what kind of man Melek Ahmed Pasha is, that he wasn't able to keep hold of you? And such a disgrace occurred! Now, recite a portion of the noble Koran." I recited in a loud voice the verses beginning, "And we bestowed on

David Solomon, what an excellent slave" (38:30). Köprülü was so pleased that he said: "You stay in our service, Evliya." He attached me to his retinue and appointed quite a substantial salary, so I was busy night and day reciting litanies and benedictions.

I remained in Istanbul for another month, before we went off to Anatolia against the *celalis*.

[1070/1660: The pasha is with his army outside Livno (Hlevne).[2] Evliya has rejoined him and has become reconciled with the treasurer.]

A Marvel: The Genuine Dream of Gazi Melek Ahmed Pasha

One morning, after the dawn prayer in the Livno plain, and in the presence of the Livno janissary agha Halil Agha, Tekeli Pasha's steward Hüseyn Agha, and myself, Melek Ahmed Pasha said:

"May it be auspicious: this night I had a dream. I was in this very oratory, built by Seydi Ahmed Pasha.[3] I had mounted the pulpit and was delivering a sermon to the troops; apparently it was Friday. Suddenly Seydi Ahmed Pasha came running up the pulpit stairs, all clad in armor and with his helmet on his head. 'My brother,' he cried, 'it is no great merit to mount my pulpit. Intercede with me before the vizier, Köprülü Mehmed Pasha, and save me from being killed; otherwise they are going to martyr me on just such a Friday as this.' And he wept.

"I left off preaching and said to him: 'Don't despair, my brother. God will save you from them, and God willing, we will meet next year in Tımışvar plain and we will resolve your affair. Now don't worry, but take up residence in Budin, repair the fortress and guard it well.'

" 'I accept this,' he said, 'but don't forget me in your prayers.'

"He started backing down the pulpit stairs, but he stumbled, fell down the stairs, and died. I decided to end the sermon in order to bury that *gazi* vizier, so I quickly uttered the prayer: 'May my rebellious and sinful and prodigal soul be straightened through obedience to God.' But then, in my distress, instead of saying 'O you who are in attendance' (*eyyuha'l-hazırun*) I said 'O you who are inattentive' (*eyyuha'l-gafilun*).

"At that moment I glanced over to Mt. Prolog opposite,[4] and there were 700 or 800 black swine, pouring down from the mountains into this plain, with chains on their necks. They rushed in among the congregation, went between the rows of those performing the Friday prayer, and began to snap at the body of Seydi Ahmed Pasha who was lying at the foot of the pulpit. But the congregation maintained their neat rows.

"Amidst the swine was a fat yellow bear who lumbered up, dragging the chain on his neck, and started to mount the pulpit. Then you, my Evliya, caught hold of the bear's chain and pulled him back down the pulpit. I was shouting from the pulpit: 'Kill him Evliya!' So you bared your sword, killed the bear, and placed his corpse next to Seydi Ahmed Pasha's body. Then I finished the sermon and performed the Friday prayer. After that I ordered the swine that had come in amongst the congregation to be killed, and they were all put to the sword.

"It seems the morning prayer was nigh. Silihdar Süleyman woke me up. Now I have performed the dawn prayer and you arrived and I uttered a *besmele* and related this dream."

"May it be auspicious," cried the janissary agha and Tekeli Mustafa Pasha's steward.

"May it be auspicious," cried I as well, and continued: "My sultan, God and His prophet know best"—*interpretation of the humble Evliya*—"but this office previously belonged to Seydi Ahmed Pasha. The office, which he gave over to us, was his pulpit. His saying, 'It is no great merit to mount my pulpit; save me from Köprülü' indicates that he is frightened of Köprülü. Your saying, 'We will save you from Köprülü' means—but God knows best—that he will cross the bridge (*köprü*) of this world and will be saved. Your saying 'Repair the fortress in Budin' is to say, 'From now on repair your religion (*din*) and your faith.'⁵

"Now you have been governing in his pulpit—that is, his office. Seydi will seek the office of (governor of) Bosnia once again—he tried to mount the pulpit. His tumbling from the pulpit and dying indicate that the governorship of Bosnia will not be vouchsafed to him; rather—but God knows best—his swine-like enemies will wound him, and he will die a martyr. Also—but God knows best—the infidels, like swine, will make a night attack and will enter among our troops; but, God willing, they will all be put to the sword, and their place will be hell fire."

"Praise be to God," cried the pasha. "Just such an interpretation occurred to me as well. There is no power and no strength but with God!" He rose and ordered all the troops to arm and stand ready.

Glory to God! The sealike army welled up in the Livno plain with a tumultuous wave, then moved off calmly toward Mt. Prolog, grazing their horses as they went. Now, by God's wisdom, that day being Friday, while all the *gazis* were playing jereed, five horsemen came galloping up. At their head was———Beg, Atlı-beg-zade's younger son, who was slightly lame. That brave youth cried:

"My sultan, *çeşteti*[6] vizier! The other day a group of soldiers went off raiding, including Ismail Alay-begi, Çoltar-oğlu, Yenge-kırığı, Nak-oğlu, Gırbo Bölük-başi, Çitineli Baba Ahmed-oğlu, and Ismail Bölük-başı. They raided and pillaged below the infidels' fortress of Split, and they were on their way back. But it seems the infidels had set an ambush over there in Mt. Prolog and were lying in wait for them. Now they have begun to do battle. Mercy, felicitous vizier! It is close by. Hasten to their aid like Hızır,[7] and answer their plea for justice."

"Well," exclaimed the pasha, "this being mounted for the jereed is surely from God." In a trice he had 1,000 men on foot mount spare horses; added these to the 2,000 picked and fully armed soldiers who were already astride their short-haired steeds; put the chief regiment officer, Arnavud Hüseyn Bölük-başı, in command; and sent this company off. I, too, kissed the pasha's hand and—*How we went as a relief party from Livno plain*—with a *besmele* (joined the troop).

When the *gazis* reached the rugged terrain of Mt. Prolog, most of them dismounted; but I and a few hundred others who had sturdy horses remained mounted. God be praised, the Herzegovinian steed beneath me could manage on the stony ground. So we 300 or so horsemen rode to the peak of Mt. Prolog and from there saw the foot soldiers ahead of us. Advancing a bit, we heard musket shots and cries of "Allah Allah!" So we too cried: "Come on *gazis!* Allah Allah!" Horse and foot, springing like deer over the bare rocks, we came up to the scene of battle.

As soon as the infidels saw us they drew up in "swine ball" formation and rushed against us. Now our *gazis* were tired and weakened with thirst, but when they saw us their thirst vanished and they found new life. They had their backs to a cliff and were fighting like that, as we emerged from the ambushes and unfurled our banners. Of the 2,000 soldiers, we had left behind 500 in the ambushes as a rear guard, with the water and biscuit. The remaining 1,500 let out a Muhammedan war cry, shouting "Allah Allah!" with a single voice. We did not give the infidels a chance to blink, but showered them with a volley of lead.

When the hell-destined infidels saw that the relief party had arrived, they turned upon us like rabid snakes. Our former troop as well, seeing this change in circumstance, found new life and rushed out of the place they had been hemmed in, whooping "Allah Allah!" and attacking the enemy from behind. Caught between two armies, the infidels were so struck down by Muhammedan swords that, as God is my witness, such a *gaza* had never before been witnessed on that frontier.

In sum, we took 1,060 infidel heads, 700 live captives, bound and chained, 70 banners with crosses, plus 70 brigand chiefs along with their drums and fifes. On our side 70 of our braves and 110 from the former troop had fallen martyrs. This former troop consisted of 2,000 picked men, commanded by the district commander of the Bosnian *sancak*, Ismail Beg, and included his own soldiers as well as other berserkers and raiders. As part of their huge loot (captured previously) were 600 women and boys and 75 heads. God be praised, the infidels were defeated and demeaned, whereas the armies of Islam were honored and victorious.

On that day, in the Livno plain, so much booty was arrayed before the pasha's tent pavilion, and so many captives, and so many heads on poles. We returned safe and sound, performed the funeral service for our martyrs, and buried them all together in a place named Şehidlik ("Martyrdom"). In celebration a volley of muskets resounded in the camp, and a cannon salute was shot from the fortress. Then the *gazis* brought the 600 women and boys before the pasha, and we presented him with 150 choice boys and girls as his fifth share. From the rest of the prisoners—those infidels who escaped the sword when our relief party attacked, and the 70 captured brigand chiefs, and the 700 ordinary captives—we gave the pasha 200 splendid captives as his share.

But when the pasha threatened to kill the other prisoners before the tent pavilion, the frontier *gazis* all objected, saying: "This is the custom of our frontier, and the price of our blood: that we share equally. If the noble vizier has to kill these, then he must also kill those captives that were given him as his share. If they were not[8] to be killed, we would have killed them all in Mt. Prolog after we captured them. And if, God forbid, we were to fall captive to them, they would kill us." There was a good deal of this kind of talk.

Eventually a different sort of argument arose in the ranks: "The prisoners should *not* be shared equally among the troops. *We* went first and risked our lives below the fortress of Split. We battled mightily for three days and three nights and took so much booty. The prey belongs to the one who takes it first. *You* came later. You were 2,000 men. The two parties made common cause, and together we slaughtered the infidels. We won't interfere with the spoils and captives taken in that battle. What's yours is yours, what's ours is ours." There was a huge quarrel which nearly turned into an all-out battle.

Finally, the pasha convened a grand council, summoning the *kadı* of Livno and the *şeyhülislam* and several hundred *ulema* and the veterans of the frontier *gazis*. The following judgment was reached in the pasha's tent-pavilion, in the presence of the noble *şeriat:*

> Inasmuch as, while you were coming back after having taken booty below the fortress, the infidels caught you up and were not sticking out their tongues but were slaughtering you; and inasmuch as these 2,000 braves came to your rescue, and so many of their number fell martyred for your sake, and they captured so many captains and brigands and *yunaks*,[9] and also did rescue you; therefore, according to the *şeriat*, all the spoils should be sold at public auction, and you should all, like brothers, receive equal shares. However, according to the dictum of the *imam* Ebu Hanifa, those who caught the prey with their sword are to be given as a prize, from the shares of the others, one goldpiece per captive; and those who lost a horse or a mule or a weapon are to be compensated for the loss from the spoils. You are to share equally in what remains after these adjustments. This is the judgment of the noble *şeriat*.

The *kadı* and the *gazis* all acceded to this, and a Fatiha was recited. So all the prisoners and the booty were piled together like mountains before the pasha's tent pavilion; and everything was sold at grand auction, to the tune of "one five" and "one thousand and five."

As for the captives that had been given to the pasha as his tithe, the pasha had them paraded before him one by one. All the women and boys and girls he put to one side. Of the murderers and brigands—like deadly poison filtered through seventy layers of stone—he kept 200 as his share and decided to send the remainder, along with the 1,130 infidel heads and the "tongues," to the imperial stirrup. So he had the captive infidels flay all those heads and salt the scalps.

But then the *gazis* all pleaded before the pasha, saying: "Noble vizier, if you send these infidels to Istanbul, they will somehow manage to escape the galleys and will return to this frontier of ours to wreak havoc and lay waste. Please butcher them right now. It will be easier just to send their heads to Istanbul."

At this point Atlı-beg-zade spoke up: "Noble vizier, do you see this damned brigand with the wispy beard? He was the regiment commander of our vizier Seydi Ahmed Pasha, but he turned renegade at the battle of Marina fortress[10] and went over to the Venetians. He also martyred several of our *gazis*. When, God be praised, Marina was finally taken, this scoundrel boarded a caique and escaped to Zadra. Now we have captured him in this battle, praise be to God. And all these infidels here in chains are scoundrels like him. If you kill them all, you will have performed the greatest *gaza*."

The frontier *gazis* consented to having them killed. This renegade infidel was the first to be struck down by the fire-steeled sword of the executioner of fate. He was cut to pieces.

Just then one of the bound infidels—he was fat and fleshy, with a thick neck and a large nose, squat and stout, and had manacles on his hands and a chain on his neck—suddenly leaped up, got free of the chain drawer, and headed toward the pasha shouting, "Now I've got you!"

As I was just next to the pasha, I grabbed the end of the chain and gave it a hard tug, leaving the fellow sprawled on the ground. He ran off wildly, fearing for his life, and went right up the pulpit of Seydi Ahmed Pasha's oratory, from where they brought him down.

"Well," said the pasha, "what a stout and plucky fellow that one is."

"My sultan," replied the frontier *gazis*, "do you see this infidel? He is a brigand chief named Vasil, which means 'bear.'[11] He has been scouring the roads and the passes for nigh unto twenty years—every since the year of Tekeli Pasha."[12] They bore witness to this effect.

"God is great!" cried the pasha. "Look here, janissary agha. This morning I related a dream to you and to Tekeli Pasha's steward and to our Evliya. I was delivering the sermon when Seydi Pasha came up the pulpit, and as he descended he fell and died. Then a bear with a chain came up the pulpit and attacked me. Evliya pulled him back by the chain and knocked him down. Then Evliya struck off the bear's head. Didn't I tell you this dream just this morning?

"Well now you see that was a genuine dream vision. Here I was, seated on the stool at the foot of the pulpit. He turned out to be my brother Seydi Ahmed Pasha's renegade regiment commander. I cut off his head and left it at the foot of the pulpit. That is what my dream portended. God willing, my brother Seydi will still have many years to live. As for the bear that my Evliya pulled back by the chain: here he is, this scoundrel who rushed upon me on the pulpit. And it turns out that his name is Vasil! Evliya, you killed this bear in my dream, now strike off his head here in the open."

"As you wish, my sultan," said I, girding my loins. "Now let your dream (vakıa) become reality (vakı)." I had a *gulam* named Receb. Removing my Şeyhani sword from my waist, I handed it to him and said: "Come on, do it." The lad, God bless him, gave that bear of an infidel such a Zulyezen[13] sword stroke on his neck that his head came rolling off like a Bosnian cabbage. As God is my witness, the dream was fulfilled in this manner.

Now it was the turn of the 200 infidels given to the pasha as his fifth share. "Come on, my wolves!" he cried to the *gazis*. In a twinkling all 200 of them were put to the sword, just like the swine that had entered among the congregation in his dream. Their heads too were flayed and salted. A total of 1,335 heads were made ready to be sent to the Porte.

But one frontier *gazi* had kept alive a certain infidel brigand. *A strange and comical story.* As soon as it was reported to the pasha that this youth had kept this infidel alive, the pasha flew in a rage and ordered both of them to be brought into his presence. When they arrived, the pasha signaled the executioner and they made the infidel kneel down in the arena of chastisement.

Now that youth flung his arms about the infidel's neck and cried: "Mercy, noble vizier! During the battle I gave this infidel my religion, and I took his religion. We have claimed each other as brothers. If you kill him he will go to paradise with my religion, and it will be too bad for poor me. When I die, the religion of this infidel, whom I have claimed as my brother, will remain with me and I will go to hell, so again it will be too bad for me." He burst out crying and would not be separated from the infidel.

"Hey *gazis*," cried the outraged pasha, "what is this man talking about?" The frontier *gazis* replied thus:

"When one of our *yunaks* on these frontiers falls captive to the infidels, while eating and drinking with them, one infidel[14] may pledge to save him from captivity, and the Muslim, too, promises to rescue him from the Turks if he falls captive to us. They make a pact, saying: 'Your religion is mine and my religion is yours.' They lick each other's blood, and the infidel and the Muslim become 'brothers in religion.'

"Now apparently this *gazi* became a 'brother' to this infidel who rescued him from captivity. Since now the infidel has fallen captive, he must save him and keep him alive in order that their pledge be fulfilled. It seems that they have exchanged religions, so if the infidel is killed now he will go to paradise, and if the other one dies he will enter hell with the infidel's mis-religion. True, nothing of this sort is found in the books of the Muslims, or of the infidels. Nevertheless this heresy is quite common in these frontier regions."

The pasha, always quick at repartee, said: "Well, I set both of these infidels free: the one is an infidel renegade by his own volition, the other is an infidel by his essence." So he gave the captive infidel to the renegade infidel, and they ran off like dogs in a field. We were all amazed at this discussion.

At last the pasha sent off the heads in custody of his trusty agha, Mustafa Agha. From the spoils of war he presented this humble one with 200 piasters, and another 50 piasters to each of my two slaves. Once again we settled down to guard the Livno plain and to carouse with all the *gazis*.

[While raiding in Dalmatia in Muharrem 1071/September 1660 the pasha and his troops, after a wearying march, have crossed the Cetina, set up camp, and gone to sleep.][15]

A Frightful Adventure

Now Ali Agha, the guard of the grand pavilion, also fell off to sleep along with his entire crew.

It so happened that a certain infidel *uskok*[16] had drunk a goblet of bubbling wine at the hands of that accursed and irreligious so-called General of Split (i.e., the Venetian commander) and had vowed unbravely to assassinate the pasha. He now came to spy out the pavilion (*seraperde*), but he could not observe what divine manifestations lay concealed behind the curtain (*perde*). What he saw was that all of the troops were lying in a drunken stupor, as though belonging to the tribe of "Die at God's command"[17] and as if to illustrate the proverb, "Sleep is the brother of death." So this cussed *uskok* seized the opportunity, broke through one of the tent streets, and headed fearlessly toward Melek pasha's pavilion.

A Comical Occurrence

Some of the pasha's Abkhazian guards—named Abaza Merşan Yusuf, Abaza Arıt Ali, and Abaza Kamış Veli—had just gone outside to renew their ablutions, and were squatting nearby. They addressed the infidel in their Abkhazian dialect:

"Look, man, it's midnight, this is no time for bringing a petition."

"What are you doing, man? The pasha is weary and lying down. There's no council tonight."

"The head of the council isn't here. What is this crap? Why have you come here at night?"

"When it's morning, and he convenes the council, and the drum and shawm go boom boom, come then and present your petition!"

While the Abkhazians and the infidel *uskok* were engaged in this conversation, it seems that the pasha overheard their impudent talk from inside the pavilion where he was lying. Peeking out, he saw that it was an *uskok* infidel commando firebrand, armed to the teeth. The pasha immediately seized his great and lusty sword, leaped lustily out of the grand pavilion, and gave the *uskok* such an angelic (*melekî*) blow that the heavens were jealous. But all this time no one, except for the two or three *gulams* just mentioned, even woke up or had the slightest inkling that this infidel's head had been cut off.

As it turned out, however, the slain infidel had twelve brave *yunak* and *çoyık*[18] companions outside, who had also managed to get inside the pavilion. Two (of the pasha's attendants)—a doughty brave named Çerkes Şehbaz, who was known as Peşkirci-başı ("chief napkin server"), and a man-of-Ali named Gürcü Zülfikar—these two champions grabbed their "Zülfikars"[19] and began to smite those twelve infidels in the pavilion. At this, all the aghas of the interior raised a hue and cry, and they cut off the heads of all twelve of the infidels.

By God's command, the felicitous, sword-wielding pasha, having regained his strength, immediately summoned Yusuf Kethüda and the rest of his officers into the grand pavilion, and held a şer'î hearing in the presence of the army chaplain and all the emirs. It was amazing! First he brought the treasurer to his knees, and was about to strike off his head. But all the aghas and emirs kissed the ground and begged that the sentence be reduced to a thousand stripes.

In sum, he had each one of his 380 *gulams* of the interior—with the exception of the Abkhazians mentioned above, and Peşkirci-başı and Gürcü Zülfikar who were ready at their posts—quaff 500 bowls of cornel-cherry sherbet (i.e., blows of the bastinado), until the bitter taste came out their heels. As for the chief doorkeeper who was the pavilion guard and his six subordinates, (the pasha) paid not the slightest heed to the aghas' pleas, but made the heads of all seven of them roll before the grand pavilion.

While some approved of this action, others cried foul, and this gave rise to all sorts of murmurrings. In this instance, they said, the pasha ought to have proceeded less rashly and have shown more clemency. The chief doorkeepers, and the forty-six regiment commanders—everyone, in short, down to the chief cook and the chief groom—turned into stinging scorpions. They were all displeased and offended with the pasha because of this immoderate punishment. The pasha realized that his officers and attendants were all sick of this campaign; and he made efforts to console them, to win them over, and to raise their hopes.

Notes

1. In 1065/1655; see IV 284b f. (288f.).

2. See Turková, notes 2 and 8. [H. Turková, *Die Reisen und Streifzüge Evliyâ Çelebîs in Dalmatien und Bosnien in den Jahren 1650/61* (Prague, 1961)]

3. He was governor of Bosnia from 1656 to 1659. See Turková, note 412.

4. The Prolog (Poroloq) is part of the Dinarian Alps separating Bosnia from Dalmatia. See Turková, note 7 and map.

5. See Ch. 10, n. 19.

6. A Serbian word meaning "just" ('ādil), as Evliya explains at V 131b.29 (439).

7. See Ch. 2, n. 41.

8. So the text: *olmasa*; perhaps in error for *olsa* "if they were".

9. A Bosnian word meaning "brave youth" (cf. Bosnian vocabulary at V 132a.16 [440]), used to indicate the frontier soldiers.

10. In 1070/1659–60—that is, the previous year (?). See V 146b.29 (489; tr. Turková, 58).

11. Cf. VIII 214a.19 (109) where Evliya states that *vasıl* is Greek for "bear." Evliya apparently derived this notion from the song of the gypsy bear-keepers in Istanbul, in which the bear is addressed: *ya Vasıl!* (I 169a.17 [561; Hammer ii, 146]).

12. The reference is to the year 1056/1646 when Tekeli Pasha, then governor of Bosnia, lost Kilis to the Venetians; see V 134b.2, 138a.1 (448, 461); also I 77b.23–78a.9 (271–72; Hammer i, 149). Danişmend, p. 403 dates the loss to 8 Şaban 1057/8 September 1647.

13. That is, Seyf ("Sword") b. Zi'l-yezen, a hero of Arabian romance.

14. The text here has *ḵāfir* instead of *kāfir*.

15. Cf. Turková, 38–40.

16. The *uskoks* were Christian Bosnians who had fled to Dalmatia before the Turks (see Turková, 87).

17. Cf. (?) Koran, 2:243.

18. For *çovik*, a Serbo-Croatian word meaning "man" (cf. Serbian vocabulary at V 116a.10 [382], Bosnian vocabulary at V 132a.3 [439]).

19. Zülfikar is the name of Ali's legendary two-pointed sword.

10

FATMA SULTAN (1662)

[In Rebiülevvel 1072/November 1661, after long campaigning
in Transylvania, Melek Pasha receives official orders in Fogarasch an-
nouncing the death of Köprülü and the succession of his son Fazıl
Ahmed Pasha to the grand vizierate; and informing Melek of his marriage to Fatma Sultan. Melek Pasha expresses his outrage at the news
by saying: "They have given me an old crone, and told me to 'feed the
state elephant' " (VI 28b.20-25). Melek and Evliya return to Istanbul.]

On 10 Ramazan 1072/29 April 1662 the nuptials were celebrated according to Prophetic custom. *The marriage of our lord
Melek Ahmed Pasha with Fatma Sultan, daughter of Sultan
Ahmed Khan, in Ramazan.* On the nuptial eve all of us retainers of Melek Ahmed Pasha celebrated in Fatma Sultan's palace at
the Ebu Ansari gate.

An hour before dawn our lord Melek Ahmed Pasha emerged
wearing his former dress. His eyes had turned to bowls of blood
out of rage. When his close retainers congratulated him, he
replied: "I am still in a state of ritual purity from the evening prayer."[1]

At dawn he called for a prayer rug and performed the dawn
prayer, then he turned to me. "Evliya," he said, "prepare Karpuzcu's four-paired caique right away. I have to go someplace."

"My sultan," I replied, "all the viziers and deputies and *ulema* and *imams* and preachers and *şeyhs* and *seyyids* and
other notables are about to come and eat wedding trotters.[2]
Where are you going?"

"Yes, where *am* I going.[3] Bring a caique right away." He
was quite incensed. I went immediately and brought Karpuzcu's
caique from the dock.

The Strange and Wondrous Adventure
of Melek Ahmed Pasha

Now the perfect pasha summoned his steward and treasurer and his other agents and gave them instructions: "Entertain my brother viziers and all the *ulema efendis* coming to the feast, show them due respect according to statute and protocol. There is something I must attend to." Four of us—the swordbearer, the valet, the seal-bearer, and myself—boarded the caique with the pasha. "Take us to the arsenal garden," he ordered, and we were whisked across.[4]

Alighting from the caique, we entered that paradisical garden on foot. The garden master came over and kissed the pasha's hand. "You stay behind," he said to him and to the other retainers, "Evliya and I will take a little stroll. Don't be concerned at all for us, and don't interrupt us!"

So the rest turned back, and the two of us entered the thickly wooded park just as the sun was rising. In the middle of the garden there is a large pool, and nearby, in the shade of five or ten lofty cypresses, there is a square grassy knoll, the size of a prayer carpet, marked off by a row of stones.

"My Evliya," said Melek Pasha when we reached this spot, "do you know this tulipbed?"

"No, my sultan."

"During the seige of Constantinople, when Sultan Mehmed the Conqueror was bombarding the city across the way, it was at this very spot, in this pleasure park, that the sainted Ak Şemseddin carried out forty-day trials and austerities.[5] He dwelt here until Istanbul was conquered. And supplications are still answered in this rosebed: by God's command, all worldly and otherworldly blessings are achieved. Come now, let us each perform two prostrations of 'need-worship' (*hacet namazı*), then I will make supplication, and you say 'amen.' "

"All right, my sultan."

Noteworthy Deeds of Melek Ahmed Pasha

We each performed two prostrations in this station of the *şeyh*. Thereupon Melek Pasha took out the dagger from his waistband and began digging the ground. He made a small hole, then lay face down, buried his beard in the hole, and covered his beard with earth. Reminding me to say "amen" he said:

"Lord, greetings from You to You. Your slave Melek Ahmed is an old beggar of Yours. Once again he has come to Your gate. You have never turned him away from Your gate empty handed. Now again he has come to You, God. For the sake of Your glory and Your majesty, for the sake of Your 124,000 prophets, and in particular for the spirit of Your beloved Muhammed el-Mustafa; for the honor of 'the boy of my home,' Your lover Veysülkarani,[6] and Your 77,000 meritorious and perfected chiefs of the saints;—accept the prayer of this slave of Yours, Ahmed.

"Evliya, say 'amen'!" he cried. But I was dumbstruck.

"Oh Lord, this is my prayer: either take my soul and my faith, and rescue me from the filth of this world, or else save me from Fatma Sultan.

"Come on, Evliya, say 'amen'!"

"Come on, my sultan! How can I say 'amen' to a prayer in this place?"

He kept rubbing his face and his eyes on the ground, uttering, "Oh Lord, Oh Lord, accept my prayer." Then he moaned and groaned for quite a while, then went into a rather lengthy mystical meditation. He stood up and sat down. When I looked at his handsome face his cheeks and eyes and beard were covered with pure mud and dirt. He must have been weeping profusely, for his tears had turned that perfumed dust into a seal of Lemnian earth, his light-filled face was stained with clay, and he glared at me like a raging lion. At last he heaved such a deep sigh, it seemed that all the trees in the arsenal garden trembled. My own body shook like an autumn leaf, and every hair on my head stood on end.

"My Evliya," he said, "you are my confidant. You are my kinsman and my brother, my dear soul! Let me tell you, but keep it secret."

"Go ahead, my sultan."

"My Evliya, there is a saying, 'Your prayer was accepted, but the arrow turned back the mark.' You needn't worry: you won't be friendless after I am gone. You have many faithful lovers. You will live a long time and travel much. Just don't forget me in your benedictions."

He recited *elhākümü³t-tekāsür* (Koran, *sure* 102) ten times. Then we stood up from that rose-garden spot and began to stroll at random in the arsenal park. The tears streamed like a river from those narcissuslike doe-eyes of his. When we came to the big pool, which I mentioned above, he washed the dirt off his face. Then we rested a while at the Conqueror's prayer ground.

"My Evliya," he began again, "do you know this arsenal park? It is an ancient garden of paradise that has served all the kings of Istanbul since Yanko ibn Madyan who founded the city. What conversations have been held in this garden, what acts of piety and worship have been performed, by Sultan Mustafa and Sultan Osman and Sultan Murad Khan. God be praised, once again our supplication has hit its mark in this place where prayers are answered."

As he said this I noticed that his wrath had dissipated slightly and the light of grace had been restored. "My sultan," I cried, "what a fine rage you are in today!"

Complaint of Melek over Fatma Sultan, Daughter of Ahmed Khan

"My Evliya, let this be a secret between us. The tortures I have suffered from that wife of mine during this nuptial night are not visited on the Malta captives. God forgive me, what a shameless immodest extravagant woman!

"As soon as I entered the harem, having uttered a *besmele*, I saw her. Now I am supposed to be her husband, and this is our first night—she ought to show me just a little respect. She just sat there, stock still, not moving an inch. I went up and kissed her hand.

" 'Pasha,' she says, 'welcome.'

" 'God be praised that I have seen my sultan's smiling beauty,' says I, and I shower her with all sorts of self-deprecating flatteries. Not once does she invite me to sit down. And she puts on all kinds of virginal airs, as though she weren't an ancient crone who has gone through twelve husbands!

"The first pearl from her lips is this: 'My dear pasha, if you want to get along with me, whether you are present at court or absent in some government post, my expenses are 15 purses each and every month. Also I owe my steward, Keremetçi Mustafa Agha, 100 purses: pay my debt in the morning. And every year I get six Marmara boatloads of firewood. And my retainers Selman Beg and Ömer Beg and Mukbil Agha and my steward get as a daily stipend 100 bushels of barley each, 10 *okkas* of coffee, 10 *okkas* of fine sugar, and nightly 10 *okkas* of camphor beeswax'—and on and on with suchlike nonsense, spouting these expenses like a talking inventory. Several times she pinched my cheeks.[7] But I was like a walking skeleton.

"Now her stewardess and treasuress and ladies-in-waiting and, in short, 300 or more women come to kiss my hand and stand there in rows. 'Well, my dear pasha, these are my servants of the interior. I also have as many or more manumitted slave girls on the exterior. Together with children and dependents they total 700 souls. You will provide all of them with their annual stipend of silk and gauze and brocade and broadcloth. And you will pay the annual stipend to all my halberdiers and cooks and gardeners and coachmen and eunuchs and *begs*, as well as those serving them, numbering 500 people. And if you don't— well, you know the consequence!'

" 'I swear by God, my sultan,' says I, 'that I have just returned from the Transylvania campaign. I am a vizier who fights the holy war. In that campaign I had 7,000 men to feed. I spent 170,000 goldpieces and 600 purses.[8] I even had to sell quite a lot of equipment and arms and armor and helmets and to borrow money from the janissary corps. I am no tyrant, that I should extract money unjustly in the posts to which I am assigned to feed you so extravagantly. I am unable to bear such expenses. Also, I have quite a few servants and retinue of my own. I am a campaigner. These expenses are too much. Please reduce them a little. I was able to bear the expenses required by the late Kaya Sultan; but this is five times as much, and I don't have the resources.'

" 'Well, my dear pasha,' she shoots back, 'do you consider me like Kaya Sultan? She was my brother's daughter. Whereas I am the daugher of your lord Sultan Ahmed Khan. Just look at this slave of my father! He considers Kaya girl and me the same!'

" 'God forbid, my sultan, that I should consider you the same. You are Ahmed Khan's daughter, a seventy-seven-year-old lady. You have lived long, have seen many men's faces, and have gone through twelve husbands.[9] Whereas I married Kaya Sultan when she was a thirteen-year-old virgin who had not seen any man's face except her father's. She lived as chastely as Rabia-ı Adeviyye[10] and she died while yet married to me. She was Kaya Ismehan, a peerless girl, a shining moon. You are an old lady, run down and used up, with wrinkles on your face. How could I even consider you the same as her?!'

" 'Look here, bridegroom! Since you consider me old, why did you marry me?'

" 'God forbid! I had no notion of marrying you. While I was away campaigning in Transylvania and completely unaware, you went ahead and married me here in Istanbul. The news of our marriage reached me in Transylvania. Just as I was thanking God for having rescued me from Kaya Sultan's expenses I heard that the late Köprülü had married me off to you. "I gave Melek an elephant, let him feed her," he said, then he upped and died. Well, here I am. It is God's to command.'

" 'My pasha,' she says, 'if you can't get along with me I will divorce you, dead or alive. Be prepared to pay my dowry amounting to an Egyptian treasure.'[11]

"We had all sorts of quarrels until morning. What a wedding night! It was a night of ———.[12] Finally, an hour before dawn I said: 'My sultan, you take all these extravagant expenditures which you have mentioned, and if I come here again may God take my soul!' I came out and performed the dawn prayer with you while still in a state of ritual purity from the evening prayer. Then we came to this spot, and God be praised, our prayer has been accepted. God forgive me, I will not go again to Fatma Sultan's palace. God willing, I will never see her face again."

In this manner, weeping the while, did he relate to me in the arsenal garden, point by point, all that had transpired between himself and the sultana.

Reboarding the caique, we crossed to the Bağçe Kapı landing where he mounted his horse and rode directly to the grand vizier, Köprülü-zade Ahmed Pasha. The grand vizier entertained him and congratulated him on his wedding, then accompanied Melek Pasha to the felicitious Padishah, who said, "My *lala* Melek Pasha, may your marriage with my aunt be blessed." He had the pasha don a sable cloak, and continued: "My *lala* Melek, I have made you second in the *divan*, just below my grand vizier. And I have granted you the *sancak* of Afyon Karahisar as an imperial grant by way of stipend (*arpalık*)."[13]

"It is my Padishah's to command," replied the long-suffering pasha. Emerging from the imperial presence, he made his way to his own palace, and began to frequent the imperial *divan* for a three-month period. I begged leave to accompany his agent to Afyon Karahisar, but he denied my request, saying, "I need you for a few days."

And indeed, a few days later, certain corrupt and irreligious slanderers and busybodies bruited it about that "Melek Ahmed Pasha and Fatma Sultan quarreled on their wedding night."

Eventually the gossip reached the royal ear of Sultan Mehmed Khan. So one assembly day his majesty the world-refuge Padishah addressed the pasha, saying: "Has my *lala* Melek Pasha quarreled with my aunt? These things happen. No one can interfere between man and wife. Still, I will try to reconcile you." He made some witty comments. When the pasha emerged from the assembly hall after the *divan*, he proceeded to his palace, performed the *ebvabin* prayer,[14] and rested.

Exploits of the Saintlike Ecstatics[15]

Despite so many gatekeepers and watchmen guarding the gates, in through the door of the pasha's cell burst a Bektaşi dervish, shaven in the "four strokes" manner,[16] beardless and heart-wounded, with a halberd in his hand and a sheepskin apron round his waist; decked with bells and plumes; his "pocketbook of love" and *palheng*-stone at his waist, his "water-pot" awry on his head, his chest gashed and shirtless; mad, wild, naked and hairless; barefoot and bareheaded; his doe-eyes tinged with collyrium. This Bektaşi saint of the Turks (*abdal-i Rum*) appeared at the door crying, "Love to you, Melek Khan, love to you!" Begging leave, he removed the trumpet from his waistband and let out several thunderous blasts with that clarion trumpet, leaving us stunned.

The gentle pasha merely smiled and said, "Dervish, you are welcome. From what land and through what gate have you come?"

"I have come from our court," the dervish replied, "from the land of our lord, and I have entered your arsenal[17] through your gate. God be praised that I have seen the beauty of your rose."

"Dede," said the pasha, "have you brought me any greetings?"

"I have, by God, my Padishah. I bring you greetings from the saints of Spain, currenty the land of the infidels. Balurba Erşek sends your noble self greetings, along with this letter and this book, saying: 'Henceforth let Melek Dede peruse the *Tarikat-i Muhammediye;*[18] let him serve in the post of Budin (or: this religion);[19] let him be free of all guile and henceforth let him wear garments of cotton cloth.' "

With this he drew out of his pocketbook a quantity of cotton cloth and some needles and thread and incense and gum benzoin and camphor and raw ambergris. Handing these over to the pasha he said, "Forgive the effrontery of presenting you with

these gifts. We will recall you in our prayers; may you, too, not
forget to pray for us for a few days. Yāhū to you!" He went out the
door and slipped away through so many servants.

"Hey, don't let the Dede get away!"

Several people searched for him, but could not find a trace.
We were all astounded. Afterwards we read the book which the
dervish had brought. It was indeed the *Tarikat-i Muhammediye*, but the copy was one of the books printed in Europe![20]

"Bring a horse!" cried the pasha. *The ominous words of
Melek Ahmed Pasha.* The vizierial pasha immediately put his
book into his bosom and, taking with him a pastille of ambergris, mounted his zephyr-swift steed and rode directly to the
şeyhülislam, Sunʿizade Efendi. He removed the *Tarikat-i Muhammediye* from his bosom and showed it to the şeyhülislam
who perused it and found it to contain passages relating to the
final gathering and the resurrection and life and death.

"A fine book, God bless us! Indeed you should read this
book at every occasion."

Melek Pasha restored the book to his bosom, gave the şeyhülislam the pastille of ambergris and a rare Kashmir shawl,
and said: "Do not forget us in your supplications. And when you
are performing the prayer service mention us with a benediction
and make our heart happy. And from time to time come to visit
us." He uttered several such ominous expressions, then took his
leave from the şeyhülislam, and they wept as though they
would never meet again.

Returning to his palace, the pasha presented all of his
aghas with several hundred precious items out of his treasury.
In the morning he returned to the imperial *divan.*

A Brief Account of the Reason for the Death
of the Late Melek Ahmed Pasha

By God's wisdom, that very day Melek Ahmed Pasha ate
too much in the *divan* and also quaffed various beverages
from strange hands. Feeling a bit queasy, he got leave from the
grand vizier to absent himself from the domed council chamber
and return to his palace, it being Sunday. He was quite weak
and listless.

That Tuesday was to be a high *divan* in which 5,000 purses
were to be disbursed to all the Ottoman *kuls.* The pasha informed
his retinue that he would not attend the *divan.* When I entered
his chamber he said, "Evliya, what are the people saying?"

"They are saying what they are saying," I replied. "But aren't you going to attend the *divan* today?"

"To tell the truth, I feel quite poorly. I can't go."

"But today is a high *divan*, and the *kuls* are to receive their salaries. If there is an uprising among the *kuls*, if they refuse their soup[21] and don't take up their salaries, it will give rise to all sorts of malicious gossip and groundless accusations. People will say that Melek Ahmed Pasha knew about the uprising and for this reason he did not attend the *divan* and that he instigated the *kuls* not to take up the purses. Aren't you a man? Now, muster your strength. Call continually on God the Strong, the Firm, the Living, the Standing. And go to the *divan*."

"By God, may you prosper, my Evliya," replied the foresightful pasha. "Hurry, bring a horse, get me dressed and drag me like a corpse to the *divan*."

So he put on his *divan* outfit, dragged himself out of bed, mounted and rode straight to the council chamber where, ill as he was, he conversed with the grand vizier. Then the salaries were disbursed to the *kuls* according to Ottoman statute, and after prayers and benedictions they all went to their barracks. At this juncture, when the viziers were about to enter the royal assembly, Melek Pasha begged leave of the grand vizier; and although horses are not allowed at the council chamber, they brought Melek Pasha's horse all the way to the mounting block of the felicitous Padishah and managed, with ten or fifteen men, to get the pasha on his horse. He returned to his palace in a daze, and lay down to rest. Later that day he began to spit up black clots of blood.

On Tuesday, Wednesday, and Thursday he continued to spit up blood and clotted matter. He kept reciting God's name. Now he would lay his blessed head upon the pillow, now upon this humble one's knee. With his own money he freed 105 slave boys, bestowing on them their mounts and gear, plus 100 goldpieces each. He made his last will and testament in the presence of all the *ulema* and notables, bequeathing 5,000 goldpieces to his servants, 3,000 for his palace in Galata, 3,000 for the large room and the small room,[22] 3,000 for his palace in Ibrahim-pasha, and setting aside 3,000 for his own laying out and burial.

> This gold, which I have given over to the endowment administrator, is a divine trust. Have complete Koran recitals performed in each of the rooms every night, for the sake

of God, and let their religious merit be a free-will offering
on behalf of my soul. Have 40,000 noble invocations be recited each Friday eve for the sake of the spirit of the
Prophet. And do not put my body in a tomb with a vault,
but bury me at the felicitous foot of my patron and master,
the sainted Kiçi Mehmed Efendi, in the vicinity of Ebu
Eyub Ansari. Do not raise a dome or other building above
my grave. Just plant tombstones at my head and my feet. I
give 1,000 goldpieces to my son Ibrahim, and 1,000 to my
daughter ———— Fatma. I commend them to God, and those
who descend from them I commit to the Omnipotent, the
Self-subsistent, the All-compelling.

Thus for seven full hours he made his last will and testament. Censers were lit, burning incense, raw ambergris, and aloes. In chorus with his personal retainers he recited the noble
Yasin (Koran, sure 36). Not once did he perform his prayers
without a congregation nor did he once miss a prayer and have
to make it up later.

Finally, on Friday evening in the year ————, toward morning, while his noble head was on this humble one's knee, and as
I was reciting the verse from the noble Yasin: "It was but a single shout" (36:29), he shouted out once: "Ya Allah!" and turned
toward the kıble, in the throes of death. Then his victorious
spirit flowed from the perishing realm to the unperishing realm,
he surrendered his noble soul to God, he reached the station of
the loftiest paradise; may God have mercy on his soul.

A Strange Story

As soon as dawn broke, a coach drove up and Fatma Sultan
emerged, saying, "He is my lawful husband, he owes me an
Egyptian treasure as dowry." She put her seal on all the rooms
and on the treasury, drove us all outdoors, and had the pasha's
noble bier left outside in the council hall. For our part, having
just begun to moan and wail, we flew into a panic when we saw
our lord treated in this fashion and realized that all our money
had fallen into the hands of women.

By God's wisdom, just then the grand vizier, Köprülü-oğlu
Ahmed Pasha, arrived. My eyes had already turned to bowls of
blood. "Noble vizier," I cried,[23] "don't leave our late lord like this.
Right now Fatma Sultan is inside. She has confiscated the

treasury and taken our money and our rooms as well, and they have left our lord like this."

Köprülü-zade, God bless him, immediately took his knife in his hand and began to break the seals on the 320 sealed rooms and the pantries and the treasuries. Meanwhile Fatma Sultan fled in disguise through the back gate, leaving her coach behind.

As soon as Köprülü-zade emerged, all of Melek's servants fell at his feet and cried blessings upon him. The vizier wept. "My father Mehmed Pasha died and I did not weep so much," he said. "This man was as dear to me as a father, and I am desolate at his loss. Take his noble bier down to the courtyard right away and wash his body."

They laid him out, having performed the *ıskat* prayer,[24] sent out calls for the funeral service, washed the body, wrapped it in the shroud, and placed it in the coffin. "We'll bury him next to my father," said Köprülü-zade. But our *imam*, Mehmed Efendi, and I told Köprülü-zade of the pasha's last wish, to be buried next to his master, (Kiçi) Mehmed Efendi.

"Gentlemen, that won't do. He was a noble vizier. We'll bury him in the tomb of Boynu-kara Mustafa Pasha, or in the tomb of the conqueror of Yemen, Sinan Pasha."

"No, my sultan, accede to his last wish."

"Well, so be it."

All the viziers and deputies and *ulema* and *şeyhs* assembled and we placed Melek Ahmed Pasha's coffin at the oratory gate of the great mosque of Aya Sofya.

Now the *şeyhülislam*, Sun'izade, said: "We are charged to perform the ritual prayer for padishahs and princes and sultanas. But five days ago this Melek Pasha came to us and made ominous utterances, saying, 'Sir, do not forget us in your supplications; and when you are performing the prayer service for us, mention us with a benediction; and from time to time come to visit us.' So we will perform the ritual prayer for this Muslim."

They went over to Melek's bier. The *şeyhülislam*, serving as prayer leader, said: "We know this vizier to be a good man. May God have mercy on his soul." And 40,000 or 50,000 men cried in response: "God have mercy on his soul!"

As they were bearing Melek's coffin in the funeral procession, this humble one gathered fifty or sixty *müezzins* and the same number of dervishes and we followers of Bilal[25] recited prayers and litanies in fine voice, crying: "Muhammed is the friend of God, Hakk-a!" The coffin was placed in a caique at the

Bağçe Kapı landing, and the cortege of several thousand viziers and friends and lovers boarded as many as a thousand separate caiques. Passing in front of Fatma Sultan's *yalı* at Ebu Ansari gate, we proceeded to the vicinity of the late Kaya Sultan's *yalı* near Ebu Eyub Ansari, where we buried him in accordance with his last wish at the foot of his master, the sainted Kiçi Mehmed Efendi, and without a sign—that is, without a dome. Tents were set up and night and day for several days this humble one, in the company of 300 dervishes, performed, each one of us, twenty complete Koran recitals. May God have mercy on his soul. . . .

*   *   *

Eulogy of Melek Pasha

[Koran verses, poems, etc., on death]

When our lord Melek Ahmed Pasha passed away, as God is my witness this humble one, because of the great love I bore him, wailed and wept so much that for a while I was stunned as though suffering an epileptic stroke. It was not merely that we were kin on our mothers' side. Rather, this was true love and admiration, "love for God's sake." When he died I was so overcome with weariness, that for me to drink a cup of venomous poison was no more than to drink a drop of purest water. Then I realized, weak slave that I am, that for a lover, dying for the sake of his beloved is everlasting life. For, aside from our kinship, I was in his service and enjoyed his favor for twenty-one years. It was he who enabled me to undertake so many journeys, and to participate in so many *gazas*. And not once during all those years did he look at me askance, not once did I hear an angry rebuke. It was never his practice to speak abusively. If he did get very upset at someone he might say, "You shameless one," or "You coward," but beyond this he would never utter an ugly word.

This humble one was always in his good graces, and I never made a move without his permission. I was his constant companion and confidant, the sharer of his secrets and the fellow on his path. I was at all times his boon companion and his interlocutor. Never did I hear him say a bitter word about me. I was all the times his servant, groveling in the ashes, and embarrassed by his bounty. May God inundate him with mercy.

Henceforth it behooves us to shower him with benedictions. God have mercy on his soul, and God be pleased with his spirit—El-Fatiha.

The Beginning and Birth of Our Lord the Late Melek Ahmed Pasha, His Growth and Upbringing, His Virtues and Excellent Deeds

It is a digression, to be sure; but it is appropriate, at this juncture in our narrative and while speaking of his death, that we relate as far as possible the course of his life, from rising to setting, and mention his noble spirit and his sterling character; in order that pure lovers who hear it may utter a benediction. Hopefully the benediction of his friends will be accepted at the divine court, and Melek's soul will rejoice in the everlasting realm. For, "What is with you perishes, and what is with God remains" (Koran, 16:96). In accordance with this definitive and evidential verse, the Living and Permanent One remains, and all else perishes. So my benedictions go to the souls passing from the perishing to the unperishing realms, because benedictions are acceptable with God at the divine court and are permanent; also, the dead are in need of benedictions.

This being the case, in order that the soul of Melek Pasha be remembered with benediction, let us recall his fine nature and sound qualities and enlightened heart, albeit a drop in the ocean and a mote in the sun. Were we to record all of his deeds and qualities it would require an entire scroll; but this humble and faulty slave, Evliya, on account of my kinship with the late pasha, and because I became so well acquainted with his secrets due to our intimate association, will record in our *Book of Travels* some part of his exploits and his exemplary character. Hopefully, those noble friends who read it will recite a Fatiha on behalf of Melek Pasha's spirit. Help is with God. "Alas, separation, separation, alas!"

The brethren of purity should know that Melek Ahmed Pasha's noble father was present at the conquest of Egypt (in 1517), serving as treasurer to Sultan Selim I's grand vizier, Kara Piri Pasha, who was a descendant of the caliph Ebu Bekr as-Sıddık. His own birth was among the Sadşa tribe, situated in the wilderness of the Elburz mountain skirt (i.e., the Caucasus), between the Circassians and the Abkhazians.[26] He was a military slave (*gulam-ı feta*). I will record here what I heard from (Melek's) own tongue by virtue of our kinship:

"My noble father was an old man. For forty-seven years he kept a coffin in his room, on the grounds that 'Today or tomorrow I shall die.' This was in his *yalı* in the village of Fındıklı, near Tophane. The coffin was made of cypress wood and stood in the closet at the head of his bed.

"My noble father served as chief of the guards to Özdemir Beg in Egypt. He was Özdemir Beg's nephew on his mother's side, and Özdemir was Sultan Gavri's nephew on his father's side. Tavaşi Süleyman Pasha, who was Süleyman Khan's vizier, departed from Egypt on a campaign to conquer Yemen and to invade the Indian Ocean. In the year ———[27] he left Yemen with 150 ships, crossed the ocean in five months, arrived in India, and with his sword took Diu, Benderabad, Dabulabad, and several other walled towns from the Portuguese Franks. Putting those cranky Franks to the sword, he captured so much booty that they threw overboard all the ballast and unnecessary gear and stuffed his ships with treasure and jewels. He turned over the keys of the above-mentioned castles to the emperor of India, who presented him in exchange with seven *leks* of money. In Turkish reckoning, one *lek* is equivalent to ——— (100,000). So all his corvettes were stowed tight with money and jewels and precious stuffs.

"Departing from India with the royal fleet, Süleyman Pasha proceeded to the port of Massawa in Abyssinia. He made Özdemir Beg commander of 12,000 fully armed troops. Of the Abyssinian ports, they took Dumbi, Burega, Meymun, Lulu, Suakin, Kif, Dehlek, Massawa, Harkova, Vula, Hindiye, Behlule, Zeyla, Vikat, Hediye, Razdan, Mogadishu[28]—in sum, 170 castles and towns were taken in the province of Habeş (Abyssinia) in seven months during the reign of Süleyman Khan at the hand of Tavaşi Süleyman Pasha of Egypt, with the help of the *gaza* of Özdemir Beg. This same Özdemir Beg became the first governor of the province of Habeş with the rank of *begler-beg*.

"After conquering Abyssinia, Süleyman Pasha returned with the fleet to Egypt, leaving Özdemir Pasha behind to govern Abyssinia, with Melek Ahmed Pasha's father serving as marshal of the guards. 'At that period,' my father used to say, 'I could shoot an eighty-seven dirhem musket from the arm.'[29] Also: 'To this age I have never known any forbidden liquors or intoxicants.' "

At a later period Melek's father served with Özdemir Pasha's son, Osman Pasha, when the latter, during the Persian campaign, conquered Gence, Şirvan, Şamaki, Tiflis, Tumanis, Serirüllan, Çıldır, ——— Tumük, Şeki, Ereş, Kars, Baku, Derbend, Gilan, and 110 other towns and castles and 9 *khanlıks*. This took place in the year 986 (1578) during the reign of Sultan Murad III. They made a treaty with Şamhal Khan, the ruler of Daghistan, whereby the coinage and the Friday sermon were in the name of the Ottomans, the Şamhals were enthroned by leave of the Ottomans, and the Ottoman troops took up winter quarters in Daghistan province. But as there was no currency in that region, Osman Pasha cut aspers out of leather and paid the *kuls* with that.

Then Melek Pasha's father, considering that his home country was nearby, got leave from Osman Pasha and traveled from Daghistan to the aforementioned province of Sadşa. Reunited with his kinsmen, he received as gifts seventy outstanding slave boys and beautiful virgin slave girls. Now, in Circassia and Abkhazia robbery is bravery; it is praised not blamed. To come to the point: among those captives was one girl, pure and lovely as the sun, whom he embraced, leaving her pregnant with Melek Ahmed Pasha in the land of the Abkhazians.

Just as the father was about to return to Daghistan with so many captives and booty, he learned that Osman Pasha had left that region and was traveling over the Kıpçak Steppe and Circassia to the Crimea, and thence by boat to Istanbul. So he proceeded with his goods from Sadşa to Abkhazia, boarded ship at the port known as Sovuk Su, and came to Istanbul where he settled in his house in the village of Fındıklı.

By the wisdom of the Creator, that year Melek appeared from the constellation of the sphere (*felek*) and from the fundament of mercy (*rahim*) when he came forth out of his mother's womb (*rahim*) as though a fairy were born; the luminous moon arose and the dark house was filled with a divine light. By God's wisdom, he and Abaza Mehmed Agha, who was İbrahim's equerry, and Abaza Ahmed Pasha—these three—were all born on the same day; and, according to the customs and usages of the Abkhazians, after being wrapped and swaddled, and without drinking a drop of their mothers' milk, they were given over to their foster mothers. For they say, "Lest our children be ridiculed as city boys, let them suffer homelessness and become men." So that very month all three orphan-pearls, along with their foster mothers, were put aboard the ship captained by a certain Kartıl-oğlu and taken to the land of the Abkhazians, where they were raised by their foster mothers in the province of———. Melek's real mother, meanwhile, stayed behind in Tophane with his father.

A Strange Fact

To this very day, among the Abkhazians of Tophane, some seventy or eighty cradled and swaddled newborns are given to foster mothers, along with travel expenses. Each year 100 or 200 infant boys and girls are sent to the country of the infidels and the Abkhazians, and their fathers and mothers cannot see their children for ten or fifteen years. This is their ancient custom.[30]

So, eleven years later, Melek Pasha, along with my own mother and forty other Abkhazian captives, were put aboard a ship at the Abkhazian port known as Sovuk Su and taken to Melek Pasha's father in Tophane. He in turn gave Melek along with my mother and fifteen bright young captives to Sultan Ahmed Khan as a gift. When Sultan Ahmed saw Melek, he kept him in the royal harem, for he appeared to him spirit incarnate, pure loveliness, as though born of a fairy. "God knows," said Ahmed Khan, "that this boy has attained perfection.[31] The beauty that is upon him sets a man's mind aflame in a moment. His form is angelic, his manner fairylike; he is well-mannered and rose-countenanced; his teeth are hidden pearls, his speech is harmonious; he has attained the pinnacle of beauty and of noble grace; with his doe-eyes, his sweet speech, and his shining face; a boy like the moon." Thus he praised Melek to the skies.

Among those present in that company was a certain Kalender Pasha, the trustee of the new mosque.[32] "My Padishah," said he, "bestow a name and a nickname on this boy."

Sultan Ahmed replied: "God must have been referring to this boy when he said in the *sure* of the Fig (95:4), "We indeed created man of the fairest stature." He created him an angel, and nobler than an angel. What name can *I* give him? He is an angel (*melek*), so let him be Melek Ahmed, with his name like my own. Let him be distinguished among my own *gulams* and the company of my viziers. May he live a long life, until his appointed term."

Thus was he called Melek Ahmed. "Names descend from Heaven."

Immediately thereupon Üsküdari Mahmud Efendi and my master Evliya Efendi said: "A Fatiha on this intention." They recited the *Muavvizeteyn* and puffed some air over Melek.[33]

"It does not seem right for this boy to be anywhere but here," said Ahmed Khan the Innocent.[34] He personally handed him over to the black eunuch Veli Mustafa, saying, "My dear *lala*, I give you this boy as a divine trust. Teach him to read and write, raise him up properly. I'll be checking to see what kind of upbringing you give him."

"To tell the truth, my Padishah," replied Mustafa, "it is apparent from this boy's face that God has made him perfect already, with no need for a tutor; He has raised him up with His own hand of power. So he will only lie down and get up with us."

Now this Mustafa Agha was actually a very religious man, suspected of being a saint. He used to assemble his servants every Friday, with Melek among them, and perform 40,000 invocations on behalf of the Prophet's spirit; and he himself would recite *Innā aʿṭaynā* (Koran, *sure* 108) 1,001 times. Then that night he would see the Prophet in his dreams. Several times he was blessed with beatific visions and celestial conversations.

Thus Melek Pasha was favored with the regard and the patronage of such a Cemşid-like Padishah, and such a blessed agha, and Üsküdari Mahmud Efendi, and Evliya Efendi, and thousands of other notables and saints.

On the same day that Melek was presented to Sultan Ahmed Khan, the sultan presented each of his courtiers with a *gulam*. And upon this humble one's father, Derviş Mehmed Agha, who was chief goldsmith of the Sublime Porte, Sultan Ahmed Khan, may his earth be sweet, bestowed my mother, saying, "Grand agha, you are an old man, but God willing, from this maiden you will have an angellike world-adorning son."

"God willing," echoed Üsküdari Mahmud Efendi, "this girl will soon conceive and give birth to a noble and upright male child."

"And God willing," piped in Evliya Efendi, "we will educate him and train him."

Praise be to God, nine months and ten days later this humble one came into the world, during the reign of Sultan Ahmed Khan, in the year ———.[35] And in ——— (1032/1623), the year in which Sultan Murad IV assumed the throne, my father gave me to the royal *imam*, *şeyh* of the readers and leader of the *şeyhs*, Evliya Efendi; I became one of his pupils, and he made me one of his spiritual sons. From Evliya Efendi I mastered the science of *hıfz* (reciting the Koran from memory), and I could recite the entire Koran in eight hours, without addition or subtraction, and without error whether open or hidden.

[Technical verses on Koran recitation.]

And every Friday eve (Thursday night) I was appointed to complete a Koran recital. God be praised, from childhood until the present, whether at home or during my travels, I have not abandoned this practice. And I performed several hundred Koran recitals on Friday eves in the presence of the late Melek Ahmed Pasha. In fact, he, too, when I was in the imperial harem, used to take recitation lessons from Evliya Efendi, and he once performed a complete recital from memory, although he did not study the reading of Ibn-i Kethir; and he heard me recite from memory many times. God be praised, I am a bearer of the Koran; "This is from my Lord's bounty." And I mastered the reading of Ibn-i Kethir from beginning to end, as well as the book of Şatibi consisting of ———— couplets and the book of Cezeri consisting of ———— couplets; and I performed it from memory in seven hours in the presence of Evliya Efendi and all the leading *şeyhs*. Subsequently I learned the seven variant readings as far as the *sure* of Yusuf (*sure* 12). When our master Evliya Mehmed Efendi died in the year ———— Şami Yusuf Efendi became royal *imam*, and I learned the seven variants from him as far as the noble Yasin (*sure* 36). When he died in the year ———— I completed my study of the seven variants with Şami Efendi, who was the *imam* of the Haydarpaşa quarter mosque in Istanbul and later became *imam* of the Sultan Selim Khan Friday mosque. Praise be to God.

Now, in the year 1051 in the month of Muharrem (= April 1641) I first set out on the world of travel with Melek Ahmed Pasha, and subsequently, he being the son of my mother's paternal aunt,[36] we journeyed together and passed through many lands. And since I have made it my duty to record Melek Ahmed Pasha's character and virtues, I have given tongue to my pen and made it speak. And although it may not seem proper to expatiate on the subject, nevertheless because of the due of bread and salt we will mention his good qualities, and from those well-disposed friends who hear the account of his fine character we solicit a Fatiha on behalf of this one of small store, Evliya the unhypocritical, and on behalf of the spirit of our lord the late Melek Ahmed Pasha—El-Fatiha!

First of all: After the death of Sultan Ahmed, the late Melek, being a vigorous youth, twice served in the imperial pantry at the accessions of Sultan Mustafa (in 1026/1617 and 1031/1622). And he accompanied Sultan Osman (II) on the Chotin campaign (in 1030/1621). During that campaign Melek's father served as chief of the guards to Karakaş Pasha, the vizier of Budin; and when this Karakaş Pasha was martyred, having been struck in the forehead by a bullet during the *tabur* battle below Chotin,[37] Melek's father left government service and withdrew to private life in the village of Fındıklı in Istanbul.

Melek Pasha returned to Istanbul with Osman Khan, who was then unjustly put to death in the fortress of Yedi Kule during the uprising of the rebels (Receb 1031/May 1622). When Sultan Murad IV became independent Padishah in the year ———— (1032/1623) Melek Ahmed Agha entered the imperial chamber (*has oda*). At that time he was a champion with his first mustache, a swashbuckling youth. He accompanied Murad Khan on his Edirne and Bursa campaigns.[38] Once this humble one was performing a complete Koran recital after the supererogatory prayers on the Night of Power[39] in Aya Sofya the great, and when I reached the *sure* of A'rāf (*sure* 7), by order of Murad Khan, the *bostancı-başı* and Melek Agha, who was then stirrup-holder, took me down from the *müezzins'* gallery and presented me to Murad Khan. He took this lowly one into the imperial pantry and appointed the chief panter Hadım Gazanfer Agha as my tutor. Evliya Efendi continued to come in and give me lessons, and I continued to recite the Koran. I became royal companion to Murad Khan, and we had all sorts of conversations together.

Later, when the sovereign went off on the Revan campaign (1045/1635), Melek Agha was valet. After the conquest of Revan, when Murad Khan stopped at Van fortress, Koca Nişancı became the object of the imperial anger and was dismissed from his office as sword-bearer,[40] and Melek became sword-bearer in Van. He remained in this office until the conquest of Baghdad (1048/1638) where, below the city after the conquest, he was made vizier of three horsetails and was sent with the grand vizier Kara Mustafa Pasha to lay down bounds and frontiers between the province of Diyarbekir and the Persian provinces of Derne, Derteng, Hamadan, Dergüzin, and Şehrezul. When the treaties were drawn up, Murad Khan returned to the capital. Kara Mustafa Pasha took the texts of the peace treaty and the boundary treaty to Diyarbekir with Melek, then followed Murad Khan to the capital. Murad Khan died in that year, 1048,[41] and Ibrahim Khan acceeded to the throne. Melek Pasha remained in Diyarbekir.

But 100,000 soldiers stood ready below Diyarbekir and Mardin for the defense of Baghdad. Melek Pasha, on the lookout toward Baghdad, stayed with his sealike troop night and day, fully armed, each man with a fodder bag on the back of his saddle, patrolling the province of Diyarbekir, hunting game and hunting down rebels and foes whom he put to death according to the *şeriat*. In fact there was one Kurdish ruler known as Sultan Yusuf, the governor of——— (Müzuri),[42] whom he captured in a night raid and brought to Diyarbekir in chains, where he was confined in the fortress. Yusuf Khan ransomed himself for 100 purses, expressed his repentance and was released.

There are many such stories and anecdotes relating to this period. We have abbreviated the account here, because we have gathered all the *gazas* and exploits and adventures in a separate volume of chronicles, entitled *The Gestes of Melek Ahmed Pasha*.

After that he again mustered an army of 80,000 from Diyarbekir and in the year ———[43] he wielded a Muhammedan sword against the Yezidi Kurds of Mt. Sincar, killing 13,000 hairy Yezidi Kurds, and thus taking revenge for the martyrs of the plain of Kerbela. He also took more than 10,000 captives, great and small, including their *bapirs* or "sultans," girls and boys and women, and returned with them in chains safely to Diyarbekir.

Things were quiet for a while, and he spent the time performing religious exercises with the saintly *şeyh* of Urmia,[44] as he had accepted the equipment of poverty[45] of the Hocagan Nakşbendis. He always used to recite their formulas and litanies, and his actions were directed to the welfare of the Muslims.

And in whatever direction he turned he was victorious. The arrow of his intention struck its mark. He brought to hand all the upstarts and rebels and highwaymen and, giving them no quarter, but according to the *şeriat* and by means of his decisive Muhammedan sword, he eradicated their persons from the page of Time.

At no time did a falsehood issue from his lips. He spoke little and wept much and laughed sparingly. In his councils he never allowed idle talk and malicious gossip. But if a tasteful witticism was uttered in his presence, he would smile so broadly that you could see his teeth. He did not every day let fall from his noble tongue such obscene expressions as "Fuck this" and "Fuck that." If he was roused to anger, as when some outlaw was either sentenced to death according to the şeriat, or else deserved such a sentence, he would only say, "You shameless one!" or, "You coward; repent your crime and save yourself from the pain of this world."

He was so scrupulous in his dress that he only wore garments sanctioned by religious law—various cotton stuffs,[46] and those silken weaves and other splendid stuffs not forbidden by the şeriat. And he was so clean and neat and elegant and refined, that he was famous among the viziers—his skirts were cleaner than the collars of his peers. In fact the late Sultan Murad used to say, "Ahmed, you are cleaner than me, and you are without fear or care; may God make your face white (i.e., keep you pure and free from shame) in both worlds and vouchsafe you the bliss of both abodes." Then Murad Khan would intone these verses:

Pak-damana yok sözüm asla
Hiz-i napake günde biñ lanet

I have nothing to say against the one with clean skirts.
A thousand curses a day on the unclean catamite.

He would look the little sword-bearer Mustafa in the face and say, "What do you think about this poem Mustafa?" and the sword-bearer would turn red in the cheeks from embarrassment. Then he would present Melek and the sword-bearer each with a sable robe of honor.

Indeed, Melek Pasha was clean skirted (i.e., chaste) in every respect, and was pure in every respect. He was very upright and pious, learned in religious sciences and active in carrying out religious prescriptions; he was virtuous and abstinent; a perfect *gazi* and brave vizier, the likes of Asaf son of Barakhya (the vizier of Solomon). He used to say, "From my childhood I have not been inclined to mingling with children and indulging in games and levity." Still, he was very skilled in archery, which is a *sünnet* of the Prophet, and in such sports as javelin throwing, swordplay, mace, and spear. And among his peers only Ipşir Pasha and Seydi Ahmed Pasha could rival him in horsemanship and cavalry exercises. Being a strong and courageous champion, he was also unexcelled in wrestling, familiar with seventy branches of that science: very few champions could bring his back to the ground. But sometimes he would have nice wrestling matches with his wife Kaya Sultan, for the propagation of the species. In the end he would overcome Kaya Sultan and bring her down. He engaged in this sort of "greatest *cihad*" forty-eight times a year—he did not indulge overmuch in sexual intercourse.

In sum, we are not acquainted with any vizier, from the time of Sultan Ahmed Khan to that of Sultan Murad Khan IV, who was so innocent and pure, so enlightened and so courageous. To be sure, Koca Bostancı and Koca Musa Pasha and Koca Kenan Pasha also had a reputation for innocence—God have mercy on them all.

As for Melek Pasha, he never took a single step without performing his ablutions. Even when he engaged in sexual intercourse, he would immediately perform ablutions, then do the nighttime supererogatory prayers.[47] He spent the capital of his precious life in the "fast of David." His associates and companions were always the *ulema*, the pious *şeyhs*, the dervishes, the weak and the poor. Among the preachers he was especially fond of Veli Efendi and Erdebili-zade. Attar's *Pend-name* was always on his tongue: he had gotten all its verses by heart.[48] He read a good many books on the science of grammar; and was without equal in the science of canon law, particularly the laws of inheritance. He had by heart over 800 problems of the *şeriat* and over 1,000 prophetic Hadiths. Because he was inclined to the dervish path, he had on the tip of his tongue several thousand verses of the noble *Mesnevi* of Mevlana (Rumi) and the *Manevi* of Ibrahim Gülşeni,[49] plus Persian and Turkish odes and mystical ghazels that he could recite at appropriate occasions.

In the science of calligraphy he (illustrated the Hadith,[50] "the best) script is what is legible." Still, he had been authorized by Sultan Murad IV to draw the illustrious *tuğra*, and under his tutelage he learned to draw it in a manner that rivaled the pens of Bihzad and Mani. Koca Nişancı Ankebut Ahmed Pasha, Nasuh-paşa-zade, Ömer Beg, and our head of chancellery Gınayi Efendi—all stood agape at Melek's *tuğra*.

In the early mornings he used to recite the litany of God's beautiful names in his private cell. On Monday evenings (Sunday nights) he performed 40,000 noble invocations together with his aghas of the interior, and on Friday evenings (Thursday nights) he would recite the noble Ihlas (Koran, *sure* 112) 12,000 times. Even now, due to a *vakf* of 12,000 goldpieces that he sent from Baghdad, every Monday and Friday evening 40,000 invocations of the Prophet and 40,000 recitations of the noble Ihlas are performed in accordance with his former practice in the small room and the large room of his private harem. This is a grand and wonderful pious establishment.

The Remarkable Pious Acts of the Late Melek Ahmed Pasha

Every year on the first day of Ramazan he would open his treasury, and his servants would remove whatever valuable garments and vessels and weapons and other precious items there were, and pile them up like mountains. Then he would "auction" these goods off among his 345 interior aghas. Thus, for example, he would sell a suit of armor for 1,000 invocations; a sword for 50,000; a sable fur for a complete Koran recital; a coral prayer bead for 2,000 invocations; a jeweled musket for a Koran recital. His treasurer would keep a record of the number of invocations and Koran recitals each person committed himsef for. Then on Monday and Friday evenings his marshals of the interior service would make a public announcement, and everyone would come and carry out his obligations. These evenings were like the Night of Power,[51] everyone eating musky sweetmeats of pistachios and almonds, drinking fruit syrups, and reciting prayers. In this fashion his treasury was completely emptied of weapons and other items; but by the following year, by God's command, it was even fuller than before.

Whenever he went off to a provincial post, in order that the seven or eight precious hours not be wasted while traversing the stages of the journey, he would assemble all his interior aghas and they would ride together as a body in the mountains or deserts or orchards, reciting aloud with a single voice the *sure* of Victory (*sure* 48) or the *Muavvizeteyn* (*sures* 113 and 114), causing the mountains and the valleys to resound.

After Koran recitations, to acquaint his interior aghas and his conscripts (*levend*) with the arts of warfare, he would line them up against one another to play forty or fifty rounds of jereed, or to show their skill in swordplay and archery or to fire guns from horseback in the Egyptian manner. Afterwards the marshals would stop these exercises, so as not to tire the horses, and they would enter camp in good order.

He had a great fondness for horses, especially Arab steeds of good pedigree, such as Cilfidan, Ma'nek, Tarifi, Seylavi, Keb-işe, Mahmudi, Musafaha, Havara, Mühre, and Mehrani; and he liked to have seventy or eighty of them put through their paces in his presence, under the awning of his tent pavilion.

Before marrying Kaya Sultan he had 700 purchased slave boys, for the most part Circassian and Abkhazian and Georgian *gulams*. He did not use to purchase Ukrainian[52] *gulams*, considering them degenerate and ill-mannered. If he received one as a gift, he accepted him, but then gave him away to one of his aghas.

He was also very fond of hunting, and used to ride out for picnics, playing all sorts of pieces on his military band according to the regulation of the viziers. When he returned from these excursions he would donate the greater part of the game right and left as largesse to the dervishes before he reached home.

Never did he accept bribes or allow others to accept them, nor did he get posts by means of bribery. Rather, he accepted dismissal from office. Of course, he did use to send some of the specialties of the regions he was governing, or some thorough-bred horses, as gifts (*pişkeş*) to the imperial stirrup and to the viziers and deputies.

In this fashion, there was hardly a lofty post in the Ottoman empire that he did not occupy. First, in the year 1048 (1638), below Baghdad, he was appointed commander-in-chief with the province of Diyarbekir. He was governor of Diyarbekir four times; of Anatolia province four times; of Özü four times; of Erzurum two times. He was deputy governor of Aleppo two times; of Damascus two times; and of Sivas one time. Once he commanded troops going to Crete and went as far as Menefşe castle. Once each he was commander (*muhafız*) of Tenedos, governor of Bosnia, lieutenant-commander of the Transylvania campaign, and governor of Baghdad. In 1060 (1650) he served as grand vizier for a year and a half.[53] During his vizierate he sent reinforcements to Deli Hüseyn Pasha on Crete, allowing him to conquer Retimo, Selina, and seven other strong fortresses. He was dismissed from the grant vizierate in 1061 (1651). Once he was deputy grand vizier for Köprülü. In sum, he held all the posts of this perishing realm and administered justice in this world. He lived for seventy-seven years.[54] Finally, in the year——, on the—— day of the month of——, in conformity with the noble rescript: "Return to your Lord" (Koran, 12:50), Melek was awarded as his

portion of the unperishing realm the post of the loftiest paradise, and he proceeded to the side of God without retinue and
without servants—may God have mercy on his soul.

Notes

1. The implication is that the marriage was not consummated.

2. For this custom, see Bobovi, p. 71.

3. Or, "Yes, I am going in blood," with a play on *kanda;* cf. II
349a.7 (403) *biz kanda gidüp kan içinde kalalım.*

4. The arsenal garden, later known as Has Bağçe, is below
Hasköy on the Golden Horn. See Evliya's description at I 124b.4–31
(414–15; Hammer ii, 42).

5. Refers to the Sufi practice of *çille,* withdrawal from the world
for a forty-day period; see Schimmel, pp. 103, 105; EI², art. "khalwa"
(H. Landolt). [Annemarie Schimmel, *Mystical Dimensions of Islam*
(Chapel Hill, N.C., 1975)] Ak Şemseddin was a renowned scholar and
mystic during the period of Sultan Mehmed II (reg. 1451–81) and
served as a kind of chaplain to the army at the siege and capture of
Istanbul in 1453. He died in 863/1459 and is buried in Göynük in western Turkey; Evliya claims to have visited his tomb forty times; see I
98b.9 (336; Hammer ii, 2), II 368a.23f. (461–63; Hammer, 241–42).

6. That is, Uways Al-Qaranī, a pious Yemeni contemporary of the
Prophet, prototype of the inspired Sufis who attained spiritual illumination outside of the regular mystical path; see Schimmel, p. 28.

7. ?—*yüzüme yapışdı.*

8. At V 32b.1 (103) Melek Pasha tells Evliya that he expended
1,060 purses during the nine months of the Transylvania campaign;
but 1,060 is one of Evliya's favorite round numbers, cf. V 141b.24
(473), etc.

9. According to Alderson, Table XXXIV, she was fifty-five years
old when she married Melek Pasha, her fourth husband, and had two
more husbands after he died.

10. See Ch. 8, n. 7.

11. See Ch. 8, notes 8 and 9.

12. Word erased.

13. Cf. III 173a (beginning of Ch. 4), V 69a (beginning of Ch. 8).

14. The *salat-ı ebvabin* or *işrak-ı ebvabin* is a supererogatory prayer performed at night. (*Ebvabin* is apparently a deformation of *ev-vabin* "penitents.")

15. For this section cf. III 175a.10 f. (Ch. 4 and n. 18).

16. That is, with beard, mustache, eyelashes, and eyebrows removed; see Evliya's explanation at II 357b.14 (431:omitted; Hammer, 231).

17. Or "classroom" (*ders-hane*).

18. A treatise by Birgili Mehmed, completed in 980/1572. See Zilfi, p. 261. [Madeline C. Zilfi, "The Kadızadelis: Discordant Revivalism in Seventeenth-Century Istanbul," *Journal of Near Eastern Studies* 45, no. 4 (1986)] For Evliya's evaluation of Birgili's works, see IX 87b.1–5 (177).

19. *Budin* (Buda in Hungary) or *bu din* ("this religion"). The same pun, in association with the same book, occurs in the *şeyh* of Urmia's advice to Sultan Murad IV at IV 209a.5 (54: omitted; Diyarbekir, p. 186); the same pun again at V 135b.17 (Ch. 9).

20. If true, this would be the earliest Turkish printed book. According to Nihal Atsız, *Istanbul Kütüphanelerine göre Birgili Mehmed Efendi . . . Bibliyografyası* (Istanbul, 1966), p. 15, *El-Tarikat el-Muhammediyye* was first printed in Istanbul in 1260/1844. Atsız lists 221 mss. (pp. 16–32).

21. Refusing their soup was the traditional signal of rebellion among the janissaries.

22. Apartments of his harem; see below, 48b.19.

23. Two words here are illegible.

24. Cf. Rd[2] *ıskat*: "alms given on behalf of the dead as compensation for their neglected religious duties." [*New Redhouse Turkish-English Dictionary*, Istanbul, 1968]

25. A companion of the Prophet and patron saint of *müezzins*.

26. On the Sadşa, cf. II 257a.33 (104; Hammer, 55).

27. Hadım (~ Tavaşi) Süleyman Pasha's Indian expedition departed in 945/1538 and returned in 946/1539.

28. Cf. X 30b, 33b, 433a f. (65, 74, 933–62).

29. That is, without the forked resting stick?

30. Cf. I 134a.10–15 (446; Hammer ii, 61), V 51b.33f. (see Introduction, "The Author and His Subject," at n. 13).

31. ?—*kadra ermiş.*

32. See Ch. 8, n. 1.

33. Both reciting the *Muavvizeteyn* (the last two *sures* of the Koran) and puffing air over a person are considered to protect from malign influence and ward off the evil eye.

34. *Masum*—an epithet of Sultan Ahmed I.

35. Elsewhere Evliya states that he was born on 10 Muharrem 1020/25 March 1611; see I 59a.1–3 (212; Hammer ii, 110).

36. *Validemiziñ amiyyesi oğlu.* This accords with V 52a.2 (168: *bu hakiriñ validesi halası kızı olmağile*); but at II 366a.33 (453; Hammer, 238) Evliya says that their two mothers were sisters (*validem de Melek Efendimiñ validesi kız karındaşı degilmidir?*).

37. For this battle, see Danişmend, p. 285; cf. Evliya's account at V 39b.8 (125).

38. Murad IV spent the first three years of his reign "paying visits now to Edirne, now to Bursa, killing all of the *zorba* brigands . . ." (IV 335b.15–16 [402–03]).

39. 27 Ramazan, the holiest night of the year, commemorating the revelation of the Koran. [Cf. G. E. von Grunebaum, *Muhammadan Festivals* (London, 1951, 1976), pp. 52, 55–57; Raphaela Lewis, *Everyday Life in Ottoman Turkey* (London and New York, 1971), pp. 122–23] Elsewhere Evliya states that this event took place in 1045 (5 March 1636); see I 68b.29f. (243; Hammer i, 132).

40. Elsewhere we learn that the reason for Koca Nişancı's dismissal was a fire that broke out in the sultan's bedchamber; see III 182a.19f. (Ch. 4), IV 260a.19f. (193; Bitlis, Part II).

41. The actual date was 15 or 16 Şevval 1049 (8 or 9 February 1640).

42. The text has a blank (later filled in by the word *eksük* "missing"). For Müzuri see IV 235b.34–36 (beginning of Ch. 6), 338a.30 (410: *Imadiyede Müzuri hanı Yusuf Han*), 339a.25 (413: *Imadiye Müzuri hakimi Sultan Yusuf Han*).

43. 1050/1640–41; see Ch. 5.

44. See Ch. 7, n. 5.

45. *Cihaz-ı fakr,* a phrase connoting spiritual initiation.

46. Enumerated in the text are *boğası, abayı, kutni, kazze, gücerat.*

47. *Teheccüd ve işrak-ı ebvabin;* see above n. 14.

48. A didactic *mesnevi* by the Persian poet Attar (d. ca. 627/1230). A Turkish translation by Emri was completed in 964/1557, but Evliya probably has in view the Persian original.

49. The *Mesnevi* of Rumi (d. 671/1273) is considered the greatest Persian mystical poem. The *Manevi,* also in Persian, was written in imitation of the *Mesnevi* by the Turkish mystic Gülşeni (d. 940/1534).

50. Cf. Âlî, *Menakıb-ı Hünerveran* (Istanbul, 1926), p. 5.

51. See above, n. 39.

52. *Rusü'l-asl*—that is, of cossack or South Russian origin.

53. See Ch. 2, n. 43.

54. Alderson (Table XXXIV) gives his birthdate as 1013/1604 and his death date as [17 Muharrem] 1073/1 September 1662. Giving Evliya the benefit of the doubt, his birth date should be corrected to 996/1588. However, this date cannot be squared with all the details above—for example, presentation to Ahmed I at age eleven or even at age fourteen (see Introduction, "The Author and His Subject," at n. 13)—because Ahmed I's reign did not begin until 1012/1603.

GLOSSARY

N.B. The spelling of Turkish terms and proper names follows
that of modern Turkish (thus, for example, Mehmed Köprülü
for Evliya's Mehemmed Köpürli). Note that *c* is pronounced
like English *j*, *ç* like *ch*, *ş* like *sh*. Words like *pasha, vizier,
khan, agha*, and *caique* that are ingrained in English have
not been altered.

agha (*ağa*): Title of officials, especially military officers; members of a pasha's retinue.

beg: A military title (= *emir*); governor of a *sancak;* the office of
a *beg* is *beglik.*
begler-begi: Governor of an Ottoman province (*eyalet, vilayet*).
besmele: The formula "In the name of God the Compassionate
the Merciful," recited when undertaking an activity.
bostancı: Member of corps of imperial gardeners, responsible for
policing the waterfront and enforcing sultanic orders for
banishment or imprisonment of high-ranking officials in
disgrace; the head of the corps is *bostancı-başı.*

çavuş: pursuivant or messenger, especially messengers in the
service of the imperial council (*divan-ı hümayun*); the head
of the corps is *çavuş-başı.*
celali: Name given to fugitive soldiers and to provincial rebels
engaged in armed insurrection against the state.
cihad: Warfare against the infidel (= *gaza*); struggle with one's
carnal nature.

defterdar: Director of the financial administration.
divan: The imperial council.

Fatiha: The first *sure* of the Koran, often recited as a prayer.
ferman: An imperial order.

fetva: A ruling or legal interpretation issued by a *müfti*.

gaza: Holy war or jihad (= *cihad*).
gazi: A fighter in the holy war.
gulam: (1) Servant boy or slave boy; (2) military slave in the palace service.

hadith: A traditional saying attributed to the Prophet.
hafız: One who has memorized the Koran.
harac: Tax or tribute; poll tax on non-Muslims (= *cizye*).
hasseki: Title given to a senior member in a branch of the palace service, especially in the *bostancı* corps.
hatib: One who delivers the Friday sermon in a mosque.

imam: (1) Prayer leader; (2) one of the twelve successors to the Prophet recognized by the Shiis, and also honored by the Sunnis; (3) one of the four founders of the Sunni legal schools.

jereed (*cerid*): A short javelin thrown on horseback as a military exercise.

kadı: judge in a *şeriat* law court.
kazıasker: Title of the two chief *kadis* of the Ottoman empire, of Anatolia and Rumelia.
kethüda: Steward; deputy.
khan: Title of Ottoman sultans, Crimean khans, and Kurdish chieftains; the office of *khan* is *khanlık*.
kıble: The direction of prayer.
kul: "Slave," a title for any servitor of the sultan, especially the janissaries.
kul-kethüdası: Title given to the deputy of the chief officer (*ağa*) of the janissary corps.

lala: Imperial tutor.

mihrab: Prayer niche in a mosque.
müezzin: Caller to prayer.
müfti: Jurisconsult; one who issues a *fetva*; the grand *müfti* is the *şeyhülislam*.
müteferrika: Title bestowed on select individuals in the palace service and in military regiments who carried out highly specialized or technically demanding tasks for the sultan.

nakibüleşraf: Officer in charge of tracing genealogies and maintaining the registry of *seyyids*.

nişancı: Officer in charge of affixing the *tuğra*.

okka: A measure by weight, approximately 2¾ lbs.

padishah: Title for sovereign or ruler, applied in literary texts to the Ottoman sultan (whose official title usually included one or more of the following: *sultan, khan, gazi*); it can be used in an honorific sense for others, notably saints and mystics.

pasha (paşa): Title reserved for high officers of the Ottoman state (*begler-begs* and viziers).

sancak: Administrative division of an Ottoman province; the officer in charge is *sancak-begi*.

sarıca: One of the irregular provincial levies, especially infantry.

şayka: A kind of flat-bottomed shallow draft boat used by the cossacks of the lower Dnieper.

segban: One of the irregular provincial levies, especially cavalry.

seyyid: Title for descendants of the Prophet, who were accorded a number of privileges including exemption from payment of taxes.

şeriat: The Islamic sacred law; the adjective is *şer'i*

şeyh: Title of the head of a religious order.

Şeyhülislam: The chief *müfti* of Istanbul, head of the religious establishment.

sipahi: (1) Timariot cavalryman; (2) member of one of the six standing cavalry regiments at the Porte.

sultan: A title of respect, used to address any superior; more particularly, an epithet for the Ottoman sultan and for his mother, wives and daughters ("sultana").

sure: A chapter of the Koran.

sünnet: (1) A practice of the Prophet (cf. Sunni); (2) circumcision.

tabur: Moving fortress (*Wagenburg*), a technique used in a defensive stance by forces operating in the open field.

timar: A grant of land in return for military or administrative service.

tuğra: The imperial cipher, drawn to authenticate official documents, etc.

ulema: religious personnel, including *kadis, müftis, imams, şeyhs*, etc.

vakf: Pious foundation.
valide-sultan: Dowager, queen mother.

yalı: A riparian mansion in Istanbul.

zeamet: A large *timar*.

INDEX

1. Personal Names

2. Place names

3. Groups (Ethnic, Military, Religious, etc.)

4. Topics

Printed in the United States
32963LVS00005B/1-18

9 780791 406410